Indian Women's Short Fiction

Edited by

Joel Kuortti
Rajeshwar Mittapalli

ATLANTIC
PUBLISHERS & DISTRIBUTORS (P) LTD

Published by

ATLANTIC

PUBLISHERS & DISTRIBUTORS (P) LTD

B-2, Vishal Enclave, Opp. Rajouri Garden,
New Delhi-110027
Phones : 25413460, 25429987, 25466842

Sales Office
7/22, Ansari Road, Darya Ganj,
New Delhi-110002
Phones : 23273880, 23275880, 23280451
Fax : 91-11-23285873
web : www.atlanticbooks.com
e-mail : info@atlanticbooks.com

ISBN 81-269-0579-4

Printed and bound in India at Syndicate Binders, Noida

Preface

Feminist literature and feminist literary criticism have grown and spread widely in scope and significance especially during the past decade. This is true also of Indian English literature—both in India and in the diaspora. More and more new women writers have emerged, expressing their creative and critical views. An important channel for these women writers has been the short story. In India, the emergence of the short story in English is closely linked to the emergence of women writers. After all, the eminent scholar M.K. Naik has claimed that it was Cornelia Sorabji who was the first Indian writer in English "with a considerable literary output."

International critical attention to this kind of writing has been growing lately but there are still far too few works that discuss Indian women's stories specifically. In a modest way, the present collection seeks to address this lacuna. While most of the writers discussed are diasporic, the themes of their stories—discussed here from a markedly feminist point of view—are also Indian. Furthermore, they reflect the international configuration of Indian English writing.

In the first article Ellen Dengel-Janic offers a comparative analysis of the ways Cornelia Sorabji in "Greater Love" and Githa Hariharan in "Revati" construct femininity. She builds an intriguing link between the early story of Sorabji and a contemporary story of Hariharan in discussing the interconnectedness of femininity and nationalism, and shows the problems involved in the connection.

Betty Govinden's article on the autobiographical and fictional writings of Jayapraga Reddy takes up a very common issue in women's writing: how writing and identity are problematic issues. The writer of fiction and autobiography is always faced with a challenge to represent the self and the other in some manner. A woman writer has to encounter further cultural obstacles. Govinden discusses how Reddy as a coloured woman in the apartheid society has to negotiate between displacement and enablement in her writing. Sam Naidu continues the discussion of Reddy in her article on Reddy's contribution to South African diasporic literature arguing that an over-arching transnational feminist aesthetic is being inscribed by women writers of the South Asian diaspora.

There are three articles that analyse Chitra Divakaruni-Banerjee's stories in *Arranged Marriage* (1995). Husne Jahan analyses the stories as narratives of immigration as they chart the complex terrain between the colonial, postcolonial and the neo-colonial. This space is full of complications and it has become a very contested one where loyalties and disloyalties are acted out, tested, and reinforced. Jahan's analysis offers an important reading of one approach to the issue. Felicity Hand's article continues this discussion by considering Banerjee-Divakaruni's stories as stories of displacement. Her contention is that South Asian diasporic experience has been dominated by the male experience. The emergence of women writers has enabled a more varied expression, of which Banerjee-Divakaruni is a good example.

Antonia Navarro-Tejero analyses Banerjee-Divakaruni's stories by comparing them with Jhumpa Lahiri's stories. The stories of both writers deal with identity and self-definition. This takes place in view of the cultural context from which the narrators spring from as hybrids of North American and Indian cultures. Navarro-Tejero sees differences between the two writers' stories: while Lahiri celebrates the hybridity, Banerjee Divakaruni is more traditional, reinforcing the binary opposition of the East and the West. Puspa Damai's article continues the discussion of Lahiri's stories. Damai looks at the ways in which these stories deal with illness and death. The connection between the art of storytelling and illness evokes a far-reaching contemplation on the communicability of human experience. Rajeshwar Mittapalli discusses Lahiri's stories from the point of view of hybrid identities of the Indian diaspora in the USA where the center-periphery polarities are blurred and instances of hybridity occur in the reverse direction. In her article, Nandini Sahu compares the ways in which Jhumpa Lahiri and Arundhati Roy approach the issue of nostalgia in their storytelling, discussing literature as a global meeting point of world's traditions through the cultural encounters and existential rediscoveries.

The Partition of India has given rise to a number of stories. Beerendra Pandey looks at the way women's stories about the violence of the Partition change from Lalithambika Antharajanan's "A Leaf in the Storm" (1948) to Shauna Singh Baldwin's "Family Ties" (1996). Pandey perceives a clear paradigm shift from the political immediacy of the Partition generation to the irony in the later writing. He sees that Baldwin's story enables the subaltern female subjectivity to voice her own concerns in times of crisis.

Rebecca Sultana discusses Anjana Appachana's story "Her Mother" and analyses the ways in which it takes up the issues of tradition and modernity. This simplistic division is challenged by the way Appachana discusses the experiences of a mother and her daughter. Andrew Hammond's article on Bharati Mukherjee adds a new dimension to the scholarship on her short fiction.

In their articles, Joel Kuortti and Mala Pandurang discuss Indian writers who do not write from a diasporic location. Kuortti discusses Bulbul Sharma's *The Anger of Aubergines* and examines the ways in which the stories in the collection challenge traditionally and culturally determined gendered positions. Pandurang looks at Lakshmi Kannan's *Going Home* as an intended critique of the stifled and insipid lives led by educated middle-class women of apparently modern families, concentrating on Kannan's use of the leitmotif of 'house' in order to raise disturbing questions on aspects of systemic patriarchal oppression within the contemporary urban Indian milieu. In the concluding article, Basavaraj Naikar and Joel Kuortti offer a narrative analysis of Anita Desai's stories in *Diamond Dust*.

It has been a challenging and rewarding experience to put together this collection. We believe that the present volume will prove immensely useful to both the teachers and students of English literature, while the general readers who are interested in women writers will find it intellectually stimulating. Our sincere thanks are due to the contributors for their learned papers which have enriched the anthology.

Joel Kuortti
Rajeshwar Mittapalli

Contents

1 Constructions of Femininity in Cornelia Sorabji's "Greater Love" and Githa Hariharan's "Revati"

Ellen Dengel-Janic

Conceptualising 'Woman'

> She was an unpleasant reminder of a world gone by. A child-widow was a thing of the past, a page from a history textbook that should be safely contained between cardboard covers. Not what she was, as large as life, walking, talking, eating huge mouthfuls of our food. (Hariharan, "Revati" 93)

The paradigm shift in the construction of femininity in 20th century Indian women's fiction in English can be traced and defined by exploring representative texts that reveal the historical transformation of gendered identity. Cornelia Sorabji's short story "Greater Love" (1901) and Githa Hariharan's short narrative "Revati" (1993) illustrate how femininity is negotiated at the beginning and at the end of the 20th century. The kind of female subjectivity which is represented in the texts is set in a frame of socially determined gender stereotyping. Cornelia Sorabji's study of female existence is rooted in cultural norms of femininity, whereas Githa Hariharan's story "Revati" discusses and transforms the culturally given stereotypes.

In a short passage from the "Introductory Note" to Cornelia Sorabji's collection of short stories called *Love and Life Behind the Purdah*, which was published in 1901, it is emphasised that certain characteristics of "Indian femininity" will be at the centre of the short narratives: "[Cornelia Sorabji's] stories are set before us, in the most attractive way, the tender, faithful, meek and lowly character of the Indian woman, combined as it so often is with quiet persistence and strength, and with an unselfishness which amounts to self-sacrifice" (Dufferin 7). The author of this note, Lady Dufferin, the wife of Frederick Temple, the Viceroy of India from 1884 to 1888, invokes the stereotypical image of "*the* Indian woman" and thus highlights the position of a "doubly colonised" subject, which, here, as if for the first time, is represented and provided with a voice, even though it seems to be a collective rather than an individual one. In order to challenge this categorisation of "the Indian woman," one needs to contextualise the literary constructs of femininity, drawing on epic-religious and political discourses that emerge in the contact zone of Colonialism and Indian culture and that produce dominant categorisations of women.

Feminist critics have argued that "woman" is produced by gendered discourses and thus is constructed according to dominant thoughts and ideologies that are present in a given culture.

Joan Scott, a historian, assumes that gender is a social category imposed on a sexed body. Similarly, Catherine A. MacKinnon argues that: "Gender, cross-culturally, was found to be a learned quality, an acquired characteristic, an assigned status, with qualities that vary independent of biology and an ideology that attributes them to nature. The discovery that the female archetype was the feminine stereotype led to the exposure of 'woman' as a social construction" (15-16).

The culturally determined conceptualisation of women can offer an in-depth analysis of the texts that are centred around female identity, and thus enriches the approach of feminist literary theory. "The ideology of ideal womanhood" is constructed in different discourses on women, in which women are positioned, defined, located and images of women are produced that might be diverse and even contradictory, but which nevertheless lead to the effect of dividing society into the binaries of male and female, the female being the dominated part. An interdisciplinary perspective allows us to interweave different discursive images of women into a "model" conceptualisation against which the literary female identities will be contrasted, compared and analysed.

Tracing the conceptualisation of "woman" in Indian history demands an investigation of dominant ideologies about women in the 19th century, at the time of an awakening nationalism and social reform movement since, within these discourses, "woman" was redefined. Kumkum Sangari and Sudesh Vaid state that, "the recovery of tradition throughout the proto-nationalist period was always the recovery of the 'traditional' woman—her various shapes continuously readapt the 'eternal' past to the needs of the contingent present" (10). Two things happen simultaneously, "woman" is used as cultural marker, against the domination of the colonial power in the present and the conceptualisation of "woman" is rooted in a supposedly glorious Hindu past and Hindu tradition. By recovering a lost Vedic-Aryan Golden Age (Chakravarti 28), the colonised man disqualifies the derogatory counter-discourses of the British. Conceptualising "woman" as the bearer of tradition becomes essential to this national endeavour: she recreates, gives birth, preserves family honour and links all this to the golden past. This is in a peculiar way enabling and controlling women at the same time. Irene Gedalof summarises these re-definitions within the nationalist discourse: "On the one hand, there is the promise of re-ordering gender relations implicit in a certain 'feminisation' of nationalist discourse, and in the political mobilisation of real women. On the other hand, there is the containing of women by the nationalist movement within its own patriarchal norms" (46-47).

The two concepts of "woman" and "nation" have been brought together in the historical moment of the formation of the Hindu middle class and its nationalism. The formation and identity of the middle class was closely connected to the effects of colonisation, western ideas of liberalism and a new nationalism. Let me briefly outline a few central concepts of the social reform movement that has spread over the country during the 19th century, and its ideas which were characteristic of the new middle class.[1]

Societies such as the Brahmo Samaj and the Arya Samaj were the agents of the social reform movements and were founded in many parts of the country. They made the legal and social positions of women their central issue. The matters which were discussed and were seen as being in need of reform, were the upper-caste Hindu widows' position in society, and the related questions of *sati* and remarriage (Chaudhuri 10). Furthermore, the question of education for women was raised, the advantages and disadvantages of education for upper-caste, middle class women was pondered by social reformers. Through redefining their women's status and role, Hindu reformers positioned themselves and their class against the accusations of the Colonial power that saw the "degradation" of women as an indicator of the standards and the degree of modernisation of a society. This argument of degradation was of course used as an instrument to justify the domination of the colonised culture. Kumkum Sangari argues that "women became subjects and vehicles through whom the retention and modernization of newly defined Hindu patriarchal forms were to be achieved" (22). The great visibility of women in this national context influences the concepts of women in the realm of literary production. Especially texts by women writers absorb these national images of women and their implied ideologies and transform them into literary constructs.

Cornelia Sorabji's "Greater Love"—A Critique of Ideal Femininity

In the case of the short story "Greater Love" it is necessary to consider the conceptualisations of women in national as well as epic-religious discourses. The national ideology combines the ideal mother with nationalist ideas in the use of the image of India as a mother. The Mother India worship, as Lata Mani argues, locates "women" as the excluded but necessary ground upon which what might be called competing national economies of the same are constructed. There are even more aspects to this image: firstly, the country, which is seen as the mother, becomes the place of origin, the pure authenticity that is untouched by the influence of colonisation and westernisation. This pure place is connected to the concept of home and family, which are seen as holy and traditional, and contrasted to the colonial and public sphere of British intervention (Sarkar 2011). And secondly, if the country is like the mother goddess, it is powerful and protective, and of course, worth to be fought for. It is a way of glorifying motherhood, more specifically an abstract form of it, and, at the same time, elevating real mothers, who, by giving birth, provide the state with new loyal citizens. Giving birth becomes an act of national, social and religious importance.

Taking the epic-religious tradition as a frame of reference it becomes apparent that the concept "woman" is firmly situated in the family and in the marital relationship.[2] The images of ideal wifehood, based on the ideals of epic figures like Sita and Savitri, and the concept of the "pativrata" are crucial for the discursive production of the female self in this socio-historical context. Defining female identity by being positioned in the familial space is secured by her otherwise non-existence as a valid member of the religious community.[3]

Taking the nationalist Mother India ideology as a frame of reference for the definition of female subjectivity in the short narrative "Greater Love," it becomes clear that childlessness has severe consequences for the characters. The protagonist is threatened to lose her position as wife and mother, since she is unable to bear a son and thus she is considered an outcast in the circle of wives. In order to conform to the religious-social norms of the Hindu upper-caste setting, she decides to leave her marital position and provides her husband with a surrogate wife, who will bear him the much wished for male heir. Her choice of an ascetic life in the mountains is reminiscent of Sita's sacrifice in the *Ramayana*, where she prefers exile to court life in order to conform to the ideal of wifehood.

The implicit critique of the marginalisation of women is detectable in the narrator's commentary of the domestic opening scene when at the Kunkun party Matha Shri, the unhappy childless wife, is openly ostracised by the present women. It becomes clear that "[t]he freedom achieved outside the domestic closure was purchased at the risk of ostracism, or at best marginalisation, while paradoxically a central position in society—as wife or as mother—could be granted only to those who submitted to the collective feminine code of conformity which erased the individual self" (Mukherjee 78). This collective identity is implicitly questioned by the narrative, which focuses on a redeeming figure, the young wife and host of the party, Kamala, who is modelled on an ideal form of virtuous and sympathetic femininity. The emphasis on positive femininity and human empathy, which is contrasted to the marginalisation of women by other women, is even further re-enforced by giving the presentation of Kamala a considerable amount of narrative space, accordingly her position is foregrounded.

A further critique is noticeable when analysing the contrasting behaviour of the young Kamala and her guests: "Kamala was silent, as became a well-mannered Hindu maiden in the presence of her seniors. But there was a viciousness in the jerk with which she anointed each virtuous forehead. 'Daub, daub,' she went, with the slimy red stuff out of the silver pot, till each guest bore her stigma of wifehood at the hands of her hostess" ("Greater Love" 64). The gendered ideology of the "silent" and "well-mannered Hindu maiden" is subtly transformed by the description of her disregard for her companions, who symbolise her collective identity. Instead, the narration criticises the limitations of wifehood by calling the bindi, the sign of wifehood, a "stigma" ("Greater Love" 64).

The configuration of the short story shows a considerable variety of female characters: Kamala, the kind Hindu wife, Sahai, a mere shadow of a young dutiful wife, the conservative and superstitious women at the Kunkun party and most importantly Matha Shri, who is ironically called the honourable mother. The second part of the narrative relates Matha Shri's story, presenting her psychological conflict, which results from her childlessness, her decision-making and eventually her choice of the life of an ascetic, making her quasi-saint. Thus giving a rendering of a fairly complex character who—although adhering to the ideal of wifehood, and thus sacrificing herself for the well-being of her husband—nevertheless shows a certain capability to act and to become the agent of her own destiny. On the level of the implied gender discourses, the narrative suggests that the ideology of the ideal Hindu wife is projected onto the female characters, but instead of being silenced and eradicated from the story that is being told, they claim a central space in it, being presented as complex and individual human beings. Interestingly, Matha Shri decides to go into exile, removes herself from the domestic setting, which would give her a female space and secure identity, in order to claim her position as an active participant in the events of the story, even providing it with a "happy ending."

The fact that Matha Shri is eager to learn about the public version of her part in her husband's happiness with new wife and child—the fulfilment of a Hindu man's wishes—hints to her claim to a place within this story. Her excitement is felt in the following lines: "'And what say they of—her? Is there no talk of—her who was lost?' 'No! None! Except—that people wonder at the great love which Nano bestowed upon her, in refraining from using, through the long empty years, his privilege as a sonless Hindu. That was her only glory, this love of Nano's' [...]" ("Greater Love" 69). The assertion that "[t]hat was her only glory, this love of Nano's" ("Greater Love" 69) shows that the villagers' version of the story about marital happiness omits Matha Shri's sacrifice that led to it. But the implied criticism of this statement can be seen in the title: "Greater Love," meaning that Matha Shri is the symbol of greater love, demonstrating her importance, and this makes her story, which is at the same time a counter-narrative to the dominant version of female existence, worth telling.

The Crisis of Being a Woman in Githa Hariharan's "Revati"

In the short story "Revati" by Githa Hariharan female identity becomes highly problematic. Being positioned within a rigid familial system results in a crisis, and even more so when this position is threatened or lost. The narrative is centred around Revati, a child-widow whose identity is constituted by the absence and loss of her marital status and consequently her position is very fragile and contested. Even though she manages to live independently, supporting herself by a teaching job, towards the end of her life she becomes a highly ambiguous figure within the family setting.

The implied religious-mythological discourse on widows can be drawn from the epic tradition. Looking at the definition of epic widowhood, it becomes clear that moving outside of the patriarchal structure of the family would result in a loss of a stable and fixed idea of the self. The practice of sati, which is not yet a widely performed custom in the Epics, but is already mentioned in the *Mahabharata*, can help to illustrate this point. Due to the loss of the vital connection to the husband's family, the position of a widow is outside the family structure.

Cases of sati show that the wife's place is with her husband in life *and* in death. Women's helplessness and powerlessness contribute to the idea of the wifely duty and obligation to follow her husband onto the funeral pyre. Women are known as *abalas* i.e. those without power, and therefore need protectors. Once the protection of a husband ceases to exist, the woman is perceived as completely helpless. The marginalisation of a widow is remarkable, thus showing the insidiousness of an "ideology of ideal womanhood," that asks women to "purify" themselves in utter self-destruction.

Different gendered discourses on widowhood are mentioned in the opening section of the short story: sati, dowry-deaths and child-widows. An alternative and possibly a counter-discourse is presented in the romanticism of filmic versions of widowhood, where the problematic situation of a child-widow is resolved by the plot of romance. Another very dominant concept of widowhood is introduced: the ascetic and saintly widow who is devoted to her family. In this case the widow's identity is completely adapted to the family's needs. In contrast to all these versions, Revati transcends all those dominant ideas on her identity, instead, she is unashamed and obstinate. Ultimately, she becomes a burden to the family: "Nobody said it in so many words, but clearly, something had to be done about Revati. It was ten years since she had retired from her teaching career. She now lived alone, at least for a small part of the year. The rest of the time she visited her brothers and sisters for long stretches, her bulky frame in the wrong place at the wrong time, always in the way" ("Revati" 95). After having begun the story by quoting different discourses on widowhood, the story continues to emphasise that Revati is a relic of the past, she does not fit in with the supposedly "modern" attitude of the family that is voiced by the narrator. But her anachronistic existence seems to be rather an excuse for the family to further marginalise this figure, and thus the ancient tradition of ostracism of widows is repeated. The past and the present are intertwined, she is "in the wrong place, the wrong time" (95), revolting against what the ideology of ideal femininity would tell her to do.

The usually silenced issue of female sexuality is raised, thus subverting the stereotypical norms of female behaviour completely. She is depicted as devouring food, instead of delicately and modestly eating. Her passion for eating and her relationship to a young retarded relative hint at her hidden sexuality, which eventually results in a scandal which is immediately hushed up by the family. The marginalisation of the other, in this case the sexual other, is paralleled by the marginalisation of the mentally retarded and therefore the marginality is doubled in the pair of these two outsiders. The normalisation produced by the microcosm of society, the family, is highly visible in the steps taken against the members of the family that are perceived as other and outside of the socially acceptable. This is even more perceptible in the sanctioning and silencing of sexuality, which is perceived as deviant and not conforming to the ideals of wifehood and marriage.

The female code is continuously undermined by the ambiguity of Revati's actions, her representation subverts the notions of female chastity, modesty and silence. The dichotomy that is established by the narrative between "us," meaning the family, and Revati reinforces her role of the rebel against the socially approved forms of womanhood. Furthermore, she leaves the safe social world of normalisation, by drifting into the world of madness. She is thus positioned outside the security and conformity of wifehood and femininity. Being perceived as mad means that she becomes the "mad woman in the attic," which is a common literary representation of the subversive female subject. Madness has traditionally been seen as a female disease, it is said to be the acting out of the "devalued female role or the total or partial rejection one's sex-role stereotype" (Chesler 56).

Nuances of Subversion—A Comparison

When looking at the two short stories and comparing the concept of the family as it is represented in the texts, it becomes clear that there are different underlying ideologies that form the structure of the fictional families. Revati is framed within a family structure, whereas Matha Shri leaves the home for the sake of the family. Both of these women are marginalised figures, one is spatially exiled, the other inhabits an internal exile within the rigidity of the familial-domestic space. The question of space in connection to the concept of femininity can be very illuminating when analysing texts by women writers. In French Feminism, Luce Irigaray states in *Speculum de l'autre femme* that "woman" is constructed as the outside in a logocentric discourse. Namely, the dislocating experience of being a woman is a consequence of never occupying a place of one's own, but rather being the empty space to be manipulated and inscribed by the male dominant discourse. Woman as an empty space and woman as a mirror have been elaborated on by many feminists, Simone de Beauvoir, for example, a pioneering theorist, and Luce Irigaray, who further investigated the thematic implications of the excluded position of woman in philosophical and psychoanalytical discourses.

Moreover, the concepts of exile from a gender perspective and from a postcolonial perspective can be used as an approach to the discourses of gender in the influential epic tradition and in nationalist discourse, both have formed the self-awareness of women in post-Independence India. The different forms of exile are delineated in Sita's exile as it is depicted in the

Ramayana. The position of the exiled in a "foreign" space that is identified with alienation, isolation and estrangement is inherent in the forming of female identity in a patrilocal society.

The domestic space as female space on the one hand and the internal or external exile as a form of female existence on the other is played out in both these short stories. Female space is defined by seclusion, religious and social duty in "Greater Love," and then transgressed by the main character, which subtly shows the agency of the female self. Whereas in "Revati" transgression is not shown in spatial dimensions, but the widow is rather portrayed as being exiled and alienated ideologically from the norms that society and the family would like to impose on her. The treatment and presentation of female space therefore illustrates how the underlying gender discourses are negotiated in the literary works.

The ideology of ideal femininity is modelled on the conceptualisations of women in the Epics, where they are positioned within the structure of the family. Considering this, the analysis of the narrative "Greater Love" demonstrates how this ideology produces a form of femininity that is both desirable and repressive at the same time. The collective identity of the group of wives is a site of longing for the main character who, by being stigmatised by childlessness, is excluded from this female space. As a reaction to this, she crosses the boundaries of her female-domestic setting to live the life of an ascetic, thus paradoxically fulfilling her "stri-dharma," her duties of an ideal wife.

In contrast to the concept of the ideal woman, we are confronted with a subversive image of womanhood in "Revati." The female code of chastity, modesty and silence is turned upside down by the bulky widow who, instead of merging with the needs of the family, centres her attention and the attention of others around her bodily needs. Consequently, her characterisation dwells on the very physicality of her existence. The shift from the ethereal female ideal of the Epics cannot be greater, as the narrative revolves around a woman's body, including its vulgarity and ugliness.

In the two short narratives the focus on the woman and her identity shows how the definition of female identity is intertwined with women's positions and roles within the patriarchal system of the family. Analysing the two stories and comparing different constructions of femininity leads to the conclusion that the gender categories produced by the texts are in a process of transformation. The idealisation of the female character in "Greater Love" is a contrast to the ambiguity of the female figure in "Revati." Towards the end of the 20th century there seems to be a greater anxiety about what it means to belong to one gender and the implications that go along with it. Negotiating the different variations of femininity shows how stories by Indian women writers in English focus on the complexities of women's positioning and re-positioning within the microcosm of culture, the family. In "Revati" the past and present discourses on women are concentrated around the figure of a child-widow, who seems to be an anachronistic creature, alienated from contemporary forms of female identity. Her exiled position is both spatial and temporal, and even ideological. She represents a form of female self-definition that subverts and transcends normative concepts of gender.

Krupabai Satthianadhan has been called the founder of a female tradition in Indian-English writing. More recently Cornelia Sorabji has been discovered as an important actor in this field, and her female protagonists have to be seen as a significant contribution to the expression of a new self-awareness of women in Indian literature. In the introduction to the re-issue of her short fiction, the editor states that: "Not only does the author pioneer the tradition of Indian-Parsee women's literature in English, but she also deserves a prominent place in world archives as one of the earliest women in India to fictionalise the Indian woman in the English language" (Lokugé xiii). Her collection of short stories *Love and Life Behind the Purdah* reveals different nuances of femininity, the female figures are immersed in stories about love and life, they are predominantly the silent and suffering actants in static tragedies. Although most of the women characters are seen as ideals following the female code, they are chaste, devoted, ready to sacrifice themselves, there is an element of a modern-liberal attitude in some of the stories. The critique of the custom of sati, for instance, can be read as the influence of the British involvement in the sati debate as well as an Indian Nationalist and reformist stance, which had a tendency towards modernisation of ancient Hindu law from within Hindu culture.[4]

The striking element of these stories is that the marginalised female positions, represented by a banned Rani, a childless woman who leaves her home to do penance on a pilgrimage, a widow, or a Parsi woman committing a deadly sin, all these women are foregrounded in the short narratives and their suffering and their positions are presented and implicitly questioned. The narratives encompass the polyphonic discourses and contexts of Colonialist criticism of indigenous custom, the missionary zeal, social reformist concepts and all this is woven into the web out of which the female identities are constructed. And furthermore, these female voices emerge from this heterogeneous texture claiming their own positions, may they be contested and fragile, but nevertheless obstinate.

In the collection *The Art of Dying and Other Stories* Githa Hariharan introduces complex female figures, which emerge from their anonymity as wives, mothers, or daughters and demand their right to have a distinct voice and a visible position from which to speak. Even though some of these characters may be portrayed in ironic or caricaturist modes, their originality and subversive potential is what redeems them. What has begun in the 19th century with literary representations of women in Indian-English literature with figures like Mantangini in Bankimchandra Chatterjee's *Rajmohan's Wife* (first serialised in *Indian Field*, a small-circulation journal in 1864) and Kamala in Krupabai Satthianadhan's *Kamala, A Story of Hindu Life* (1894) has developed further into a tradition of portraying women beyond stereotyping and marginalisation. The gendered categorisations and rigid social relationships founded on gender norms are subtly questioned, re-defined and negotiated with every new literary version of female subjectivity.

NOTES

1. Maitrayee Chaudhuri suggests that the "women's question," the emerging Hindu middle class and the social reform movements were closely connected (9).
2. Shakambarai Jayal states that: "Marriage as a social and biological necessity was given religious sanctity even in the Vedic age. In the epics marriage as a prelude to life is of the greatest importance i.e. domestic life gradually became an important and obligatory sacrament" (40).
3. In the Epics a woman's identity is intertwined with her role as wife and mother, even concerning her role in religious duties. Outside marriage she has no religious status (Jayal 40).
4. See, for example, Maitrayee Chaudhuri, who explores the topic of social reform and its roots in Hinduism (11-12).

WORKS CITED

Chakravarti, Uma. "Whatever Happened to the Vedic Dasi?" *Recasting Women: Essays in Indian Colonial History*. Ed. Kumkum Sangari and Sudesh Vaid. Delhi: Kali for Women, 1990. 27-87.

Chatterjee, Bankimchandra. *Rajmohan's Wife*. Foreword by Meenakshi Mukherjee. Delhi: Ravi Dayal, 1996. [In *Indian Field* 1864.]

Chaudhuri, Maitrayee. *Indian Women's Movement. Reform and Revival*. New Delhi: Radiant, 1993.

Chesler, Phyllis. *Women and Madness*. New York: Avon Books, 1973.

Dufferin, Lady. Introductory Note. *Love and Life Behind the Purdah*, by Cornelia Sorabji 1901. New Delhi: Oxford University Press, 2003: 7.

Gedalof, Irene. *Against Purity. Rethinking Identity with Indian and Western Feminisms*. London: Routledge, 1999.

Hariharan, Githa. "Revati." *The Art of Dying and Other Stories*. New Delhi: Penguin, 1993: 92-97.

Irigaray, Luce. *Speculum of the Other Woman*. Trans. Gillian Gill. Ithaka: Cornell University Press, 1985. [*Speculum de l'autre femme* 1974.]

Jayal, Shakambarai. *The Status of Women in the Epics*. New Delhi: Motilal, 1966.

Lokugé, Chandani. Introduction. *Love and Life Behind the Purdah*, by Cornelia Sorabji. Ed. Chandani Lokugé. New Delhi: Oxford University Press, 2003: xiii-xlii.

Mani, Lata. "Contentious Traditions: The Debate on Sati in Colonial India." *Recasting Women: Essays in Indian Colonial History*. Ed. Kumkum Sangari and Sudesh Vaid. Delhi: Kali for Women, 1990: 88-123.

MacKinnon, Catherine A. "Feminism, Marxism, Method, and the State: An Agenda for Theory." *Feminist Theory. A Critique of Ideology*. Ed. Nannerl O. Keohane, Michell, Z. Rosaldo and Barbara C. Gelpi. London and Chicago: University of Chicago Press, 1981: 1-30.

Mukherjee, Meenakshi. *The Perishable Empire*. New Delhi: Oxford University Press, 2000.

Sangari, Kumkum. *Politics of the Possible. Essays on Gender, History, Narratives, Colonial English*. New Delhi: Tulika, 1999.

—— and Sudesh Vaid. *Recasting Women: Essays in Indian Colonial History*. Delhi: Kali for Women, 1990.

Sarkar, Tanika. "Nationalist Iconography." *Economic and Political Weekly* 21 (1987): 2011-15.

Satthiandadhan, Krupabai. *Kamala, A Story of Hindu Life*. Madras: 1894. [2nd ed. *Kamala: The Story of a Hindu Child-Wife*. Ed. Chandani Lokugé. New Delhi: Oxford University Press, 1998.]

Scott, Joan. *Gender and the Politics of History*. New York: Columbia University Press, 1988.

Sorabji, Cornelia. "Greater Love." *Love and Life Behind the Purdah*. 1901. New Delhi: Oxford University Press, 2003: 61-69.

2

Narratives of Disablement and Enablement: Jayapraga Reddy's *The Unbending Reed* and *On the Fringe of Dreamtime and Other Stories*

Betty Govinden

> [...] we are not gods but wounded creatures, cracked lenses, capable only of fractured perceptions. Partial beings, in all senses of that phrase. Meaning is a shaky edifice we build out of scraps, dogmas, childhood injuries, newspaper articles, chance remarks, old films, small victories, people hated, people loved; perhaps it is because our sense of what is the case is constructed from such inadequate materials that we defend it so fiercely, even to the death. (Rushdie 12)

In this essay I consider Jayapraga Reddy's unpublished autobiography, *The Unbending Reed*, and her short stories collected in the volume *On the Fringe of Dreamtime and Other Stories* (1989). I read the two texts contrapuntally, drawing attention to the complex connections between the double narratives of disablement and enablement at work in these two examples of her writings, the one autobiographical and the other fictional. I explore issues of identity, self-representation and representation, drawing attention to differences in spatial configurations in the two writings.

Background to Reddy's Career as a Writer

Reddy was born in 1947, and until her death in August 1996 lived in Durban, KwaZulu-Natal. She began writing from the time she was twelve years old, when she published her first story, "The Lost Tube of Toothpaste." When she was in the fourth standard she wrote a short story which she sent to the local magazine, *The 1860 Settler*, where it was published without acknowledgement. Her first play, "The Balloon Seller," was also written at this time.

Reddy was fortunate to enjoy a prominent career as a writer, and the story of her publication success is unique among Indian women writers in South Africa. A chronological survey of her achievements shows a slow but steady incorporation of her work into the mainstream of South African writing. In 1975 the BBC broadcast her short stories, "The Love Beads" and "The Stricken Land." "Nandi's Secret Friend," a short story for children, was also accepted by the BBC. In the 1980's these stories were published by *Staffrider*, as well as new ones, such as the "The Slumbering Spirit," "Market Days," and "A Gift for Rajendra." This last story was later broadcast by the BBC.

Reddy's short story, "Web of Persuasion," was adapted for radio and television by Franz Marx in 1984, and was hailed as a success, although Reddy complained that the script had been changed considerably. In the same year *The Reader's Digest* published "The Slumbering Spirit" under the title "The Awakening Spirit." The story was translated by *The Readers' Digest* for its international editions in several languages, including Hindi for its readership on the Indian sub continent. In 1987 her short story collection, *On the Fringe of Dreamtime and Other Stories*, was published by Skotaville. In 1988 the retrospective edition of Staffrider, *Ten Years of Staffrider*, included her short story, "The Spirit of Two Worlds." In 1989 Reddy also presented a further script to the SABC, entitled "Release to the Wind." In 1991 Annemarie van Niekerk's anthology of South African women's short stories, *Raising the Blinds*, included her short story, "Two Friends," which had appeared in the collection *On the Fringe of Dreamtime and Other Stories*.

All these publications were by well-known local and international publishers, and were aimed at a wide reading public. It is noteworthy that the short stories that were selected for anthologising were those that provided a variety of South African contexts, dealing with race relations ("The Slumbering Spirit"), experiences in an Indian extended family ("The Spirit of Two Worlds"), and domestic tension related to race, class and gender ("Two Friends"). Reddy notes, in her introduction to her collection of short stories, that writing is determined inevitably by living in a particular place: "One derives one's creative spirit from this land of a myriad contrasts. There is no 'typical' South African way of life" (Reddy, 1987: Foreword). It would seem that her work has been included in various anthologies for its very contribution to the "myriad contrasts" that constitute South African life. While the short stories are not directly autobiographical they do draw on some of the experiences that she records in her autobiography. Some of these are experiences of being uprooted through the Group Areas Act ("On the Fringe of Dreamtime") and of being confined to a wheelchair ("A Gift for Rajendra").

Reddy's autobiography, *The Unbending Reed*, was submitted for publication to Skotaville. Later, it was also sent to two overseas publishers, but she had yet to hear from them when she died in 1996. A publisher had actually requested that she write the autobiography, presumably anticipating a great deal of interest in her story on the strength of her creative work. A short extract from the autobiography was published in the COSAW collection of writings, *Like A House On Fire—Contemporary Women's Writing, Art and Photography* (Horn et al.), in which the autobiography was described as "forthcoming," but to date it has not been published. The autobiography, a simple, linear account of her life, with a great amount of detail concerning her illness, may not have been considered as interesting as her short stories. What seems to have been ignored is that the very act of writing, rather than the content itself, was the real achievement.

In her autobiography Reddy—unlike Dr Goonam in her *Coolie Doctor*—presents a narrow, almost self-absorbed, personal narrative. She recounts her early childhood, and events of her life as she grew older, up to a few years before she died. The physical disease she suffered from—muscular dystrophy—is centrally placed in her life story. In some ways the autobiography might be seen as a one-dimensional text, in which her disability and her concern for her physical condition are central pre-occupations. A parallel and related strand is that of her development as a writer, of the difficulties and successes she experienced in getting herself into print. It is her desire to overcome the restrictions imposed on her by her infirmity, her physical bondage that influences her intention to become a writer.

Although Reddy asserts in the Foreword to her short stories that she is not readily disposed to speaking of herself, in the autobiography she does give important personal details about her life, details that would have otherwise remained unknown. In the Foreword to the short story collection she speaks of her inclination as a writer to be "a very private person" (Reddy, 1989: 1). She observes that "solitude teaches one the beauty of silences, those long silences that deepen and stretch into eternity" (1). There are large tracts of her emotional and psychological life about which she remains silent, but she does focus on the physical details of her diseased condition with almost obsessive concern. Her ambivalence about telling her story and being reticent about it is perhaps best captured in the anecdote of photo-taking that she recounts early in the autobiography in which she quotes her grandfather's caution against capturing "an image of oneself" (2).

Her story begins with an account of Kesa, her elder brother, and herself growing up apparently normally. She then describes how the family gradually confront the truth that Kesa has muscular dystrophy. His death is movingly described, and Reddy tells how the finality of the separation is brought home to her when Kesa's pet cat walks away, never to return again:

> Then Prill walked in. Through the front door he came, tail erect and marched with a purpose towards the coffin. He put his front paws on the coffin and peered in. The mourners were sufficiently roused out of themselves to stop weeping, and watched as he turned and walked out

> the way he came in. We never saw him again. If anything... succeeded in bringing home to me the finality of death and the rending pain of loss, it was that. (Reddy, *Unbending* 15)

Reddy and her younger brother, Mags, are also stricken with the disease, and spend their entire lives valiantly coping with it. Her physical disability is the controlling element in Reddy's identity; it determines how she is accepted and what life experiences she will enjoy. If there is a "preoccupation with self," as there usually is in black woman's autobiography (Watts 108) due to the systematic diminishing of a sense of self, in *The Unbending Reed* it is particularly so because of Reddy's having to live with muscular dystrophy as a black person and as a woman in South Africa. She is conscious that she is positioned peripherally because of her physical disability. She constantly observes, with amusement and sadness the attitudes of those around her towards her disease: "Over the years I have become used to being treated as some kind of curiosity specimen" (Reddy, *Unbending* 17). She writes of the prejudices towards her, conscious that she is a spoken subject, and treated as if she were totally ignorant and lacking an independent self. These attitudes, she constantly reiterates, are only due to the lack of awareness and education on the part of others on how to respond to her condition. Reddy is all too aware of the ambivalent attitudes of those around her to her handicapped condition. In her autobiography she writes:

> In different societies, people react to the disabled in different ways. In the Indian community, the reaction is usually one of sincere concern and sympathy. When discussing the disabled child in his presence, it seldom occurs to people that he is perfectly capable of understanding every word and that he has feelings. For instance, a typical reaction from visitors would be, after scrutinising me thoroughly, and tut-tutting in sympathy, 'Shame! What can you do, it's God's will.' (16)

Reddy refuses the image of victim, and in this she is supported by her grandparents and parents, who were strong adherents of the Jehovah's Witnesses church. The door-to-door evangelising approach of this church would have appealed to Reddy in her confined condition.

There is strong family support for Reddy, as she is loved and affirmed by her immediate as well as extended family. From her side there is deep admiration and love for her parents, her aunts and uncles, who provide her with the emotional and psychological nurturing to develop a positive sense of self. In this respect her story is reminiscent of that of Noni Jabavu who, in *The Ochre People*, also speaks of the moral support of family, although in her case her problems were social rather than physical (see Watts 115). A strong sense of family is also evident in the writings of Mayat, Sam and Goonam, with different members of the family being decisive influences in the authors' lives. These writers speak of their mothers in particular as having been influential. Reddy constantly refers to her mother as a "pillar"; her image of her mother as a strong woman is captured in the epigraph, "A woman is like the reed, though she bends with the wind, she does not break," from which the title of her autobiography, "*The Unbending Reed*" is drawn. In the "Dedication" of the autobiography she notes: "To the memory of my Mother, Esperi (Bommie) whose dedication, discipline, far-sightedness, courage and endurance made life a lesson in grit." Reddy also claims a nurturing role for herself, and this is seen particularly in her relationship with Mags, as she assists him in coping with his own muscular dystrophy.

Her parents and grandparents, who believed strongly in the liberating power of education, and of education for girls in spite of much prejudice against this, encouraged her in her striving to be independent. They saw 'education' as a means of her attaining independence. Her mother's moralising tone has a familiar ring about it: "If you have wealth, you can lose it. Fine things can be stolen. But nobody can take your education from you" (47). It is the need to improve, to develop, to cope with her handicap, that makes it imperative for Reddy to gain an education.

Reddy describes how she experienced great difficulties in securing an education owing to her physically disabled state, and how this was exacerbated by her being black and female. Her disability made going to school difficult, and there are graphic accounts in her autobiography of her seeking admission to a school. It was the time of the 'platoon school system,' deployed to cater for the lack of adequate schooling facilities for black children. The principal's refusal to admit her, shows the extent to which prejudice against handicapped individuals went unquestioned. The efforts of an African nurse from "Cripple Care" paid off as she insisted that the principal admit the new pupil. Reddy describes the attitudes of people towards her, and the unsuitability of the school for children like her—there were "stairs everywhere," and the toilets were far away. Further, there were forty pupils in a class; and the teacher had been teaching from the age of fifteen, with no suitable teaching qualifications. In spite of all the 'inconveniences' she endured, she managed to be at the top of her class, and enjoyed many friendships while at school. When completing her education at the normal schools proved difficult, she continued with her studying through correspondence courses. She used this educational background to develop self-sustaining careers, such as part-time teaching at her home and free-lance journalism.

More importantly, 'education,' in whatever form it took, is seen as a pre-requisite for writing books, and this is for Reddy a way of asserting an identity that is undermined by the prejudices of those around her, and a way of claiming her freedom (van Niekerk 70). The lack of education has presented black women writers in South Africa with significant hurdles, as Daymond points out: "For black women who chose to write stories (as against telling them) and to write in English, questions of education and opportunity are what would have first controlled their activity; attaining literacy and a general education was even more difficult for them than it was for black men" (Daymond 193). In Reddy's case, education provides the route to writing, which in turn provides a way of overcoming the debilitating effects of muscular dystrophy.

Reddy's strong urge to read whatever she could lay her hands on was an important part of her preparation in becoming a writer. In reading voraciously she responded to the available colonial education of the time. Shirley Chew and Anna Rutherford, in their book, *The Unbecoming Daughters of Empire* (1993), shows the ubiquitous nature of colonial education in different contexts. Ironically, such an education is usually a Eurocentric one, and this was true for Reddy as well. Unlike Zoe Wicomb, in *You Can't Get Lost in Cape Town* (1987), and Tsitsi Dangarembga in *Nervous Conditions* (1991), Reddy does not develop a critical attitude towards the language and culture of the coloniser. Indian women writers, such as Zuleikha Mayat and Dr Goonam, try to find a balance between an English, colonial education and an Indian, traditional one where the family languages, cultural values and, in Mayat's case, religion, are assiduously learnt and assimilated. Agnes Sam, in the short story, "Jesus Is Indian," describes the need to assert non-western cultural values and reinterpret the kind of Christianity that is transmitted to her. Reddy, however, embraced and assimilated her colonial education with alacrity and in an uncomplicated way, and this English cultural affiliation shaped her identity almost entirely. English Literature provided her with an alternative world; in the autobiography Reddy, who describes herself as "an incorrigible book lover," writes:

> Reading was a road to discovery. I discovered the great English writers, Jane Austen, Dickens, D.H. Lawrence, Graham Greene, H.E. Bates, Hardy, Noel Coward and Bernard Shaw and Somerset Maughan. I have read every one of Shaw's plays and love them all. I remember the day I first saw a picture of him on the back of a paperback. I studied it for a long while. Why, it resembled exactly my childhood image of God! (Reddy, *Unbending* 41)

She recalls that the close identification she enjoyed with the English language and its literature instilled in her a desire to visit England:

> My favourite subject was English. I loved words and always waited for a suitable opportunity to use the new words I'd learnt. I loved the English language and for this

> reason I could never get enough of the great English writers [...]. Reading Dickens brought London alive to me. I could feel the harsh cold of the English winters, taste the Christmas dinners, feel the warmth of the wood fires. How I longed to visit London, Dickens' London and experience the beauty of the English countryside! For years I had a recurring dream in which I would find myself roaming the streets of London. I would be gripped by wonder and incredulity and then I would awake, frustrated. How I yearned to make that dream a reality! (43)

Reddy did make a trip to England with members of her family and ten others, as part of a special sponsored tour for handicapped persons. Her journey made her all too aware of the differences between Britain and South Africa, especially for disabled persons. Although the arrangements for the tour were poor, Reddy speaks of a dream come true as she visited all the familiar sights that she had known from her reading of English Literature—Oxford, Stratford-on-Avon, the Lake District, Abbotsford (the home of Sir Walter Scott). She even managed to visit the BBC for an interview.

In her critical reading of selected South African black women's autobiographies, Sarah Nuttall writes of "recognition" in reading, whereby identities are constructed outside the framework of apartheid through exposure to the world of English literature. Phyllis Ntantala, for example, Nuttall points out, records in her autobiography, *A Life's Mosaic* (1992), that when she was in England she visited familiar sites from her reading of English Literature. In living in the world of mainstream English Literature Reddy, like Ntantala, was presumably enjoying escape not only from "South African social realities" (Nuttall 6) and her own physical handicap, but was expanding her imaginative world, as "books and reading [are] adopted by the narrating self as signs of an 'intellectual' identity" (9). This world provided Reddy with "other shells for living in," to use Doris Lessing's words as pointed out by Nuttall.

"Writing the body"

In spite of, or perhaps because of, the tendency among some people to be inured to a handicap such as hers, in her autobiography Reddy constantly draws attention to it. She frequently gives many factual details concerning her illness, almost to counter any denial of or ignorance about it. As part of her natural curiosity about everything around her, she learnt a great deal about her muscular dystrophy. It was also a way of coping with her illness:

> But I tried to live with it all and did everything I wanted to. All this took years. It was a time of self-discovery too. I was learning about my abilities and my limitations [...]. I became my own physician. I understood my body better than any doctor. (Reddy, *Unbending* 70)

At a stylistic level, in Reddy's autobiography, writing about her body is more evident than "writing the body," where the latter is a "distinctively feminine kind of writing," referred to as "ecriture feminine" by Helene Cixous. In this type of writing the "sexual, psychic and physical identity of the female gender is given voice" (Gray 97). However, I am using the term to suggest that in Reddy's writing there is an attempt to "write the body" in another sense, where a body which is scripted with a certain negative identity in society is re-scripted wilfully and deliberately, and given a new and alternative identity, value and 'voice.'

In order to overcome her constricted reality, and the identity associated with such a condition, Reddy created an alternative identity through writing. "Writing the body" is indeed a way of transcending the body's 'infirmity.' In an interview with Annemarie Van Niekerk, Reddy states: "I especially enjoy creating a whole world of my own which outreaches any possible confinements" (in van Niekerk 74). Ironically, writing, in her condition, she points out, was a "profession that was highly suited to me" (Reddy, *Unbending* 10). (And given her frailty she writes short sustainable pieces. The autobiography follows the style of her short story writing in that it comprises vignettes of various incidents in her life.)

Writing gave her the satisfaction of "putting down your thoughts on paper and seeing a whole new world taking shape. A world you created" (Reddy, *Unbending* 10). Not able to participate more actively in that world, she was able to observe it, comment on it, and develop an imagined fictional world out of it. It was by watching the world around her, as her family moved from place to place, that prepared Reddy to eventually create fictions. In her autobiography she records that this predisposition started at a very early age:

> Hampson Grove, Warwick Avenue, Ajax Land, Wills Road, I knew it all. Sometimes Mother would place me on the balcony, seated on high pillows so that I could see the passing life on the street below. I was just four, but even then people fascinated me. I would watch the people moving up and down and wonder about them. Where did they go to and what did they do? Did they have children? Did they go to work? These were some of the questions that intrigued me and I would provide my own imaginary answers. (18)

Her personal condition did indeed enable her to become an acute observer of events and persons around her. As she writes in her autobiography: "Memories, impressions and thoughts all form part of the process. Then there is the observer in you, the observer that sees too much, whose perceptions are sharper than normal, whose heightened awareness enables him to sense things beyond the obvious" (10). Kathleen Komar states that many women writers "exploit an interior space that is not biological but psychological, a space that is eventually re-exteriorized in the form of the literary text itself" (Komar 97). The limitations that women generally experience make them use the literary text as a public space.

While very different from other women writers in respect of her physical disability, there is still an interesting resemblance between Reddy and the other South African black women autobiographers that have emerged of late. These writers validate their experiences through writing and, gaining narrative control and discursive power, write of the very experiences that were marginalised by apartheid history. The political role of autobiography for South African women writers that Jane Watts describes is, I believe, a view that has direct bearing on Reddy's writings:

> Autobiography is the South African writers' answer to [...] interference with their consciousness—they use it to try to reverse the conditioning process in order to free themselves, through reassessment of their entire growth and development, of their mental subjugation, to remake their consciousness [...]. Writing becomes a request for reassurance that they in fact have an identity, that they have rescued the fragments and shards of a personality from the systematic official attempt to eradicate it. (Watts 115)

South African black women writers have used the genre of autobiography to recreate identity. We see this explicit political purpose through 'life-writing' in black women's autobiographies such as Sindiwe Magona's *To My Children's Children* (1991), Emma Mashinini's *Strikes Have Followed Me All My Life* (1989), and Ellen Kuzwayo's *Call Me Woman* (1985). Jane Watts sees the autobiography as a "self-making process" for the South African black writer. She points out that it is "a means by which they can find the balance between themselves and the outside world and investigate that tension between the subjective and objective that orders our whole life" (114). We notice in Reddy's case a very specific version of this identity-creation: it is through her defining her identity as a writer, an identity that is part of and an extension of her 'life writing' that she is able to transcend the circumscribed spaces that she as a black woman with a physical disability is forced to endure. She is able to accept her physical condition with great equanimity, and make others do so as well. She goes even a step further in making her physical disability the very reason for her attempts to create an important literary space for herself. To achieve her ambition to become a writer, besides valuing her education, she bought a typewriter, assisted by her mother, took a course in journalism, joined a writing school, tried her hand at writing on a variety of issues and in several genres, and was not daunted by initial publishing disappointments. Accordingly, Reddy encourages others who are disabled to work hard to succeed: "If independence and dignity matter to you, then you'll surely work your fingers to the bone to achieve and retain it" (Reddy, *Unbending* 58).

Reddy's attempt to "write the body" then has two main facets. One is a narrative of bodily disability, exacerbated by the fact that she is black and a woman; the other is a narrative of enablement. Her increasing disablement as a person, the unfortunate bodily inconvenience she experienced, is juxtaposed with her increasing enablement as a writer. Writing affords her imaginative compensation and affirmation at the same time that she is enduring increasing physical deterioration.

There is a contrast between the confined world that she has to inhabit as a person, and the imaginative world that she is able to portray in her fictional writing. The physically straitened space which she inhabits is quite different from the unconstrained spaces of her imagination. She fashions an alternative self through her writing: in extending her sense of self, she is able to realise her social being in a measure that is quite remarkable—because of and in spite of her illness. Reddy transcends the limitations of her physical body to inhabit diverse racial, gendered, social, religious and cultural bodies.

At times Reddy uses experiences that surrounded her illness as grist for her fictional writing. Some of her short stories depict confinement that is similar to her own. In the short story, "Celebration," an old woman is confined to her room. In "A Gift for Rajendra" we encounter an itinerant barber who despairs because modernised services have now made him redundant. However he soon discovers a mother wanting to give her son, named Rajendra, a gift of regular haircuts. Rajendra is confined to a wheelchair and the barber's itinerancy is seen as a blessing. The character of the barber is based on a real-life person Reddy knew in Clare Estate. Other short stories are set in hospitals; it is evident from her autobiography that, owing to her condition, she was taken to hospital on several occasions. Conversely, she develops the silences in her autobiography into fictional accounts in her short stories. For example, private, emotional longings or experiences of love, marriage and childbirth, which are not alluded to in the autobiography, are dealt with in her short fiction. Ironically, in her autobiography, which foregrounds her body, she presents a "bodiless woman," to use Whitlock's phrase in another context (Whitlock 171), where sexual desire is not spoken of. Reddy probes this, however, vicariously in her fictional writing.

Spatial Restrictions and Apartheid Society

While the dominant trope that determines her narrative self-construction in the autobiography is that of her disability, her story is also located in the context of the racial divisions of the apartheid state. Alongside her physical constriction, Reddy is also restricted to the separate spaces dictated by apartheid.

The space that is depicted in Reddy's writings is a racially hierarchised one, and highlights the "spatial politics of difference" (Blunt and Rose 19) in South Africa, with the personal and the public being interwoven. The spaces in her narratives are to be seen in the context of the socio-political economy of apartheid and the Group Areas Act. Durban was the site of the original Group Areas legislation, designed specifically to keep the movement of Indians in urban areas in check, and to separate Africans, Whites, Coloureds and Indians from one another. Reddy recalls the previously integrated living that was destroyed: her aunt, Mutha, had a farm in New Germany, now an African township (Clermont); and an African woman with a large family—who owned a cow and supplied milk to the neighbourhood—lived in the neighbourhood in Clare Estate but had to sell her house and move out of the area.

The attempt to separate racial groups on the basis of cultural differences influences identity construction. Robert Thornton's observation in this respect shows the calculated severity of apartheid. He states that South Africa was—

> known for its apparent totalising system of social engineering in which the vision of 'apartness,' apartheid, was implemented through massive and violent spatial dislocation of much of its population in terms of a rationalised bureaucratic master plan of a total differentiation of

> spheres of life based on race and (what was the name for its architects) culture. (Thornton 142)

The places that one could call 'home' and that shaped one's identity were not mere accidents or the result of personal choice and means. The autobiography shows Reddy and her family confined to separate areas set aside for Indians. The existence of separate schools, separate libraries, and other facilities are well documented in the writings by Indian women. Ela Gandhi recounts a similar story in an interview with Diana Russell:

> Ever since I could remember, I was aware of living in the apartheid system. I travelled to school by train, and I always had to use the nonwhite compartments. Often I would see that the white compartments were empty, while ours were full, sometimes necessitating my standing all the way from Phoenix to Durban, which is about a forty-five minute journey. The amusement parks were only open to whites, the beaches were separate, and so on. These things made me bitter and aware that the whole system is inhuman. And the Africans suffered more than the Indians. (In Russell 135)

The tendency to "collapse space" began in the early indentured years, where Indians of different languages and castes, were forced to live together. In the "new leavening process" that inevitably evolved, a pan-Indian culture began to emerge, alongside internal differences (see Haraksingh 8). With this kind of segregated and compartmentalised living during the apartheid era, what occurred was a consolidation of this constructed communal life, where 'community' was developed and reified on essentialist notions of race and ethnicity.

Is Reddy, then, constructing an "ethnic autobiography," to use a phrase of Kamala Visweswaran's, where the story of a separate community is presented (Visweswaran 8)? And is this kind of writing, with its own demography of 'Indian areas,' peculiar to Indian writing in South Africa, and in this study, to that of Indian women writers? Linda Warley (1993) points out that spatial location is a crucial dimension in autobiographical self-representation in postcolonial writing, that self and identity are intimately tied up with where one lives in relation to other groups, especially since separated living is mapped out by the authorities. While the residential boundaries are becoming blurred in the new South Africa, it is still possible to think of different areas as being racially marked: Soweto, Chatsworth, Grey Street, Clermont, to name just a few, immediately conjure up racial territorialisations, and provide textual identity. This is clearly evident in Reddy's autobiographical writing, where she writes of the confined apartheid areas in which she and her family were forced to live.

Reddy may not strive to be overtly political, but her work is situated within the larger questions of race and apartheid. In conversations about her writing, she states quite simply that she writes, and does not reflect on her identity as a writer in any self-conscious way in terms of gender, race or class, or political affiliation. She does point out, though, that "if you are reflecting life in this country and the effect change and restrictive legislation has had on its people, then your work inevitably becomes political" (in van Niekerk 71). Encountering some of the evils of apartheid personally, she writes: "Not for the first time, I seethed at the idiotic laws that strangled life in this country" (Reddy, *Unbending* 108). At the time of her growing up—the 1950s—'separate development' became entrenched. Black Consciousness was to become more firmly established by the '70s, when a younger generation of Indians would identify with a larger black identity (Reddy's cousin, Saths Cooper, became a stalwart in the Black Consciousness movement and an ardent anti-apartheid activist, and was imprisoned on Robben Island).

Alongside her personal story of her physical trauma, Reddy recounts a wider story of socio-political constraint. She herself is poised on the "fringe of dreamtime" as she recalls in the autobiography a lost world that she enjoyed with her extended family, and the anguish of being uprooted from it. In this the autobiography may be seen as documenting both a personal as well as a collective history. In the autobiography there is a strong sense of communal memory, intertwined with personal memory. With constant control of individuals by apartheid policies, many communal memories were scripted as personal memories. Memory is especially potent in Reddy, who writes: "So many things stand out sharply in my mind, as sharply as peaks against a winter sky" (11).

Reddy's story traces the family's continual movement from one place to another. She writes of the constant removal and relocation that they were subjected to as a result of the Group Areas legislation. Reddy's family moved to different places in Durban and its surrounding areas. Her story begins with her growing up in the 60's in Briardene, a semi-rural area then outside Durban. Her father was born in Briardene, and worked for Bakers Limited as a "van boy," delivering bread by horse cart. This place, where she spent the first four years of her life, has a strong hold on her imagination. She remembers that Briardene "was a place full of rugged hills and valleys with deep mysterious shadows," with an unreality about it: "Today Briardene is no longer an Indian area but it still retains that haunted quality reminiscent of *Wuthering Heights*" (11). In addition to literary references she also occasionally claims a wider world of the cosmic and infinite through her writing. Her love of storms, the wilderness, and hills becomes evident and shows a desire to reach beyond the ephemeral, mundane, and local.

From Briardene the family then moves to the city, to live with her "granny." Reddy writes of life here—the hustle and bustle of life in this urban area—Hampson Grove, Warwick Avenue, Ajax Lane, Wills Road, where many Indians lived in the 50's. She notes that the "area in which we lived no longer exists as I remember it. A freeway runs right through it, flattening the quaint, interesting roads. Long before that however, people were forced out of the area through the Group Areas Act" (18). These are the same places that Phyllis Naidoo recalls in her writings, although Naidoo gives a different feel to these places through her experiences of shebeen life there and its vibrant multi-racial character.

Because of the uprooting, a sense of loss, and the memory of that loss, become inevitable motifs in Reddy's writing. Hints of the ancestral motherland from which they are uprooted, and of a "lamenting for their motherland" (Rooke 10), are particularly evident among the first generation of Indians who set foot in South Africa. While Reddy's father was born in South Africa, her grandfather came from "farming stock [...] in India" (Reddy, *Unbending* 22). This general sense of loss was then exacerbated by colonialism and apartheid, or at times, by personal tragedy. Her grandmother, Mungamma Reddy, for instance, had to move from their farm at Roosfontein, which was situated beyond the city in the suburban spaces of Westville, to the city on the death of her husband. She was an emotionally strong woman who earned her keep by selling her wares at a stall in the Indian market, and the account of her having to leave her old family home is heart-rending:

> Mungamma returned to Roosfontein, the day the old wood and iron house was pulled down. An old tree grew on the road, a silent witness to events. She stood under its familiar comfort and wept. For a home is more than brick and mortar, it's laughter and memories, pain and joy, warmth and sharing, living and being born, growing and developing. It's togetherness. It's a place to return to when everywhere else has palled, an eternal truth so poignantly made in the parable of the Prodigal Son. (23)

Memory in Reddy's writing is often linked to a sense of place, particularly those places from which her family are removed. There is a longing for the lost countryside. Flora and fauna are an intrinsic part of Reddy's story. There is regret that the quality of existence they knew has to make way for inevitable, creeping change: "The beautiful wilderness was carved up and sold [...]. Everyone lauded the changing environment, labelling it progress and improvement" (29). The wilderness and the bushes gradually recede, and Reddy recalls: "We no longer see that many birds and butterflies. Fireflies used to be so common but I no longer see them. Spiders, frogs and snakes have all become rare" (29). It was the time when an iguana would come to bask on a neighbour's front lawn. What emerges through the descriptions in the autobiography is a strong sense of violation of the idyllic countryside.

The experiences of dislocation due to apartheid policies and practices are not peculiar to Reddy, but are a common theme that runs through many examples of South African literature by black writers. Ronnie Govender in the Epilogue to his collection of short stories set in Cato Manor, *At the Edge and other Cato Manor Stories*, writes of the loss that so many Indians experienced when they had to move from Cato Manor to Chatworth:

> CATO MANOR
> silence now and bush
> no more Discovery Road
> no more Trimborne Road
> no more hopscotch
> no more ripe mangoes from Thumba's yard
> Cato Manor, you have done your penance
> amid crumpled eviction notices.
> (Govender 159)

This "death of Cato Manor," as recorded in literature, is similar to that of Sophiatown described by Bloke Modisane and Can Themba, or of District Six by writers such as Alex La Guma and Richard Rive (*see* Ehmeir 27-28). These separate places become symbolic of the spatial location of apartheid society. These scenarios are also taken up in Farida Karodia's *Daughters of the Twilight*, and in Goonam's autobiography, *Coolie Doctor*. The recent memoir of Pushpam Murugan, *The Lotus Blossoms on the Eastern Vlei* (1997), documents the history of Indian families living in Magazine Barracks in Durban before the removals between 1964 and 1966. While Ronnie Govender depicts the effects that Cato Manor had on men, Reddy and Karodia show the loss that both men and women experienced through such relocations. Similarly, in her autobiography *Call me Woman*, Ellen Kuzwayo tells of the world that was lost by her family when they were forced to move in 1974 from their freehold farm which they had owned from the 1880's. And Pippa Green (1998) speaks of the "bulldozers and jackhammers of apartheid" that destroyed Ozzie Docrat's home in Pageview around 1978, a story that is recorded by David Goldblatt in *South Africa the Structure of Things Then*, referred to already.

A Range of Subject Positions

In her short stories Reddy attempts to transgress the ethnically and racially constricted spatial world that she depicts in her autobiography. While Reddy does not present a wide regional landscape, as do Sam and Karodia, she moves from crowded city sites ("Market Days"), to peri-urban and suburban settings ("The Spirit of Two Worlds"), to rural ones in Natal ("A Gift for Rajendra" and "A Dream at Sunset").

Although she is generally the omniscient narrator in the short stories, Reddy does develop her plots around protagonists from different racial and gender positions, and moves into "Group Areas" quite different from those she is personally accustomed to. The short stories show a range of subject positions and identifications in her attempt to constitute a new ethical whole as she recreates and restores a sense of community destroyed by apartheid. Drawing from the peculiar socio-political aspects of life in South Africa as a rich narrative resource, she presents situations confronting persons of all population groups.

The short story "The Slumbering Spirit" is about a young Coloured boy named Terry who grows in confidence and self-awareness through the love and attention of a surrogate mother. It is set in the period before the Group Areas Act in a neighbourhood where Coloureds, Indians, Whites and Chinese live together. Terry's family are sceptical of his friendship with a White woman, but Terry appreciates that the woman has time for a young person such as he, lost in a large family of ten:

> Miss Anderson had given him something, something more precious than anything material. Years later, he was to recognise it for what it really was. But standing there in the cool night air, with a lift of the heart, he remembered a gentle old woman on a sun-warmed step. She had given

> him time and friendship, and something else which his fourteen-year-old mind was too young to analyse. It was awakening, an awakening of the slumbering spirit to mutual sharing and communication and sympathetic understanding. And that was something he would carry with him for a lifetime. (Reddy, 1987: 120)

The picture of a caring woman in "The Slumbering Spirit" is similar to the kind of neighbours Reddy herself had when her family lived in Hampson Grove. In her autobiography Reddy notes that "the woman of the house, a plump motherly woman, loved children, even though she had four of her own" (Reddy, *Unbending* 19). As pointed out earlier, Reddy was also loved and affirmed by the women in her family—her grandmother, aunts and her mother. She understands well the transfiguring effect that such love can have on an individual.

Reddy takes a critical view of those who show race and class prejudice, and portrays complex inter-race relationships, as in the short story, "Two Friends." In this short story, the 'madam,' Sadhana, who has been married for eleven years, is trapped in a boring marriage. She watches films on television to pass the time. Her domestic employee, Bessie, brings her little daughter, Phumza, to work, and Sadhana's daughter, Asha, and Phumza become "two friends." Asha, who seems angry at being neglected by her mother, tramples her doll, while Phumza looks on with horror, especially since she nurtures a secret desire to own a golden-haired doll of her own. Phumza nurses the doll, putting it on her back "in the manner of generations of African mothers" (Reddy, 1987: 110). She is bonding with the 'child' in a way that Sadhana does not seem capable of in relation to her daughter. When Asha sees this she demands her doll back, and Bessie, all too aware of the limits of a 'friendship' tempered by class and race differences, tells her daughter to return the doll. Sadhana, in the meantime, watches the scene with amused detachment and is unable to see that she is caught in a conflict in which she is both estranged and estranging. She is oblivious to the dynamic between madam and servant, self and other, and the way this is played out between herself and Bessie and their children.

Bessie's silence and acquiescence show her in the role of non-person or subaltern, and Reddy is suggesting a racial and class polarity that prevents a sisterhood across these divisions.

The short story, "The Stolen Hours," also depicts the experiences of a domestic employee, who dreams of wearing a much-coveted dress owned by her employer. The employee wears the dress when the family are away on holiday, and spends a few glorious hours imagining herself in another world. Domestic employees, mainly African women, with no institutionalised other to oppress, are a permanent underclass, and Reddy is conscious of their plight. In her autobiography, she speaks a great deal about her relationship with her domestic employees, as she is dependent on them. She also describes her own reservations and prejudices, although in her short stories she transcends them (It is worth noting that Rosemary, mentioned in the autobiography, still works in Reddy's home in Clare Estate, and is the housekeeper for her brother Mags).

Reddy does not confine her short stories to experiences peculiar to Indians (as is generally true of her autobiography), but is also able to write imaginatively and empathically of relationships among Africans themselves. In her short story, "The Love Beads," the typical love triangle is given a new twist. Jacob, a rickshaw driver, is involved in an accident and taken to hospital, where he meets Mandy, a nurse. In a world of hardship and impoverishment, and separated from his wife by apartheid laws, he feels a strong attraction to the nurse—"her sweetness reminded him of the sweetness of swiftly flowing streams. Her warmth was like the warmth of the sun in winter, gentle and welcome" (22). He luxuriates in the attention he receives at the hospital, and imagines fleetingly that he is falling in love with Mandy. He soon comes to realise that the nurse is going to get married, and that he has to live his own life, and value what he has. He begins to appreciate his wife's faithfulness and gentleness towards him, symbolised by the love beads, of red, yellow and black, given to him by her: "He fingered the beads absently. Then he realised what an important link the beads were between his life in the city and his life in the Transkei. It was a link that was umbilical" (23).

At the same time as Reddy writes of other race groups, her personal experiences make her sensitive to the experiences of other Indians, especially in relation to dislocation and loss. In the title short story, "On the Fringe of Dreamtime," Reddy shows how the strong bonds between people and the places they have cultivated are severed. She tells the story of an Indian man (it is significant that he is nameless) who returns to his old homestead, now turned into a "Group Area" for whites:

> He ran his hand along the arm of the branch which was still as strong as ever. Here his father had hung a makeshift swing, by tying two ends of a rope to the branches and placing a sack over it for a seat [...]. To him it had been more than an ordinary tree. He had come to love it in all its moods and it became a symbol of safety, a source of strength like a sturdy and reliable friend. (61)

The tree stands as a link to a lost life, as it conjures up memories of the past:

> The mistiness of memory cleared and he became aware that everything else about the place was strange and unfamiliar. Only the tree remained, a silent witness to time and its pain. There, on the fringe of dreamtime, he could hear echoes of past laughter and knew once more the searing pain of heartbreak. (62)

The evocative description shows the extent to which it was possible to dream unhindered of a time when there was a tacit connectedness with all things:

> Down at the stream, he imagined he heard his mother slapping the washing on the stones and singing the folk songs of her youth [...]. The crabs would crawl out of the water [...]. He and his brother would sit on the rocks and watch them, fascinated [...]. They were at one with all of creation [...]. (65)

The description also heightens the dereliction of the present, and the alienation is further exacerbated by the new White occupants who see the Indian man as an intruder. Narratives such as these show how the Group Areas legislation and subsequent disruptions in its living arrangements were to directly influence the creation of identities: Zoe Wicomb has argued, referring to District Six, that "ethnicity was constructed within a politics of nostalgia that sentimentalised the loss" (Wicomb 95), where such "loss" was directly related to "group areas" from which groups and communities were removed.

Undergirding all her short stories is the unmistakable reality of apartheid life in South Africa, and all that comes with it: racial tension and conflict, bigotry, dislocation, a yearning and desire to be accepted in an alien world. Highlighting the "ordinary" rather than "spectacle," Reddy writes of quotidian reality rather than of the macro-political world. She shows the effects of racism at an individual, domestic and personal level. There are both fissures in racially-defined relationships as well as courageous attempts to bridge such schisms. We see a tension between acceptance of conventional racialised thinking—of white dominance as part of the order of things—and of incipient resistance to it. Like Sam and Karodia, there are instances of prejudice and discrimination among oppressed groups themselves, and also empathy with other oppressed race groups.

Gendered Spaces and Identity: Living in the Yard

In Reddy's writings, identity is spatially defined not only in terms of race, but also of gender. In her autobiography there are descriptions of racially separate spaces, but in many instances these are also gendered spaces, with their own 'female subculture.' When the family moved to Clare Estate, Reddy describes a striking picture of communal life, of "living in the yard," a common space between homes that is usually used for social interaction. "The yard" is at once a private and public space—private, as it is peripheral to dominant White places, and public, as it provides interaction for those who are marginalised. It is also a gendered space, where women gather together to converse or pursue domestic tasks traditionally assigned to them. Reddy describes the daily, ordinary routine and rituals of Indian women who are juxtaposed in such communal spaces.

In the autobiography there are vivid scenes of women working at daily, ordinary, gendered chores—winnowing rice, cooking on open fires, cleaning vegetables or preparing sheep heads for consumption (Reddy regrets the fact that a scene of the singeing of a sheep's head was left out of her script, *Web of Persuasion*, when it was sent for publication. It is likely that this was seen as too culturally idiosyncratic for Western readers). Life revolves around food, and with this, the sharing of taboos, such as those pertaining to the eating of pork and beef. We read of an itinerant seamstress, with her treadle sewing machine, who periodically becomes the focus of attention. Modern luxuries are sparse, with all the neighbours using the only fridge in the yard. In the need to survive, women play a central role and act, as usual, as stabilisers of communal living. During their time together they share gossip, but also details of their own personal lives, of abuse or disappointment.

In relation to the yard-space, Brinda Mehta ponders on a "reconfiguring of the politics of the household" in her interesting analysis of the Indo-Caribbean home. Mehta argues that "serving as community space, the yard also provides the necessary space to establish a centre for political and social advising for women, resembling a village panchayat or council.... Female power is thus located in the dual capacity to negotiate one's way through the inner machinations of the home as well as through life's forces, represented by the yard and its capacity to function as a microcosm of a more global, external exchange" (Mehta 10).

These liminal, communal spaces, then, help women create, shape, modify and claim identity. Are these recuperative spaces as Kathleen Komar suggests, enclosed female spaces, reminiscent of the womb? Are they seen as places of confinement in which women are contained and separated from male social space (Komar 91)? In Karodia's *Daughters of the Twilight*, the kitchen becomes the space where the women meet and strategise about dealing with the world. While recuperative in terms of gender and class, it also provides community in the face of a dehumanising public life in terms of race. Dorothy Driver notes that the "search for a self-constituting community is important because of the damage done to black South Africans in an apartheid culture" (Driver 232). This is particularly so for black women, given their marginalisation at several levels. In Reddy's own case these intimate communal spaces provide the security she requires in an alienating world; they also symbolise the doubly constricted world to which she is confined by apartheid as well as by her handicap. These spaces play a complex, contradictory role in the formation of her career as a writer: she is nurtured in these familial spaces to become confident enough in herself to be a writer; at the same time she is able to transcend these very confined spaces in and through her writing.

In the closed communal context we see a preclusion of any introspective, psychological probing of living in a segregated society. Dr Goonam, for example, is only able to claim a critical, interpretive voice against alienation from the wider South African community when she has moved out of the false security of a confined, racially-constructed, communal space. And paradoxically Phyllis Naidoo appropriates an apartheid gaol as the liberatory space for the creation and celebration of racial solidarity and a sense of community with persons of different racial groups.

It is this implicit critique of racialised and gendered spaces that makes Reddy in her short stories, in contrast to her autobiography, depict a wider and more intricate canvas of social relations in the context of racial and gender divisions. The women in Reddy's autobiography are resilient and assertive, supporting their men in decisions that have to be made. In her short stories a more complex picture of women in domestic spaces emerges; they are found in varying and diverse social relationships, some stifling and others liberating. The women may be seen as struggling between individualistic inclinations to be free and independent, and traditional, conservative influences that pin them down. There is a negotiation and appropriation of private, gendered spaces, or an attempt to transcend their confines to recreate female identity. For example, in "Celebration," Shamala resolves to leave a suffocating marriage and start a new life with her young son; however, in "A Time to Yield" a young bride, Zainab, acquiesces, as the title suggests, to the pressure from her family into entering a marriage about which she has grave doubts.

The dire effects for women of the changing times on family and communal relationships are alluded to constantly in the short stories. In "The Spirit of Two Worlds," seething conflict between an older, conservative mother-in-law and a younger, modern, daughter-in-law develops. Reddy draws on the narrow conformity and claustrophobic atmosphere of the extended family, or *kutum*, the gendered roles that are usually assumed in these domestic contexts, and the pressures, both internal and external, that come to bear upon it. The story takes us into the world of South Africa's cramped council-house and tenement living. Sharda, the daughter-in-law, longs to be independent, to live on her own, and to go out to work. She wishes to claim an alternative space, both literally and metaphorically.

In this short story family life is centred around the domineering figure of the mother-in-law, who expects compliance. This matriarch works hard to keep the family together, running a market stall in the city, and resisting any threat to a carefully constructed and 'stable' sense of family. Her own work outside the home is based on sheer survival; she cannot understand why her daughter-in-law should choose to work to escape "boredom." A state of boredom, the mother-in-law reflects, is surely a modern disease: "Her mind went back over the years searching for something which remotely resembled this malady, but there was nothing. There had been hardships, countless sacrifices which had been made willingly, much pain and heart-break and some rare and memorable moments of joy and happiness, but never boredom" (Reddy, 1987: 11). After the son and daughter-in-law leave to make an independent home, and their first child arrives, the mother relents, thereby preserving the ritual bonds of the extended family.

In her TV drama, *The Web of Persuasion* (1984), written especially to present a South African Indian setting (there were other scripts in the series that were written by other writers presenting "English, Afrikaans, Coloured and black" settings), Reddy explores this question of women's independence in the face of traditional constraints. The play, deftly juxtaposing the old world and a new emerging one, begins with several conversations among guests at the scene of an Indian wedding. There is a stark contrast between the conversations of the adults and those of their children. The women talk of the way children behave "these days"; they recall how weddings were conducted previously, and of the times when there was more land for the joint family system. They are conscious of differences in linguistic preferences, wealth and even complexion—"best to marry your own kind" (Reddy, 1984: 4).

Mrs Singh wishes for an arranged marriage for her daughter Indira, while Indira prefers instead to go to university to study law. The mother asserts, "I know what is best for you and my plans are made" (7). Indira sees the way her sister-in-law is trapped in an unhappy marriage. When the two families meet and the ritual of serving the tea is endured, Indira begins to realise that Anil, the "arranged" suitor, feels just as uncomfortable as she does about the whole affair. The two resist their family's overtures, and find that they could be friends by fighting a tradition that is mindlessly perpetuated. "My mother is doing what her mother did, and her mother. Daughters must be married off. I wish I were a man" (18).

Indira wishes to assert her independence: "I'm not a parcel to be wrapped up and handed over as a gift, Ma. I have a mind. I have feelings and I have a right to choose [...]. If you wanted to sell me for the best offer you should have kept me in purdah" (25). The mother is the voice of tradition, sectarianism and patriarchy: "Rights, rights. You talk about rights. You are a child. You are a girl, and you are a Hindu" (25). Indira tries to run away, but is resigned in the end to her marriage, when she is presented with two options only: accepting the partner that has been chosen for her, or being abandoned to a life of loneliness, thereby bringing "disgrace" to the family. The play ends with the prospect of the two, Indira and her husband, beginning to understand each other, and accommodating each other's ambitions.

In the short story "A Time to Yield" (referred to already) in the collection *On the Fringe of Dreamtime and Other Stories*, however, a woman's resistance is not accommodated but transformed into acquiescence. We witness a domestic scene before a wedding day, mainly involving the chief women players of the occasion—a bride, her mother, sister, and grandmother. Zainab, the young bride, is experiencing doubt, anger, reluctance, bitterness and dread at the prospect of being forced into a marriage against her wishes. The rest of the women around her play ambiguous roles, forcing her to be submissive, to endure, and accept her lot, in the hope that she will be happy and that love will grow during the marriage. An inverted sisterhood is evident as pressure is exerted on the bride to adapt and acquiesce. For women caught between tradition and modernity, and seen as the pillars in social relations, conformity and compliance is the expedient route. Here Reddy writes of the restlessness, the conflict and anxiety that women experience over traditional roles, but does not depict outright revolt. However, in the short story, "Celebration," referred to above, Shamala the female protagonist, trapped in a restrictive marriage, realises that she can give the story of her life a different ending if she wills it. Beginning a new life by leaving her marriage and transforming the gender roles imposed on her is her "celebration."

Conclusion: Infirmity, Identity, Writing, Voice and Power

In her autobiography Reddy constantly returns to the problem of her helplessness. Yet hers is also a powerful story of the overcoming of the body's infirmity, of claiming power through carving out an identity as a writer. Constantly interspersed with the accounts of her muscular dystrophy is a detailed chronological account of her progress as a writer. She describes her early successes and failures, her sustained effort to continue writing and to get her work published. In this it is important to note that the power and influence that she claims is not social (her passing away in 1996 went almost unnoticed), economic or political, but moral. Visweswaran argues that identities are constructed by power:

> Autobiographies are, of course, fictions of the self, but in my view, this emphasis on pluralism leads to a notion of "trying on identities," which obscures the fact that identities, no matter how strategically deployed, are not always chosen, but are in fact constituted by relations of power always historically constituted. (Visweswaran 8)

Reddy claims the power of the word and power and agency through the word because of and in spite of her physical privations. Her life shows a struggle against any such deterministic, "historically constituted" identities that might have been conferred on her, especially in view of her physical condition and her racialised and gendered experiences. She engages in a powerful and persuasive "politics of articulation"—to use the term coined by Pratima Parmar in writing about the empowerment of black women in Britain—both in her life and in her writing, and in representing elements of the 'self,' which are considered 'other' by dominant systems of representation she reclaims, empowers and defines (and redefines) herself (see Parmar 116). In spite of her physical handicap, Reddy is able to traverse different worlds, and wield immense power especially in "the world of the imagination." As she writes in her autobiography:

> I live in three different worlds at once. The real world in which I live and move, the world of the imagination peopled by characters of my choice, where I play god the creator, retainer, disposer and destroyer, and the world to come which the Bible promises as the second Eden. (Reddy, *Unbending* 76)

She has extended the "autobiographical pact" by creating an "autobiographical space" that also includes her fiction, prompting us to read the one in relation to the other (see

Lejeune 1989). Reddy's muscular dystrophy directly determines the assertion of her identity through writing, the need to inscribe a 'self' contrary to the one ascribed to her. In most South African black women's writings—Bessie Head, Zoe Wicomb, Gcina Mhlophe—the body, gendered and racialised, plays a significant part in the formation of subjectivity. Sidonie Smith's cogent observation from the point of view of the politics of the body has particular relevance to questions of identity in these autobiographical writings. Smith notes that "those positioned peripherally to the dominant group, those claiming and/or assigned marginalised identities, find themselves partitioned in their bodies" (Smith 10). But the "double jeopardy" (through race and gender) that feminists have usually talked about in relation to these "partitioned" bodies is extended to a *multiple* one in Reddy's case, making her work a unique and classic study in the "politics of otherness" among autobiographical writings by black women in South Africa.

3

South Asian Diasporic Women's Short Fiction: The South African Contribution

Samantha Naidu

This article examines the short story genre and how it is deployed by women writers of the South Asian diaspora. The general argument is that an over-arching transnational feminist aesthetic is being inscribed by women writers of the South Asian diaspora. In particular, the article focuses on short story writing by South African women of South Asian descent. To facilitate this focus I provide an overview of South African women's writing, and give a brief historical account of the South Asian diaspora in South Africa. A close reading of some stories from Jayapraga Reddy's collection, *On the Fringe of Dreamtime and Other Stories* (1987) is then presented.

Genre, History, Context

The short story genre is highly favoured by women writers of the South Asian diaspora. Many collections from different diasporic locations have been published in the last decade. Perhaps most notable has been Jhumpa Lahiri's *Interpreter of Maladies* (1999) which won the Pen/Hemingway Award and the 2000 Pulitzer Prize for fiction. Lahiri was also selected for *The Best American Short Stories* and the O'Henry Award. Although these collections contain stories with a wide range of themes and subjects, many of the stories deal with feminist and diasporic issues. The question here is why do these writers use the short story form of narrative, and further, is there anything distinctive about their use of it?

The classification and categorization of the short story is extremely contentious and difficult. The general understanding that the short story is a short fictional, prose narrative, has over the years, been challenged by many arguments about the porousness of the generic boundaries of the form. J.A. Cudden stresses the formal diversity of the short story which derives from other forms such as myths, legends, fables parables, fairy tales, anecdotes and even the essay. He concludes that in "the end the form has shown itself to be flexible and susceptible of so much variety that its possibilities seem almost endless" (Cudden 1970: 623). Nirmal Verma has placed the short story in the liminal space between the novel and the poem and identifies its distinguishing feature as the 'imaginative potency of language" (Verma 1984: 48-50). Other critics, such as John Metcalf, have commented on this "potency" of the form, linking it to its intensity, brevity and striving for a single effect (1981: 110).

However, this distinguishing feature does not obliterate other constitutive features. As Verma concedes, the "structures have surely loosened but they have not disintegrated" (*ibid.* 43). Surely, short stories, despite innovations and experimentation, contain the basic element of narrative—a plot. Ian Reid expands on this notion of a basic framework for the form. He argues that a well written short story evinces three essential qualities: "it makes a single impression on the reader, it does so by concentrating on a crisis, and it makes that crisis pivotal in a controlled plot" (1977: 54). Reid does admit that these qualities are essential to novels too, but contends that they have to make a more striking impact in a short story in order to be moving and aesthetically satisfying (*ibid.*).

Not all writers and critics will subscribe to these three essential qualities of a short story, but on the whole, they seem to agree on the potency, intensity, and concentrated *effect* of the form. Notwithstanding the ongoing debate, this effect, it seems, derives mainly from the structural imperatives (such as a single focal point in the plot) which result from, and contribute to, the concise form of the short story. For prose writers seeking this kind of maximum impact with minimum dimensions, the short story then is the ideal form. Alka Kumar has noted that "the short story genre, with its structural use of the spotlight technique, and often the epiphany, to create heightened effect, is an appropriate form to attain concentrated focus" (2002: 56). For writers also a highly concentrated strategy is used when producing a short story, as Anita Desai confides in an interview: "a short story demands something quite different, you have to have the whole of it quite clear in your mind and just put it down at one throw" (1987: 13). The women writers of the South Asian diaspora are grappling with two main thematic areas: the oppression of women within patriarchy; and the dislocated diasporic identity. Both these themes have intensely personal significance for the writers who often incorporate lived experience into their fictional accounts of gender discrimination and diasporic tensions. Their writing is therefore self-representing, politicized and often aimed at liberation and self-empowerment through a hard-hitting form. For these reasons it is apparent why the short story which is "at once concise and evocative in its linguistic/grammatical usage and imagistic pattern respectively, [and] allows its writer to combine compression with an effulgence" (Celly 2002: 45), is favoured by these writers.

The short stories by women of the South Asian diaspora are often located in the present and they deal with immediate social realities, but they also contain personal memories or they traverse the space between the homeland and the diasporic location. In the evocative and poignant instances of female oppression narrated in these stories, a transnational resonance is evident. Not only are there similarities between women from different South Asian diasporic locations, but also many patterns of subjugation and gender discrimination common to other cultures and nations is apparent. The plurality and specificity of lived moments and everyday reality are captured in these stories.

The South African South Asian Diasporic Context

The specificity of the South African South Asian diasporic context is of particular relevance in this article. To contextualise the close reading of Jayapraga Reddy's short stories which follows, a brief historical account of the South Asian diaspora in South Africa, and an overview of South African South Asian women's writing, is provided.

Between 1860 and 1911, 384 ships carried 152,184 indentured immigrants from India to the British colony of Natal. These immigrants were contracted to their employers, white farmers, who were experimenting with sugar production, for a minimum of five years. Not quite slaves, these labourers were not quite free either. They worked under harsh conditions, were subjected to floggings and pass laws, and were undeniably exploited. After the period of indenture they had the option of a free passage back to India or they could remain in the colony as "free Indians." About half the immigrants decided to stay (Dhupelia-Mesthrie 10-11). But in 1895 a three pound tax on every ex-indentured Indian was imposed, with the desired effect that many Indians returned to India and many re-indentured (*ibid.* 16). Writers such as Jayapraga Reddy, Agnes Sam and Farida Karodia are descended from these indentured immigrants. For the women writers of the South Asian diasporic community, the "story of Indian indentured labour" formed the "the inevitable historical backdrop" (Govinden 2001: 23) for much of their work.

The 1895 three pound tax was just the beginning of many restrictive laws, which controlled Indian trade, Indian movement, education, and marriage, for over a century, until 1994, and the establishment of a democracy in South Africa. These restrictive laws formed part of the national *apartheid* regime which, based on segregation of the races, was designed by the white minority government in the 1940s and 1950s to subjugate and exploit the black races. For most of the twentieth century these immigrants, together with the indigenous black population and the 'Coloured' population of the country, lived under an increasingly intransigent and repressive white regime. Writing by women of South Asian diasporic community strongly reflects the exigencies of living under the regime's segregationist policies which resulted in widespread dislocation and relocation for the already transplanted South Asian immigrants. Betty Govinden describes the writing by women who were also political activists as "important historical documentation of the narratives of resistance against apartheid" (2001: 26). She singles out Dr Goonam, Phyllis Naidoo and Fatima Meer as authors whose "personal itinerary is assimilated into a larger historical narrative of resistance and struggle" (Harlow 1994: 117). But Govinden is most concerned with the marginalisation of Indian women writers in South African literary historiography and criticism:

> Indian women's writings in South Africa have obviously been smothered in the larger politics of marginality that has attended the production and reception of literary texts historically, to the extent that the marginalisation has gone unnoticed even in corrective archaeological work.... This may have been caused by several factors. Given the separation of racial groups historically, and the dominance of male writers, the literary achievements of Indian women have not been widely known by local Western audiences. Since these efforts have been relegated to the margins of South African society, anthologists, publishers and researchers have been inclined to gloss over them. (2001: 3-4)

It is certainly the case that literary practice has reflected wider social dynamics and works by South Asian women have not been widely published, read, studied or critically examined in South Africa. Until the 1980s very few works by black writers, male or female, were published in the mainstream literary market, but in this decade which saw two States of Emergency in South Africa, local black writers began to be more pointedly represented. Govinden describes this development, on the part of a handful of publishers and critics, as "a self-conscious attempt at this time to see the literary establishment become less elitist, to recover forgotten indigenous texts, and to encourage the enterprises of new local literary publishers in anthologies" (Govinden 2001: 8). But, according to Govinden, the decade of the 1980s ended with scant critical attention being accorded to Indian women's writings. The late 1980s saw some attempt to include the writings of Indian women, but this occurred selectively and unevenly. Govinden points out that the

> only female writer who seemed to have enjoyed any critical attention in these years was Jayapraga Reddy. In the retrospective edition of *Staffrider*, *Ten Years of Staffrider* (1988), Reddy's short story, "The Spirit of Two Worlds" was included. Later anthologies were to continue with this trend. Percy Mosieleng and Temba Mhambi have included Reddy's short story, *Friends*, in their collection, *Contending Voices in South African Fiction* (1993). (2001: 11)

Reddy's inclusion in a climate of exclusion and marginalisation for black women writers is unusual and fascinating, and warrants further exploration.

In 1990 Annemarié van Niekerk published *Raising the Blinds: A Century of South African Women's Stories.* In her introduction to this anthology Van Niekerk attempts to challenge not only the socio-political restrictions which had crippled literary practice in South Africa, but also the generic boundaries which limit short story writing. Her marrying together of literary critical discourse with anti-apartheid rhetoric is indicative of the broader processes of resistance and transformation which began in South Africa in the 1990s. Van Niekerk's project also includes a gynocritical element in that she is concerned with "ending the confinement and culturally induced blindness concerning women as storytellers and writers in South Africa" (1990: 11). In this respect, Van Niekerk is anxious to include women writers from every cultural and racial category in South Africa, although she does recognize the disparity between the opportunities which were available to white middle and upper class women and black working class and peasant women (*ibid.*). The anthology contains Jayapraga Reddy's ubiquitous story "Friends" and Farida Karodia's "Something in the Air." These two prose narratives, which adhere in many ways to the definitions of the genre offered by Cudden, Verma and Kumar, are placed alongside indigenous oral narratives and works by internationally acclaimed authors such as Doris Lessing and Nadine Gordimer. In addressing the imbalances of the past at a cross-roads moment, South African literary critics like Van Niekerk have had a tricky path to negotiate. How could they be inclusive and fully representative of a multi-cultural society which is acutely sensitive of its historical divisions? How could they conduct comprehensive and affirmative scholarship without generalizing and eliding differences which implicated them with a nationalist discourse of facile unity and solidarity? In an unwitting contradiction, Van Niekerk stresses her ambition to be all-inclusive: "This anthology, however, intends to bring together a representative selection of all the South African women short fiction writers, *disregarding* their race and class or the dominant aesthetic tradition" (1990: 17 my emphasis).

In order for Van Niekerk to edit, introduce and publish "a representative selection of all the South African women short fiction writers" she would have to pay particular regard to the race, class and aesthetic tradition of the writers. Five pages before the above statement is made, Van Niekerk clearly asserts her desire to recognize difference by compiling "a representative selection of work by women narrators from the country's wide spectrum of social and cultural positions and endeavours to compare divergent and interrelated themes, and the various narrative forms and styles" (1990: 12).

Elsewhere, for example in her article "Feminist Aesthetics: Aspects of Race, Class and Gender in the Constitution of South African Short Fiction by Women" (1993), Van Niekerk emphasises *difference* as a crucial analytical tool which, if re-articulated positively, would help South Africans to live "with incommensurability through new ethical and democratic frameworks, within a culture that both recognizes difference and is committed to resolving its antagonisms" (1993: 26).[1] For difference to be recognized and celebrated it has to be described. This is precisely what Reddy achieves in her short stories—an accentuation of difference in the national context using the intense, concise, high-impact style of the short story genre. In the transnational context, an analysis of the differences *and similarities* between women writers of the South Asian diaspora serves to increase our understanding of the dynamics of diaspora, as well as of the feminist causes of women of South Asian descent.

Migrancy: A New Form of Aesthetic Freedom?

Jayapraga Reddy is remarkable for a number of reasons. She is one of the first Indian woman short fiction writers to publish a collection of short stories in South Africa. Added to the disadvantage of being both a woman and black in *apartheid* South Africa, she suffered from muscular dystrophy and grew up in a poor, working class home. But by the time of her death in 1997 Reddy's writing had become largely representative of Indian women's writing in South Africa (Govinden 2001: 16). The publication of her collection of short stories by Skotaville, the first black publishing company in South Africa, is heralded as a highly significant moment in the country's literary history because it "exposes the silenced world of the South African Indian woman as a world riven with ideological ruptures" (Van Niekerk 1993: 77). In addition to this gynocritical achievement, Reddy also entered the wider forum of race and class politics in South Africa. For this heterogeneous political commitment Reddy receives unreserved praise:

> Her narratives reflect a far greater awareness of the dynamics operating within gender, race and class intersections than the early white women short fiction writers. She positions her characters in confrontational relations, but analytically examines the nature of this interaction, instead of blindly reproducing dominant ideology. (Van Niekerk 1990: 24)

Thus far critical studies of Reddy's work have focused almost entirely on the political and social significance of her writing, but very little analysis of the literary aesthetics employed by Reddy has been conducted. What follows is an assessment of her "grounded aesthetics," that is, the textual strategies she used in her short story writing which serves as a form of personal and cultural survival (Flockemann 1998: 12-13).

In Jayapraga Reddy's work, as will be shown later, the primary tensions are within the diasporic home where the horrors of apartheid supersede any discomfort or difficulty characters might experience as a result of cultural dislocation or patriarchal oppression. On the whole the most distinctive feature of the literature produced by women of the South Asian diaspora in South Africa, is the precedence the issue of racial discrimination takes over affiliations to homeland or a traditional cultural heritage. At the same time, Reddy, like her counterparts in other diasporic locations, does address the topic of "Indian-ness," and the plight of women labouring to be free from diverse forms of oppression. But in Reddy, similar to other fiction produced during the *apartheid* era, the grappling with imposed categories of race, is imperative.

As a descendant of indentured labourers, Reddy's history is a complex one fraught with oppression, discrimination, displacement and marginalization. She was born in Durban in 1947, three years before the infamous Group Areas Act (which separated residential areas according to race) was introduced. She fought a life-long battle against muscular dystrophy and was wheelchair bound. She cites her family, in particular her mother and her grandmother, as the main support and influence in her life, and indeed, much of her writing is dedicated to the diverse strengths and plights of her gender. This is an obvious commonality with other women writers who originate in the South Asian sub-continent. To add to Reddy's heterogeneity, her family were staunch Jehovah's Witnesses in a predominantly Hindu community, a faith which she embraced. The subject of disparate cultures and religions co-existing in one household is not dealt with explicitly by Reddy, but other writers explore this theme compellingly, for example, Agnes Sam in the title story of her short story collection, *Jesus is Indian* (1989).

Uncommonly, for the time, Reddy received an education, but not without enormous struggle. It was not common practice for Indian females to be educated, and due to separate education policies for the different races in *apartheid* South Africa, black schools were ill-equipped, let alone for a handicapped child. But Reddy persevered with her colonial education and discovered that she had a strong attraction for English culture. In her unpublished autobiography, *The Unbending Reed*, this affiliation is celebrated as a form of imaginative liberation from her own constrained life:

> I discovered the great English writers, [...] I loved the English language and for this reason I could never get enough of the great English writers [...]. Reading Dickens brought London alive to me [...]. For years I had a recurring dream in which I would find myself roaming the streets of London. (Reddy *Unbending*: 41)

Reddy began writing when she was twelve, but only received recognition as a writer in 1975, when the BBC broadcast three of her short stories. Significantly, this exposure in Britain heralded her launch as an acclaimed creative writer in South Africa. Again, Reddy's role, however small, in a much wider scenario, this time of a former imperial authority versus the literary adolescence of the postcolony, is worth noting. As with other women writers of South Asian descent, it was in the metropole, with its economic and intellectual resources, that Reddy was able to truly begin her career as a writer.

This cursory biography of Reddy raises some pertinent questions. How is it that Reddy felt deeply patriotic as a South African, despite being treated as a second class citizen for most of her life, and why did she feel a strong cultural affiliation to Britain, the former coloniser of India and South Africa? Even more puzzling is the lack of identification with India. The answer possibly lies in Steven Vertovec and Robin Cohen's social-anthropological theory about a necessary strategy of synthesis and adaptation which enables survival (and evolution) in the diasporic location, a notion very similar to Pierre Bourdieu's *habitus*. According to Vertovec and Cohen transnationalism results in the "fluidity of constructed styles, social institutions and everyday practices" which are described in terms of "syncretism, creolization, bricolage, cultural translation, and hybridity" (2000: xxiii). This positive reading of migration and diaspora is echoed by literary scholars such as Roger Bromley (2000), and Susheila Nasta, who in her text on literature of the South Asian diaspora in Britain, describes the

"the heroic potential of migrancy as a metaphor for a 'new' form of aesthetic freedom" (2002: 4).

For Bourdieu, *habitus* refers to socially and culturally acquired, embodied systems of dispositions and/or pre-dispositions. *Habitus* underlies certain human characteristics and their infinite possible variations in different historical and cultural settings. Significantly, Bourdieu insists on "the *generative capacities* of dispositions, it being understood that these are acquired, socially constituted dispositions" (Bourdieu 1990: 12-13). He also emphasises that this "'creative,' active, inventive capacity was not that of a transcendental subject in the idealist tradition, but that of an active agent" (*ibid.*). For Reddy, her creative, inventive capacity led to a patriotism to her diasporic location, which meant criticising its neo-colonial evils and celebrating its diverse beauty in her writing. As for the affiliation with Britain, Reddy received a colonial education, an acquired, socially constituted disposition, which, contrary to politically correct views, offered her liberating, imaginative forays into unconfined and enabling spaces. The break with India might very well be the result of Reddy's *habitus* in South Africa, the site of her ancestors' struggle to lay down roots and the site of her ongoing struggle for a home and an enabled, empowered subjectivity.

Reddy's short stories, generally speaking, engage with two types of oppression: the neo-colonial, in the shape of *apartheid*; and what I call the 'traditional' in the shape of rigid and unequal gender roles within the South African Indian community. This is not to say that these are Reddy's sole focuses. Reddy's collection, published in 1987 at the height of the liberation struggle in South Africa, reflects Reddy's keen engagement with the diversity of South African society. She attests to this in the Foreword to the collection, pointing out that she takes her cue from her milieu: "One derives one's creative spirit from this land of a myriad contrasts" (np). Annemarié van Niekerk has also noted the range and variety of the protagonists of the stories:

> In the fourteen stories included in *On the Fringe of Dreamtime and Other Stories*, nine are told from Indian

> perspectives, one from a "Coloured" perspective, and four from black perspectives. Seven of the stories are told from a woman's perspective, three from a man's perspective, and four from a child's perspective. (1992: 36)

But despite the diversity of subject matter, characters and plots, the complex dynamics of oppression, be it racial, class or gender oppression, feature prominently as a theme in these stories. The plots often contain "cross-confrontational relationships" (Van Niekerk 1992: 36), forming an axis on which the plot pivots, and also a means to explore the notion of difference. Further, this theme is conveyed through the literary strategy of using a single focus and concentrated effect in the social realist mode.

Many of these stories poignantly evoke life in Durban, especially the Durban of the 1950s which was the site of the original Group Areas legislation. The Group Areas Act was devised by the *apartheid* government to control the movement of Indians in urban areas (it was, in fact, an extension of the restrictive Asiatic Land Tenure Act of 1946), and to separate Africans, Whites, 'Coloureds' and Indians. This was a national policy based loosely on the principle of "divide and rule." The effects of this social engineering on identity are consequently of great concern to Reddy whose family was uprooted from a semi-rural area outside Durban in the 1960s.

Reddy's Narratives of Enablement

Reddy uses an autobiographical style of writing, relying heavily on memory and a nostalgic tone. Many of these short stories are very personal narratives, which sometimes give the impression that they have purgative value, as well as operating as a record or a tribute. This element affects the tone of the writing, imbuing it sometimes with a mournful or wistful mood, and sometimes with a celebratory, commemorative mood. Reddy uses the former tone in the title story of *On the Fringe of Dreamtime and Other Stories*. In this story the unnamed central character experiences the pain and loss of forced removals in Durban in a dream-like state. He returns to his childhood home to reminisce but is met with suspicion and fear by the new white owners. The past, the joy of ownership, the sense of home and security, the connectedness to place, all become a dream and he is cast into the periphery of his world. Here Reddy captures the tragedy of a past injustice which will haunt generations to come. In her autobiography, we learn that Reddy's family had been settled in an area which was also claimed by the government for re-population by whites: "Roosfontein was a beautiful scenic area in Westville which became a White area" (*Unbending*, 21). Here her family had farmed bananas just as the protagonist of the story had on his farm: "This is my land!" He insisted. "We lived here for thirty years! The farm, the bananas, such bananas! Then they took it all from us!" (1987: 63). The story has as its central focus the visit of the old man to his former place of dwelling. This visit is traumatic for him as powerful memories transport him back to happier times. The past, so strongly contrasted to the present, appears like a dream. Roughly, the story is divided intro three parts: it begins with a description of a tree, a tangible symbol of all that has been lost; this description is followed by a confrontation between the old man and the new white female owner of the house and her companion; it ends with the man narrating his anecdotes about the past in the local general store, and finally his departure. This simple structure is bolstered by the interspersion of idyllic childhood memories. The highly charged confrontation between the protagonist and the two white women reveals the horrors of the racist ideology which divided people and positioned them as adversaries. The encounter emphasizes the differences between the two parties and the processes of 'Othering' which both employ.

The women are stereotypically they racist. They regard the old man with contempt and suspicion, oblivious to his grief and profound sense of loss. He, on the other hand, is horrified that they eat beef, smoke, wear trousers and totally and callously misunderstand him. The result is that they appear to one another as an "alien intrusion" (1987: 62). Throughout the duration of this encounter, the old man is filled with memories which sharply contrast with the harshness of his current situation. This short story is an economical and powerful rendering of the theme of loss and displacement in the *apartheid* era, using memory and elements of autobiography to achieve its effect.

In addition, the story also contains the image of the revered and mythologised female figure:

> Her careworn face, bereft of make-up except for the traditional dot on her forehead, bending over a bed of herbs. Mother had known the earth and its powers intimately. She had known every healing plant and herb. Like a true daughter of the earth. (1987: 2)

This clichéd description of the protagonist's mother which highlights her simplicity, gentleness and fecundity, is in direct contrast to the hardness and masculinity of the white women. In another description the mother is described as "slapping the washing on the stones and singing the folk songs of her youth" (1987: 65). She is revered as the nurturer and the custodian of traditional values and practices. This reverence of the protagonist is indicative of his own position within the patriarchal structures of a traditional Indian community.

Another aesthetic element employed in this story is the description of ritual and ceremony. The old man pauses dramatically in front of the ruins of a Hindu temple as he shuffles away from his former home:

> Nothing remained of it now except the ruins for the inner sanctum. He stood there and heard once more the prayers and songs of a thousand devotees. The blackened ruin conjured up the fragrant smoke of incense and fruit offerings. Here he had accompanied his family during festivals and special occasions. At such times, the spirit of sharing and oneness was strengthened. (1987: 66)

This description too serves to contrast with his present status as intruder and alien. In the past he belonged and was secure in the bosom of his family and community. The details of this description serve also as cultural information, reinforcing the cultural identity of the protagonist.

Finally, the aesthetic element of depicting the paradoxes of diasporic life is also evident in this story. The narrator offers us a glimpse of continuity and change reside side by side in the diasporic family. The old man's sons have adapted, severed ties with past and are unable to empathise with their father's sense of loss and displacement: "But he had never really adjusted. His sons understood his pain but didn't share it" (1987: 66) and "His son's impatient blaring on the horn broke into his memories and thoughts" (*ibid.*). The younger generation is emphatically in the here and now while the older generation immigrant is immersed in the past, estranged and lonely. The closing lines of the story are curt and brutal, echoing the brutality of the protagonist's reality: "He must shed his pain and crush the desire to return to a land where he was now an intruder" (*ibid.*). Reddy's short story displays some of the elements of an over-arching aesthetic, as well as some of the typical stylistic components of the genre.

As mentioned previously, much of the literature by women of the South Asian diaspora is drawn from personal experiences and deeply intimate concerns. Thus it often relies on personal memory, and sometimes on the synthesizing of facts, events, people, settings from the author's own life, with imagined/ fictional characters and events. This overt blending of fiction with autobiography results in a hybrid literary form. As is evident from reading of "On the Fringe of Dreamtime" above, some of Reddy's short stories definitely employ this form, especially the stories which paint Durban as their vivid and real setting, and the stories which deal with spatial confinement. In another story, "A Gift for Rajendra," the young man confined to the wheelchair is sparingly but poignantly described as "sitting in a wheelchair, reading. He was young, probably in his early twenties. He was very much like his mother. But the eyes that he turned upon the barber were sombre and painlined" (1987: 7). This description could well be of Reddy's brother, Mags, who was also stricken with muscular dystrophy, and the reference to reading is a definite link to Reddy herself, who, in her autobiography valorises the act of reading as a form of liberation. This story too is simple and stark, and it is set in the Indian community of Durban. It brings together two characters who are restricted: the itinerant barber by the dissipation of his trade; and the isolated, disabled Rajendra. But the emotive impact of the story is concentrated in the quite grace and compassion of the character of Rajendra's mother, a female figure of outstanding dignity and strength who brings the two needy men together.

Revered Female

In literature by women of the South Asian diaspora, female relationships, the praise of female relatives, and the image of the revered female figure, is a widespread and complex aesthetic element.[2] Sometimes this praise or reverence is in the form of characterization (the older female relative, often a grandmother or widowed aunt who is the fount of wisdom and the narrator of life-shaping tales), and sometimes it takes the form of overt tribute. Reddy uses both means to praise female relatives. In interviews and in her autobiography, Reddy discusses at length the inspiration and support she received from her mother and grandmother. Her short story collection is dedicated to her mother who she has praised for her "dedication, discipline, far-sightedness, courage and endurance" (*Unbending*: n.p.). The short stories are scattered with older female characters who display similar noble qualities. In the short story discussed below, this aesthetic element is accompanied by another: the critique of arranged marriages and the circumscription of women's bodies and sexuality. Often in literature by women of the South Asian diaspora, these two aesthetic elements overlap and act in tandem to articulate a feminist standpoint.

In a "A Time to Yield," Zainab, a headstrong, ambitious and intelligent young woman is forced into an arranged marriage. She remains defiant but is disempowered and her attempts to assert her desires are futile. The action of the story occurs on the day of the dreaded wedding, or more specifically, in the few hours leading up to the nuptials. Zainab is imprisoned in her room, seething with anger and frustration and we are privy to her private thoughts and passionate emotions. The narrator leads us through Zainab's painful memories of the struggle she put up against the marriage. Then a series of female relatives visit her in her captivity. First is her beloved younger sister Zubeida who is sympathetic but naïve and even more powerless than Zainab. Zainab's defiance does not abate. Then follows a violent confrontation with her mother who is fearful that Zainab's unconventional behaviour will bring disgrace on their family. She strikes Zainab and forcefully drags her out of bed, undresses her and propels her into a bath. The mother's anger matches the daughter's. The mother is explicit in her denunciation of Zainab's attempt to deviate from the prescribed role of a traditional Muslim female of their class and social standing:

> 'Let that be a lesson to you! I blame your father for this. He spoilt you. He gave you everything. And what good has it done? All that education, wasted! I never believed education was good for women. But your father never listened to me. And now, what does he get? A proud and headstrong daughter!' (1987: 99)

What is more is that the mother strongly condemns the father for indulging the daughter in this deviation. The wrathful mother appears to wield power in this instance, a power to demand that her daughter conform. But as Irene Gedalof tells us in her study on the complicity of women in Indian patriarchies, this "is power in its capillary mode, at its most insidious" (1991: 184). According to Gedalof women are "produced in visible ways. It is this production of women as (impure) subjects—managed, contained, but also valorized, enabled and empowered—that helps to make their subordination so persistent" (*ibid.*).

Zainab's mother has been "produced" within a system which deems her a secondary citizen, a vassal of her male relatives. She has a semblance of power but it is allowed to be directed only at other women. Thus Zainab too is "produced" in this mould of the impure, subservient, demure woman who will obey the commands of her elders. But Zainab rebels against this system. Her father, the patriarch, humoured her as a child but as soon as she reached marriageable age he "concluded an important business deal with the Khans, and now Khan and Joosab were partners" (1987: 95), thus sealing her fate and wielding actual power. It becomes clear then that the mother is a mere instrument of this patriarchal power, her complicity rendering her both victim and oppressor.

In this story Reddy highlights the physical objectification of the young woman who is bartered in the marriage transaction. After the mother's brutal visit, a "string of old aunts followed in her wake" (1987: 100). Their invasion of her private space and abhorrent appraisal of her body is described as molestation. The scene is sinister and threatening, heightening Zainab's sense of aggravation and disempowerment:

> They surrounded her. They ran their eyes greedily over her fresh young body and touched her with creepy hands. They cackled lewdly. She shuddered and shut her eyes. She felt their stale breath on her, reeking of betel leaves and soiling her. Their raucous voices filled the room. She felt someone's hand on her, feeling the smooth lines of her body. With an exclamation of disgust, she sprang up, and thrust the person violently from her. (1987: 101)

Zainab's response to this assault on her person, which mirrors the assailment of her subjectivity, is met with disapproval because this "was no way for a shy, young bride to behave" (1987: 101). The odious aunts function as a vivid symbol of the oppression Zainab faces, rather than as loving, supporting relatives in a network of female solidarity. Reddy does not in this instance simplify the machinations of patriarchal oppression, nor does she shy away from the often shameful and complicit roles women play in it.

The story climaxes with the grand entrance of the grandmother. Zainab's grandmother is a strong commanding figure but she is also described as gentle and compassionate. This is the ubiquitous figure of the revered, older female relative who is the fount of wisdom. She immediately takes charge of the situation and calms Zainab with her firmness and empathy. She recounts her own arranged marriage and how it turned out to be a success: "I submitted to everything they required of me. And in time, I did learn to love your grandfather. We were really a very happy family" (1987: 102). She advocates that Zainab also submit to the demands of her family and socio-cultural milieu. The grandmother, it seems, subscribes to a feminism born of necessity and which involves compromise rather than outright rebellion. Her argument centres on the notion of power. She regards women as powerful, not disempowered, as agents not victims and she urges Zainab to "work at making [her marriage] a success" (1987: 103). This power is seen as universal and timeless, something intrinsic to women and not culturally determined:

> Women are the same today as they have been over the centuries. All the education and modern thought hasn't changed them much. Women have the same needs, the same desires, the same hopes and dreams, the same roles and abilities [...] and the same power, as women throughout the ages. (1987: 102)

On the one hand, the grandmother may be praised for her sagacity and her recognition of women's agency. Her encouragement of Zainab in the face of unassailable forces is admirable. But on the other hand there is something dangerous and insidiously deceptive about her argument. She is advocating that Zainab succumb to the pressures of her community, and in so doing, repress her own individual aspirations and desires. Within the circumscribed parameters of Zainab's life, she will wield a semblance of power, but ultimately she will be subject to the will of her husband. Further, when she remarks that "[...] there is power in beauty too" (1987: 103), she is asking Zainab to fight with a double edged sword. Zainab will be subject to the standards of beauty within this traditional social system and as long as she adheres to the codes which regulate her behaviour, she will be able to use her feminine attributes to wield power. The grandmother's position does beg the question: what form will Zainab's power take, and for someone who she describes as having "a strong will and a strong mind" (*ibid.*), how tenable will it be to always walk within the carefully delineated parameters of patriarchy?

The theme of marriage and the conflicts which arise from the enforcement of 'traditional' gender roles is also explored in

"The Spirit of Two Worlds," and in her television screenplay, *Web of Persuasion*, which is about the intricate net which operates to secure an arranged marriage. Reddy deviates from the stereotypical depiction of the mother-in-law as cruel domestic tyrant by portraying the mother-in-law in "The Spirit of Two Worlds" in a highly sympathetic light. It is the older woman who experiences loss and sadness at the hands of her daughter-in-law who breaks from 'tradition,' not the other way around, as is usually the case in this literature. Although the mother-in-law, in contrast to the revered grandmother or aunt, has become a stock character in this literature (like-wise in popular Hindi cinema), a symbol of the internalization of patriarchal law and complicity, there are notable exceptions. Sometimes the mother-in-law too is a figure of pathos, a downtrodden household drudge who does not have the heart to continue the cycle of oppression. In "The Spirit of Two Worlds" Reddy creates a mother-in-law who forsakes her own beliefs and needs in order to facilitate her daughter-in-law's freedom and independence.

Domestic Spaces of Women

A common aesthetic element in South Asian diasporic women's literature is the description of everyday, sensuous scenes and domestic spaces. Small objects or trivial events are described in minute detail. The richness of home living and the domestic spaces of women are evoked. In these spaces women are shown to have knowledge, expertise, traditional skills, and here they are free from oppression albeit temporarily. These spaces are often offered in contrast to other male-dominated, often public, spheres where women are either silenced and abused, or complicit in the structures which oppress their gender. In her autobiography Reddy addresses the theme of spatial confinement due to physical disability and the restrictions of the *apartheid* regime. In almost obsessive detail she describes her struggle to overcome the spatial and kinetic restrictions of her physical condition, linking this with her struggle to become a writer. Accompanying this narrative are descriptions of restriction and confinement imposed by *apartheid*. In particular, she tells the story of a community of women who are confined to the "yard," a communal space in the midst of tenement houses used by Indian women to perform daily chores and for social interaction. This "yard-space" (Mehta 1997: 10), paradoxically, symbolizes both restriction and marginalization due to *apartheid* laws and traditional Indian gender roles, and a lively, interactive, recuperative area where women can share their experiences. In the short stories these descriptions contribute to the realism of the texts which are aimed at capturing the hardships of life under *apartheid* in a 'traditional' Indian community.

"The Spirit of Two Worlds" opens with an evocative description of the old mother-in-law performing her domestic duties in her own private space:

> The old woman pounded the spices in a wooden mortar. She sat on the grass mat in the sartorial position adopted by generations of women before her [...]. Out there it was quiet and she could think her thoughts in peace as she prepared the mangoes for pickling. (1987: 9)

This opening description is significant because it shows the woman in her designated gender role of nurturer, one "adopted by generations of women before her." But it also indicates that the woman has a private space, a place of respite from the "cramped living conditions of the council house" (10) she shared with her extended family. Dissension in her home arises when her youngest daughter-in-law, Sharda, announces her decision to escape from this domestic space. Sharda first seeks employment in the city and then insists on moving into her own home. This fleeing from the confines of the family home is Sharda's declaration of her repudiation of the 'traditional' roles imposed on wives and daughters-in-law. She will not join the long line of women who, wearing a sari, sat on a mat pounding spices with a pestle and mortar. But the rift between Sharda and her mother-in-law is healed when Sharda has a son. The old woman, realising Sharda's desire to continue working, offers to care for the baby, taking him into her nurturing, domestic space where the spirit of two worlds can merge.

Elsewhere too Reddy describes the mundane duties of women to evoke their humble dignity and devotion to their families. For example, in "On the Fringe of Dreamtime," the mother idealised in a memory is described as tending a bed of herbs, washing clothes in a stream and cleaning sheep's tripe (1987: 62-65). The class status of the women in these stories is alluded to by the descriptions of them preparing offal. In "Market Days" the hardworking, tireless mother purchases a sheep's head in the market, much to the chagrin of her young son:

> When he glimpsed the sheep's head in her basket, his heart sank. Now he will have to spend the afternoon gathering firewood. She would insert long, flat irons into the fire and use the heated irons to singe the sheep's head. It was a lengthy process and would take the whole afternoon. (1987: 43)

Reddy's intention is not to provoke disgust, but to realistically portray a community living under adverse conditions, and to show the effort of its women who were determined to produce culinary delights, even from dubious sources. Significantly, Reddy does not pander to a western readership by censoring what might be perceived as unpalatable sensory details. Nor does she attempt cultural translation for the benefit of a foreign reader. Further, unlike, for example, Sara Suleri in *Meatless Days*, she does not treat these everyday, gastronomical activities as loaded with cultural significance. Her achievement, with this aesthetic, is to authentically capture the textures and flavours of life for an Indian woman in Durban during the 1950s and 1960s.

Enacting Culture

One of the most widely used aesthetic elements in literature by women of the South Asian diaspora is the use of mythology or ancient literature, 'traditional' religious practices, and descriptions of ritual and ceremony. This is an effective way to capture the richness of a culture, and to enact its preservation through writing, to allude to esoteric concerns, to set up contrasts, or to zoom in on sensory details. The themes of cultural continuation and perpetuation are thus highlighted. Reddy, being a second-generation Indian settler in the diasporic community in Durban, differs somewhat from other writers with regards to the use of this aesthetic. For Reddy the preservation of 'traditional' South Asian culture is not a foremost concern. Instead she is more concerned with representing cultural differences in the South Africa context. In interviews, and indeed in her literature, Reddy emphasises that it is the diversity of South Africa she wishes to represent, not one specific group. In an interview with Annemarie van Niekerk, Reddy claims that she does "not see the necessity of bringing in eastern influences in an African setting" (1994: 73). Rather, Reddy describes the Durban Indian community as *part of* a distinctive South African multiculturalism.

Hence, when the short stories contain cultural references specific to the Indian community, such as Hindu rituals at the temple, arranged marriages or the preparation of spices for pickling, Reddy's primary aim is to describe life in the diasporic location, and her secondary aim is to provide the culturally specific details of her characterization and settings. Furthermore, life in this specific diasporic location is about life under *apartheid*. Rather than weave the ancient cultural laws imported from India into her narratives or make intertextual references to ancient South Asian literature and mythology, Reddy addresses the laws of the *apartheid* government in South Africa. This is not say that Reddy is not aware of the continuing stranglehold or positive value of some of those ancient laws and 'traditional' practices. But her stories are not a means of perpetuating the homeland culture, but rather a means of questioning how this culture fits into the complex cultural matrix of South Africa.

For example in "Market Days" which is told from the perspective of ten-year-old Anil, the Durban Indian market is colourfully evoked. During the course of the narrative of Anil's weekly visit to the market with his energetic mother, we learn of the historic significance of the market which is threatened with shut-down by the *apartheid* authorities. The market was (and still is to some extent) the hub of Indian commerce and a symbol of the immigrants' mercantile spirit and resourcefulness. In a vignette typical of Reddy's socio-politically attentive style, the "stream of humanity" (1987: 40) which flowed through the market is described:

> A White woman sailed out followed by her African maid bearing heavily laden baskets. African women with baskets balanced on their heads moved with an enviable ease. There were trussed fowls in many of their baskets. A few beggars straggled along and further down, a group of Hindu swamis stood in their saffron robes, holding out brass trays containing ash and flowers which they handed out at random. (1987: 40)

In this scene Reddy is successful in suggesting, quite economically, the race relations and power dynamics of *apartheid* South Africa. The supremacy of the white woman is conveyed through the verb "sailed" and the servility and exploitation of the maid is captured in the image of her "heavily laden baskets." Reddy also manages to imply the dignity and the endurance of the African women who "moved with an enviable ease" even though they are burdened, in the immediate sense, and more pervasively in the their life situation. Pertinent to the current argument is the description of the Hindu swamis. They are described in sartorial detail, their act of religious devotion and piety sparingly but vividly illustrated. But these swamis, members of the South Asian diasporic community, adhering to the culture and religion of the homeland, are not of singular interest. They are part of a scene which is quintessentially South African, thus accenting the heterogeneity of South African culture, not the sacredness of homeland customs.

Heritage and Change

Diasporic literature in general, and literature by women of the South Asian diaspora in particular, often deals with the paradox of cultural continuity or the preservation of a cultural heritage versus change. The immigrants' dislocation and adaptation in the diasporic location is a primary theme. In Reddy's short stories the focus is not so much on the process of adaptation but rather on the specific exigencies of the diasporic location. Reddy differs from other writers in that the preservation of Indian culture is a peripheral concern. Rather, she is eager to capture the Indian immigrants' role in the struggle for anti-racism and justice in South African. Further, many of her stories explore this same struggle as experienced by characters of a different racial or ethnic background. For example, in "The Slumbering Spirit," she highlights the injustices and loss of forced removals in Durban and she recreates and restores a sense of community, the richness of an organic, multi-cultural, pre-1950 Durban, which has been disrupted by *apartheid*. She achieves this through narrating the unlikely friendship between a 'Coloured' child, Terry and an old white woman, Mrs Anderson. Reddy is frank and emphatic about this focus and commitment in her writing. In an interview with Van Niekerk she says "I am a South African with Indo-African links. I derive my creative spirit from the land of my birth, not from the land of my origin" (1994: 73). Hence Reddy is not, like many diasporic writers, "haunted by some sense of loss, some urge to reclaim, to look back" and her short stories do not create "imaginary homelands" (Rushdie 1991: 12). She is instead deeply embroiled in her immediate and present home.

Where Reddy does concentrate on Indian characters, she links their struggle in this immediate and present home to characters with different backgrounds, and thus explores the complex dynamics of oppression. For example, the story, "Friends," deals with the intricate and often hostile racial and class relations between Indians and black Africans. As mentioned earlier, Reddy's stories often contain "cross-confrontational relationships" (Van Niekerk 1992: 36), forming an axis on which the plot pivots. In this story the confrontation occurs on two levels. Reddy creates two pairs of characters comprising of a mother and daughter respectively: Sadhana, the indulged and disillusioned Indian 'madam' and her neglected daughter Asha; and Bessie, the hardworking, downtrodden domestic worker and her deprived daughter Phumza. Sadhana, unhappy in her traditional Indian marriage, is a neglectful and abusive mother. The five-year-old Asha, like her mother, is materially indulged but emotionally neglected. Sadhana is overtly racist and oppressive towards Bessie who is a devoted and gentle mother. The two mothers have a highly charged but muted confrontation when Bessie expresses her desire to buy Phumza a dress like one that Asha owned. Sadhana is angered by this challenge to a hierarchy which affords her some supremacy in her otherwise disempowered life. She is disdainful and uncomprehending of Bessie's aspirations to provide "good things" (1987: 107) for her child, displaying none of the stereotypical female empathy or solidarity one would expect from a mother. But Bessie is quietly defiant: "Bessie had given her a strange, unfathomable look before replying loftily. 'The shops are for everybody'" (*ibid.*).

A much more dramatic and violent confrontation occurs between the younger generation characters. Asha and Phumza are ostensibly the eponymous "friends" of the story but their relationship is also tainted by the racism and segregation endemic in their society. Phumza silently and passionately desires a doll which Asha is playing with and when Asha recognises this desire in Phumza she brutally attacks and breaks the doll, finally discarding it. When Phumza attempts to rescue and care for the battered doll, Asha savagely reclaims her property. Reddy's representation of Asha's sadism and Phumza's defeat is a powerful indictment on the dynamics of power within *apartheid* society. In the microcosm of the domestic setting Reddy shows how the Indian mother and daughter (they themselves victims of *apartheid*), act out their respective anger and frustration on those more vulnerable and less privileged than themselves. Using her signature technique of "cross-confrontational relationships," Reddy creates a tightly focused yet emotionally rich short story which explores the notion of difference amongst South African women, and Reddy is not afraid to reveal that the South Asian immigrant is so deeply immersed in the diasporic location as to sometimes become complicit in its injustices.

Conclusion

Reddy's use of the genre and the aesthetic differs significantly from their deployment by other women writers of the South Asian diaspora. She is less concerned with the continuity of South Asian culture and much more invested in the project of creating an egalitarian and multicultural South African society. Nevertheless, aesthetic similarities with other South Asian diasporic women writers are discernible. Reddy therefore comes to occupy a unique position in 'Indian' women's writing. She shares with her compatriots in South Africa a profound involvement with the country's troubled history, and with her compatriots in the South Asian diaspora, an ardent interest and concern for the condition of women in modern and post-modern society.

NOTES

1. Van Niekerk echoes Trinh Minh-ha who defines difference as "not opposed to sameness, nor synonymous with separateness ... [D]ifference is not what makes conflicts. It is beyond and alongside conflict.... Difference can be a "tool of creativity to question multiple forms of repression and dominance" (1995: 372-73). Van Niekerk and Minh-ha both argue that difference is not opposition and not predicated on a fixed binarism.
2. Examples of short fiction which use the figure of the revered female relative are Uma Parameswaran's novella, *The Sweet Smell of Mother's Milk-Wet Bodice* (2001); Padma Perera's "Mauna" (1978); and Agnes Sam's "Jesus is Indian" (1989).

WORKS CITED

Bourdieu, Pierre. *In Other Words: Essays Towards a Reflexive Sociology.* Trans. Matthew Adamson. Stanford: Stanford University Press, 1990.

Bromley, Roge. *Narratives for a New Belonging: Diasporic Cultural Fictions.* Edinburgh: Edinburgh University Press, 2000.

Celly, Anu. "Attics, Courtyards and Horizons: the 'Inscape' of Female Sensibility in the Indian and Canadian Short Story." In Jain and Agarwal (eds.). 45-55.

Cudden, J.A. *A Dictionary of Literary Terms.* Harmondsworth: Penguin Books, 1970.

Desai, Anita. "Interview, 16th November, 1979, Jaipur." In Jasbir Jain, *Stairs to the Attic: The Novels of Anita Desai.* Jaipur: Printwell, 1997. 7-5.

Dhupelia-Mesthrie, Uma. *From Canefields to Freedom—A Chronicle of Indian South African Life*. Cape Town: Kwela Books, 2000.

Flockemann, M. "Aesthetics of Transformation: A Comparative Study of Selected Writing by Women from South Africa and the African Diaspora." Unpublished Doctoral Diss. University of Natal, Pietermartitzburg. 1998.

Gedalof, Irene. *Against Purity: Rethinking Identity with Indian and Western Feminisms*. London: Routledge, 1991.

Govinden, Devarakshanam. "'Sisters Outsiders'—The Representation of Identity and Difference in Selected Writings by South African Indian Women." Unpublished Doctoral Diss. University of Natal, Durban, 2000.

Harlow, Barbara. "Sites of Struggle: Immigration, Deportation, Prison, and Exile." In Margaret R. Higonnet and Joan Templeton (eds), *Reconfigured Spheres—Feminist Explorations of Literary Space*. Amherst: University of Massachusetts Press, 1994. 108-24.

Jain, Jasbir and Supriya Agarwal, eds.. *Gender and Narrative*. Jaipur and New Delhi: Rawat Publishers, 2002.

Kumar, Alka. "Narrator as Archaeologist: Feminist Communities in Margaret Atwood's *Wilderness Tips*." In Jain and Agarwal (eds.). 56-70.

Mehta, Brinda. "Reclaiming Home in Lakshmi Persaud's *Sastra* and *Butterfly. In the Wind* and Ramabai Espinet's *Indian Cuisine*: Women and Space in an Indo-Trinidadian Household." Unpublished Paper. Mills College, California, 1997.

Metcalf, John. Cited in Arnold E. Davidson and Cathy N. Davidosn (eds.) *The Art of Margaret Atwood*. Toronto: Anansi, 1981.

Nasta, Susheila. *Home Truths: Fictions of the South Asian Diaspora in Britain*. Houndmills/Basinstoke: Palgrave, 2002.

Reddy, Jayapraga. *Web of Persuasion*. Script of play, adapted by Franz Marx. Unpublished. 1984.

——. *On the Fringe of Dreamtime and Other Stories*. Johannesburg: Skotaville, 1987.

——. *The Unbending Reed*. Unpublished autobiography. n.d.

Reid Ian. *The Short Story*. The Critical Idiom Series. London: Methuen, 1977.

Rushdie, Salman. *Imaginary Homelands: Essays and Criticism 1981-1991*. London: Granta, 1992.

Trinh T. Minh-ha. "Writing Postcoloniality and Feminism." In Bill Ashcroft, Gareth Griffiths and Helen Tiffin, eds. *The Postcolonial Studies Reader*. London: Routledge, 1995. 264-68.

Van Niekerk, Annemarié. "Aspects of Race, Class and Gender in Jayapraga Reddy's *On the Fringe of Dreamtime and Other Stories.*" *UNISA English Studies*. 30.2 (1992): 35-40.

——. "Feminist Aesthetics: Aspects of Race, Class and Gender in the Constitution of South African Short Fiction by Women." *Journal of Literary Studies* 9.1 (1993): 69-79.

——. "An Interview with Jayapraga Reddy." In Annette Horn, Susan Mabie *et al*, eds. *Like a House on Fire—Contemporary Women's Writing, Art and Photography*. Johannesburg: COSAW Publishing, 1994. 69-74.

Van Niekerk, Annemarié, ed. *Raising the Blinds: A Century of South African Women's Stories*. Cape Town: AD Donker Publisher, 1990.

Van Niekerk, Annemarié (comp. and ed.). *The Torn Veil: and Other Women's Short Stories from the Continent of Africa*. Cape Town: Queillerie Publishers, 1998.

Verma, Nirmal. "Short Story as a Pure Literary Form." *Word and Memory*. Bikaner: Vagdevi Prakashan, 1984.

Vertovec, S. and Cohen, R., eds. *Migration, Diasporas and Transnationalism*. Cheltenham and Northampton USA: Elgar Reference Collection, 2001.

4 Colonial Woes in Postcolonial Writing: Chitra Banerjee Divakaruni's *Arranged Marriage*

Husne Jahan

Relocating from a site with a history of confrontation between colonial and indigenous forces to a nucleus of neo-colonial power confronts a writer with the difficult challenge of negotiating between a heritage of resistance to colonialism and the pressure of adapting to the colonial or imperial "Other" as the new home. This essay focuses on *Arranged Marriage*, a collection of short stories by Chitra Banerjee Divakaruni, a writer who immigrated to the United States from a postcolonial Indian background. My intent is to explore how the inevitable tension between postcolonial origins and an adjustment to a country viewed as the centre of neo-imperial power[1] plays out in these short stories, many of which focus on the trope of immigration, and can thus be characterized as narratives of immigration.

The tensions that arise in works of immigrant writers come not just from simple longing and loyalties divided between the original and adopted homelands, but also from immigration's link to colonialism and neo-imperialism. Colonial powers exerted the influence of their culture and language on colonized peoples through both forceful and artful transmission. They also initiated migrations of large populations from one colonized place to another in the interest of their vast transcontinental economic ventures. Neo-colonial or imperial powers continue these legacies through the global dissemination of their politics, culture, language, and business enterprises. In the process, they also attract immigrants from various parts of the world to the centre of imperialistic power, with promises of better opportunities and rights, in comparison to their less developed homelands. From the Nobel Prize winning V.S. Naipaul, whose career began in the middle of the 20th century, to the Pulitzer Prize winning writer Jhumpa Lahiri, who emerged on the English literary scene at the end of the 20th century, migration or immigration has directly or indirectly affected several generations of contemporary writers writing in English, engendering hybridity and cultural complexity within them, and urging them to grapple with multiple cultures and countries and the tensions between them. Chitra Divakaruni is among those writers affected by immigration as well as by its corollaries: colonialism, postcolonialism, and neo-imperialism. However, Divakaruni's immigrant narratives focus on celebrating immigration as a liberating agent at the expense of overshadowing the influence of any other agency. While they rarely get declaredly into issues pertaining to colonial or postcolonial politics, they do reveal striking parallels to Orientalist perceptions of many aspects of Indian culture and society. Why one may expect to locate postcolonial politics in Divakaruni's texts and what may be the implication of their neo-imperialist messages need to be understood in relation to the dynamics between postcolonial writing and American literature.

When mapping out the literary and theoretical terrain of postcolonial writing in their 1989 book, *The Empire Writes Back*, Bill Ashcroft, Gareth Griffiths, and Helen Tiffin hesitate to include within that terrain the writing produced in the United States since its independence from Britain. They observe that the American experience and its attempts to generate a new literature can be seen as the model for all subsequent postcolonial writing. Yet they point out that they do not include the "post-colonial" literature of the United States within the category of the literatures produced by cultures affected by imperial processes, since, due to its "current position of power, and the neo-colonizing role it has played, its [U.S. literature's] postcolonial nature has not been generally recognized" (2).

Around the same time (1970s and 1980s) that postcolonial theory emerged out of the shadow of European theories of post-structuralism and post-modernism, and postcolonial literatures emerged from the peripheries to disrupt the literary canon of the old colonial centre, Indian immigrants in the United States began writing their versions of immigrant narratives, adding to the diverse voices of hyphenated Americans in the chronicling of the immigration experience. Among these texts are the American literatures whose interests intersect with postcolonial literatures produced in other parts of the world and which could be the American literatures with true postcolonial characteristics. As the predominant culture of the United States remained Anglicized due to the influence of the early settlers from the English colonial centre, newer immigrants have found themselves struggling to adapt to those pre-existing cultural norms. White immigrants with linguistic differences sought to merge into a "melting pot" through linguistic assimilation, but immigrants with linguistic and racial differences found themselves twice removed from the normative standards of the country. The immigrants from India, coming to the United States in significant numbers, between 1904 and 1924, and again after 1965, following amendments to restrictive immigration policies (Grewal 96), found themselves among those twice removed populations.

While immigration brought new opportunities for these Indian-American immigrants, it also brought them challenges such as dislocation, isolation, identity crisis, and a sense of differentiation that could easily bring back colonial memories. The writers emerging from this population were poised to portray these crises, but they also found themselves susceptible to an existing dominant tradition of immigrant narratives that characterized immigration as pure opportunity and the adoptive country as a mythical paradise. Gilbert H. Muller confirms that "The idea of America as a New World, an Eden, an El Dorado, a Gold Mountain—the pure representation of desire—

is embedded in all cycles of immigration history" (2). However, those immigrant writers who arrived with the legacies of their original countries' struggles with Euro-based colonial domination and were part of a differentiated "Other" in their adopted country with its own history of Euro-derived racial exploitation have also questioned this notion of the promised paradise. Noting the intersections of the forces of colonialism, imperialism, and immigration in some immigrant writings, Muller observes:

> In their new imperial habitats in the United States, those immigrants who were formerly colonized challenge the myths and symbols of the nation. Their heterogeneous otherness and racial difference force an interrogation of American identity and accepted national norms. (15)

In light of this comment, the texts of two immigrant writers, Bharati Mukherjee and Meena Alexander, come to mind. Both are immigrant writers with Indian ties like Divakaruni, and both have grappled with the promises and the problems embedded in immigration. Mukherjee's novel *Jasmine* interweaves the forces of immigration, transformation, violence, and regeneration in the multiple reinventing of its immigrant woman subject.[2] Alexander clearly identifies traumas inherent in immigration as she writes of herself as "a woman cracked by multiple migrations" in *Fault Lines* (3) and weaves biography, theory, and literature in a book tellingly named *The Shock of Arrival: Reflections on Postcolonial Experience.* Chitra Divakaruni's materials stride multiple cultures and nations as Bharati Mukherjee's and Meena Alexander's narratives do. But, unlike the works of Mukherjee and Alexander, the problems, pains, and erasures brought about by immigration are downplayed in Divakaruni's work, while the celebrations of the promises of immigration are emphasized to the point where some aspects of her work strongly promote neo-Orientalist and neo-Imperialist projects. I would like to note here that, compared to Mukherjee and Alexander, Divakaruni has received little scholarly attention thus far.[3]

Divakaruni writes about women from India, and sometimes also about women from Pakistan and Bangladesh, as her first major English-language publication, her volume of poems *Black Candle* states in its sub-title. However, as Divakaruni's poems in *Black Candle* attempt to speak for women of three South Asian countries, it also seeks to limit women's lives in these places only to experiences of pain. The book is inhabited by women facing different types of oppressive conditions: being in purdah, forced into detrimental arranged marriages, enslaved by a husband's extended family for childlessness, socially isolated because of premature widowhood, forced to abort female fetuses, burnt for dowries, beaten by husbands, made to co-exist with a husband's second wife, compelled to burn at the funeral pyre of a husband, and expected to sacrifice life to the service of the temple as a living goddess. Among her fiction, her volume of short stories *Arranged Marriage* and her novel *Sister of My Heart* disturbingly reconstruct the colonial binaries of East versus West as primitive versus civilized. Many of the short stories in *Arranged Marriage* celebrate Indian women's immigration to the United States as a journey from oppressed or depressed conditions to freedom and discovery of self with the inspiration of western influences. In demonstrating her indebtedness to western feminist notions and in voicing criticism of women's subjugation in India, Divakaruni repeatedly maligns far too many facets of Indian society and culture. In this aspect, her work is akin to the ideological product of that educated class in the modern Orient, which, as Edward Said observes, borrows ideas about "modernization, progress, and culture" from Europe and the United States, and "participates in its own Orientalizing" (325). The Manichean[4] polarity of colonial discourse,[5] endowing the colonizer with positive qualities and the colonized with all its opposite negatives, is relived in Divakaruni's texts. Once again, the culture and people of a once-colonized nation are represented as primitive, outmoded, inferior, and evil, in comparison to the Euro-derived culture and values of the new centre of the world, towards which all the characters of Divakaruni's stories and novels gravitate. The Manichean binaries found in her texts echo similar constructions in British colonialist and Orientalist discourse, as demonstrated through some examples in the latter part of this essay.

For all of the pain and oppression of women in the traditions, myths, and histories that Divakaruni invokes in her poetry, short stories, and novels, the writer hardly finds anything that could be redeeming, inspiring, or liberating. It seems that the literary, cultural, and political traditions of the Indian sub-continent have never produced any resistance to oppression in its entire history, which is, of course, far from reality. Indian women in past and contemporary history and Indian male and female writers have spoken up for women's rights, in many cases, long before feminism became a fully realized notion in the West.[6]

In her reading of a series of Zed Books publications about women in the third world,[7] Chandra Talpade Mohanty, in "Under Western Eyes: Feminist Scholarship and Colonial Discourses" (196-220), criticizes what she terms as analytical traps, presuppositions, and strategies "which take as their primary point of reference feminist interests as they have been articulated in the United States and western Europe" and construct "the 'Third World Woman' as a singular, monolithic subject" (196). Mohanty writes of this construction:

> This average third-world woman leads an essentially truncated life based on her feminine gender (read: sexually constrained) and being 'third world' (read: ignorant, poor, uneducated, tradition-bound, religious, domesticated, family-oriented, victimized, etc.). This, I suggest is in contrast to the (implicit) self-representation of western women as educated, modern, as having control over their own bodies and sexualities, and the 'freedom' to make their own decisions.
>
> The distinction between western feminist re-presentation of women in the third world, and western feminist self-presentation is a distinction of the same order as [...] the characterization by developmentalists of the third world as being engaged in the lesser production of 'raw materials' in contrast to the real productive activity of the first world. These distinctions are made on the basis of the privileging of a particular group as the norm or referent. (199-200)

Mohanty explains that such subject/image-construction of third world women is practiced not only by women who identify with the West, geographically and culturally, but also by women from the third world living and writing in the West, and women writing and publishing in the West, while living in the third world. Although Mohanty focuses her study on ethnographic discourse, which is in a different field from the fictional texts of Divakaruni, Mohanty's critique can be applied to Divakaruni's fictional discourse as well.

As the name of the book implies, the stories in *Arranged Marriage* are all about marital relationships. According to the custom of arranging marriages, still prevalent in countries like India, Pakistan, and Bangladesh, most of the marital relationships in these stories are arranged by the families of the people who are getting married, and almost all of them involve some oppositional encounter of Indian and American values and customs. One obvious premise of the book is that arranged marriages do not work because they are based on an invalid and unfair custom. The other premise is that in an encounter of Indian and American values and customs, the latter would be sure to prevail by virtue of an inherent superiority and progressiveness.

I would, however, begin my discussion of *Arranged Marriage* with the one story in this book that problematizes the Indian-American encounter to a certain extent and does not portray America as a simplified and glorified land of freedom and fulfilled dreams. "Silver Pavements, Golden Roofs" (*Arranged* 35-56) is perhaps one rare example among this collection of stories in which there is an attempt to look at the complexity of America, although this story too is plagued by some typical colonialist binaries. In this story, a young Indian girl goes to the United States as a college student with many dreams, which are complicated by her encounter with her immigrant aunt's unsophisticated husband (both of Indian origin) and the racist slurs of the neighbourhood boys. Although the heroine Jayanti Ganguli appears to stand up for a postcolonial way of thinking in response to her encounter with racism, her thoughts and words are imbued with colonialist binaries. She carries within her prejudices that make her judge people according to hierarchies of caste, colour and class. She and her aunt come from an upper-class, upper-caste Bengali family and both are described as fair-skinned; while her uncle, who is drawn as an unsavoury character, is described as dark-skinned and lower class. He is also said to be ugly, rude, uncultured, and rough, yet vulnerable. The uncle is seen from the perspective of Jayanti, the narrator of the story, and Jayanti's perspective of her uncle is inscribed with European colonialist notions of equating dark skin-colour with a lower breed of humans characterized by traits of brutality, vulnerability, and a lack of sophistication. In contrast, the fictive white professor Jayanti fantasizes about is drawn as the uncle's polar opposite; he is handsome, refined, and romantic. He is the one Jayanti imagines as a husband, the man with whom she will fall in love when she breaks away from the Indian tradition of arranged marriages as she declares, "No arranged marriage like Aunt's for me!" (45). When the neighbourhood white boys' racial slurs of "nigger, nigger" remind her of British colonialism and American slavery, Jayanti's American experience is problematized, but only briefly. She thinks that the slurs may have been suitable, "[i]n the mouth of a red-faced gin-and-tonic drinking British official, perhaps, in his colonial bungalow, or a sneering overseer out of *Uncle Tom's Cabin* as he plies his whip in the cotton fields" (51), but she did not imagine they could come from the mouths of boys who are young, poor, and no figures of authority. So in Jayanti's experience of the United States, racism is not an issue of exploitative policies and power struggles, but only a street prank of young boys in a poor neighbourhood. At the end of the story, while Jayanti thinks of all the many-coloured hands she has encountered in America and the complexities of race and class, white snow falls to soften "forgivingly, the rough noisy edges of things" (55). She concludes her story with this pacifying statement:

> I notice that the snow has covered my own hands so they are no longer brown but white, white, white. And now it makes sense that the beauty and the pain should be part of

> each other. I continue holding them out in front of me, gazing at them, until they're completely covered. Until they do not hurt at all. (56)

The snow becomes an anesthetizing agent, a symbol of the kind of erasure that Jayanti is about to embrace in order to survive in America. However, in this story, the author does not simplify Jayanti's entire experience as much as she does with the characters of the other stories, many of which unabashedly simplify the opposition between the Indian and the American ways of life in terms of oppressed and backward versus free and full of promise.

The story "Clothes" (*Arranged* 17-33) depicts an arranged marriage that works well until external calamity strikes. In this story, Sumita marries Somesh, an Indian immigrant who owns a 24-hour convenience store in California. For Sumita too, America is made of desire and promise: "a kingdom beyond the seven seas" (18). After she comes to America, her husband buys her American clothes through which she discovers more of the sexuality and exuberance of her body than she ever did when wearing a sari. Though she cannot wear these clothes while she and her husband live with his parents, she models them for him in the privacy of their bedroom and dreams of wearing them when they move from their joint-family situation to an American-style nuclear family life, minus his parents. When, in an unfortunate turn of events, her husband gets shot by a gunman, Sumita, the docile wife who mostly stayed at home with her in-laws, makes this resolution:

> I know I cannot go back. I don't know yet how I'll manage, here in this new, dangerous land. I only know I must. Because all over India, at this very moment, widows in white saris are bowing their veiled heads, serving tea to in-laws. Doves with cut-off wings [...] I am standing in front of the mirror now, gathering up the sari [...] I straighten my shoulders and take a deep breath [...]. In the mirror a woman holds my gaze, her eyes apprehensive yet steady. She wears a blouse and skirt the color of almonds. (33)

The clothes in this story are symbolic: the Indian sari is a symbol of entrapment whereas the western attire of skirt and blouse are symbols of Sumita's liberation. Sumita seems to be poised to liberate herself only by giving up such Indian customs as wearing saris and caring for elderly in-laws. Interestingly, in Sumita's judgment serving tea to in-laws in India is worse than getting shot by a gunman in a country she terms as "new" and "dangerous."

Through the numerous male and female characters in *Arranged Marriage*, Divakaruni criticizes qualities that she sees as typically Indian and glorifies those that she sees as European-American. Divakaruni's feminism causes her to speak against Indian men in various ways in these short stories. In several stories such as "The Bats," "The Maid Servant's Story," "The Disappearance," "Doors," and "The Ultrasound," the Indian male characters, who often play a hegemonic role in a patriarchal society, are shown to be responsible for constricting, entrapping, cheating, brutalizing, and failing to understand women. In "The Bats" (*Arranged* 1-16), an abusive husband repeatedly gets his wife to return to him, exerting on her a power analogous to the poisonous traps in a mango orchard that lure bats to their deaths in the same story. In "The Maid Servant's Story" (*Arranged* 109-68), a respectable banker seems to have a loving relationship with his wife, until it is revealed that he tiptoes in the privacy of night to seek a sexual liaison with the wife's maid. Both of these stories are set in India, and the wives portrayed in them are overpowered by the males in their lives, as they are unable to free themselves from their undesirable marriages. On the other hand, the wife in "The Disappearance" (*Arranged* 169-81) is a Calcutta woman who lives in America with her husband and manages to get out of a marriage that she dislikes, due to no apparent reason as the husband sees it, other than the husband's exercising of his normal authority. So the immigrant woman in an uninteresting marriage exercises greater freedom of will than the women who are non-immigrants and stuck in marriages that are far worse. But while Divakaruni sees the failings of Indian patriarchy and Indian men, she mostly fails to notice any flaws in American men and American patriarchal society. In fact, she creates clear binaries between men from "the old countries" (*Arranged* 187) and American or Indian-American men. In "Doors" (*Arranged* 183-202), Preeti, an Indian girl who has been in the United States since the age of twelve, is warned against marrying Deepak, who is "straight out of India" where "men have a set of prehistoric values" (184), according to Preeti's mother. And sure enough, even after a good start, Deepak proves the mother's warnings "true" by falling into such Indian ways as inviting an old friend from India to live in their house, enjoying Indian snacks and movies, and neglecting the value of privacy and closed doors as much as his Americanized wife. So even a love match between an Indian and an Indian-American does not work because of the mismatched values in which the American values are the privileged and overwhelming norm in the Indian-American heroine's life.

In "A Perfect Life" (*Arranged* 73-108), Meera, an Indian-American professional woman, describes her concept of desirable men in terms of Hollywood hero charms:

> Richard was exactly the kind of man I'd dreamed about during my teenage years in Calcutta, all those moist, sticky evenings that I spent at the Empire Cinema House under a rickety ceiling fan that revolved tiredly, eating melted mango-pista ice cream and watching Gregory Peck and Warren Beatty and Clint Eastwood. Tall and lean and sophisticated, he was very different from the Indian men I'd known back home [...]. When I was with Richard I felt like a true American. (73)

The images from Hollywood movies projected on the screen of the "Empire" (note the imperialist name) Cinema dictate notions of desirability, good looks, and true Americanness. Meera's idols are Peck, Eastwood, and Beatty of Hollywood, not Dilip Kumar, Uttam Kumar or Amitabh Bachchan of Indian cinema. Also, Richard's distinguishing qualities are tallness, leanness, and sophistication; and as he is described as "very different" from Indian men, the latter are voided of such qualities by implication. Indian men are, thus, culturally, ideologically, mentally, and physically diminished in comparison to their American counterparts. To become a "true American," the woman of Indian origin must associate herself with a man who looks like an archetypal Hollywood hero. All the other kinds of Americans avoided or marginalized by Hollywood are not seen to be qualified as a so-called "true American."

Indian women are also characterized by many limitations in Divakaruni's short stories unless they already are, or in the process of being, westernized. In many of these stories, among other things, women readily accept being cheated, dominated, devitalized, and sexually manipulated. The wives in the "The Bats" and "The Maid Servant's Story" surrender to the manipulations of their husbands with little resistance. They stay in their abusive marriages to maintain the sham of social respectability while the cores of their lives are being eroded. But the stories end differently for Indian women who have immigrated to America and are ultimately able to embrace what Divakaruni characterizes as western values. In "Affair" (*Arranged* 231-72), Abha, an Indian housewife in Northern California, spends most of her time cooking and housekeeping. She suffers from what her husband Ashok describes as her "prudish Indian upbringing" (234) and cannot enjoy life as Ashok and her friend Meena seem to do. Abha does not wear stylish clothes or makeup, not caring whether her husband's heartbeat speeds up (235) on seeing her, as she has learned from seeing her mother that most Bengali wives wore simple cotton saris and were too busy with their household duties to care for their looks. When Ashok dances with Meena at a party, "Travolta-like" (248), Abha can just stand and look at the pair with envy. Only when Meena gets out of her lifeless arranged marriage with the mismatched Srikant, Abha realizes that her own marriage with Ashok is an arrangement that does not really work for either one of them. Only through Meena's decision to start a new life with her co-worker turned lover Charles, does Abha come to know that she herself has to start a new life, freeing herself and Ashok from the ties of a futile marriage. In "Meeting Mrinal" (*Arranged* 273-300), Asha, a divorced wife, carries around the shame of her husband's abandonment of her. Never truly loved by her husband, Asha is desperate to cling to her marriage and later to the appearance of being married, to maintain the façade of a perfect life, until the realization dawns on her that she has to face the imperfections of life, including the fact of her failed marriage. Both Abha and Asha are oblivious of their own true needs for half of their lives, until they can liberate themselves from their allegedly worn-out Indian values. They are seen as the victims of the Indian custom of arranged marriage until their changing lives in America free them from their exhausted marriages and they can wake up to the so-called blessings of westernization. When Divakaruni's female characters in any of these stories stand up for themselves, America is given a definite role in their awakening. As Anju, one of the two protagonists in the next story "The Ultrasound," attributes her sense of justice and feminism to America, it is a clear articulation of the way in which every liberated female character from *Arranged Marriage* seems to find freedom and awakening by discarding India and embracing America. In "The Ultrasound" (*Arranged* 203-30), two cousins, Runu and Anju, are pregnant at the same time. Runu lives in India and Anju lives in California. They both undergo ultrasound and amniocentesis tests during their pregnancies. When it is revealed that Runu is pregnant with a girl, her husband and mother-in-law pressure her to have an abortion, because they would only accept a male child as the family's firstborn. Runu opposes this and leaves her husband's home with the guidance of Anju, who thinks that Runu's immigration to America will be the only panacea for all her problems. The story is told by Anju in the first-person narrative voice, as are many of Divakaruni's stories. Anju describes her cousin Runu as the traditionally feminine type, who studied Home Science, while Anju studied English and American literatures. As children, when they visualized their futures through their rudimentary drawings, Anju cast herself in the roles of explorer, scientist, and adventurer, while Runu imagined herself as a wife and mother. As Runu decides to end her marriage to save her child, in a fleeting moment of apprehension, Anju questions herself about her part in taking away Runu's traditional Indian womanly qualities by her own "misplaced American notions of feminism and justice" (227). Although Anju's feminism is actually expressed through her childhood drawings about her future occupations, which predate her readings of English and American literature in college and her migration to America, she declares that her notions of feminism and justice are "American." So in spite of the story's flashback device showing Anju as a budding feminist in her childhood drawings, the authorial voice denies that pre-existing feminist and places her feminism in the geographic and cultural boundaries of America.

America itself is seen not only as the country that holds many opportunities, but also as a mythical "promised land" (293) along with England, on occasions. In most of the stories of *Arranged Marriage*, the United States of America stands for freedom, enlightenment, and promises of fairytale fulfilment. But in "Meeting Mrinal" both the old colonial centre and the new centre of the so-called first world make up the landscape of this "promised land." The character of James Bond, the English spy with global reach, becomes an apt symbol for a world where neo-colonial control is exercised through methods even subtler than those of colonial times, as international political, cultural, and commercial power struggles continue in newer manifestations. Bond's capacity to seduce the world is felt through the admiration of two of Divakaruni's Indian-born heroines:

> We'd been avid James Bond fans all through high school, fascinated by his violent, magical world—so different from ours—of golden guns and intricate machines and bikini-clad beauties. If we ever escaped our conservative, teetotaler parents, we had vowed, if we ever made it to the promised land, England maybe, or America, we would celebrate by drinking Bond's special drink. (*Arranged* 293)

It is ironic that the sexist James Bond is made to be a role model for two women characters, one of whom evidently lives by feminist principles. In the same story, in Divakaruni's brief one-dimensional reading of them, characters of Hindu religious mythology, Sita and Kunti and Arjun and Bhim, are blamed for perpetrating stereotypes of female sacrifice and male power respectively, while gun-wielding, womanizing Bond is elevated to the stature of the magical and admirable liberator. As could be expected, such denigration of Indian culture and elevation of British culture was routinely a part of the official and unofficial colonialist propaganda of the British Raj in India.

The United States is re-designated as the promised land in Divakaruni's novel *Sister of My Heart*,[8] which is an expansion of the short story "The Ultrasound." The novel creates an intriguing background, set mostly in India, to lead up to the situation depicted in "The Ultrasound." In *Sister of My Heart*, we see the cousins Anju and Sudha (Runu from "The Ultrasound" re-emerges here as Sudha) growing up together and developing a bond that is stronger than any other bond in the world. Whereas "The Ultrasound" ends with the expectation of Runu's migration to America, in the story's novelistic incarnation we are given more insight into the rationale and the promise of this immigration. The United States again becomes the promised land, "as amazing as the fairy kingdoms of Pishi's tales" (179), the land across the ocean at the end of the rainbow (309-10), where Sudha decides to go, to save her unborn daughter from being aborted, as determined by her husband and mother-in-law. Although, in India, Sudha gets the unending, unselfish support of Ashok who is her first love, and stands by her throughout her troubles, the plot weaves its way to an American airport where Sudha arrives with the support of the "Sister of [her] Heart," her cousin Anju who is married to Sunil, a computer programmer who has migrated from India to the United States. The same Sunil had once desired the exceedingly beautiful Sudha even as his marriage ceremony to Anju was proceeding. Yet Sudha's long road of suffering leads her to America and to Sunil and Anju, not to Ashok, who loves her unselfishly through her marriage (to someone else), pregnancy, and divorce. Being situated in India, Ashok is not seen as being able to provide the safe harbour that the American cousins are expected to provide. In the following excerpt, we see America through the eyes of both sisters: "America has its own problems, she [Anju] said, but at least it would give me [Sudha] the advantage of anonymity.

No-one in America would care that I was a daughter of the Chatterjees, or that I was divorced. I could design a new life, earn my own living, give Dayita everything she needed" (294). In Sudha and Anju's expectations of the United States and in the novel's almost forced migration of Sudha to America, it is too easily forgotten that anonymity and newness may also mean a loss of identity and socio-cultural isolation.

Divakaruni's idealization of America makes her ignore the possibility that when migration pulls people away from their known environment and culture and places them in a culture that puts a tremendous emphasis on homogeneity and assimilation, they could be socially outcast even if they are technically accepted in their new home. All the complexities of America's past and present race and class relations are also brushed aside with nothing more than a few passing references in Divakaruni's narratives of immigration. America becomes this unique, exceptional, magical country which offers a safe refuge to the female characters of Divakaruni's fiction, mostly middle-class Indian women oppressed by Indian traditions and having the means of passage to European-style advancement in the "exceptional" promised land of the United States. Divakaruni's western critics repeatedly reiterate the notion of America being the rejuvenator of her Indian female characters and endorse the binaries the writer creates between India and America. Rose Kernochan makes the following comment about the characters of the short stories in *Arranged Marriage*:

> Recently arrived from Calcutta, unsettled in Chicago and San Francisco, Ms. Divakaruni's heroines are still half-submerged in the dream world of Indian femininity, in an innocence as still and dark as lake water. As America revives them, they rise to its challenges; the new freedoms of their chosen country act on them like extra oxygen. (20)

Reviewing the novel *Sister of My Heart*, Peter Nazareth writes, "In Divakaruni's work, despite sex, class, and caste oppression, women need not end up as victims. America chips away at ossified Indian tradition, for people to see, as Krishna shows, that the imperative of life is deeper than arranged marriage. America and India are twinned" (819). What Nazareth does not explicitly say, yet his comment leads us to the notion, is that in this twinning process, America is the more powerful and empowering of the two.

Whether intended or not, Chitra Divakaruni's work can participate in the task of promoting America's neo-imperialistic role and propagating the doctrine of American exceptionalism,[9] along with replaying the British colonialist propaganda of the superiority of European civilization in comparison with the backwardness of Indian civilization. Here, I would also like to refer to Donald Pease's discussion of the exceptionalist doctrine's influence on United States history, whereby the United States, with the help of its cultural, academic, economic, and political sectors, has shaped its image as a haven of liberty and egalitarianism, even while colonial and imperial practices have been used by its European settlers in their encounters with other races and nations throughout its history. As Pease says, the country's white settlers collaborated with Britain's "colonial domination of indigenous populations" (209) and continued those practices through policies of racial discrimination even after its independence from Britain. In relation to its newer immigrant populations, cultural domination, stereotyping, categorization, and assimilation continued to maintain Euro-white supremacy internally (Pease 215). When immigrant narratives ignore these neo-colonial practices and set off on a mission to glorify immigrants' lives in the United States, beyond reality and reason, they participate in popularizing and validating the exceptionalist doctrine. To quote Pease:

> Immigrant narratives that represented the US as a haven from colonial and political oppression closed this circle [of imperialism] by authorizing indirectly immigration policies of exclusion and denaturalization. Each story that represented the United States as safe haven from colonial oppression abroad eclipsed the history of U.S. colonial relations. The myth of the United States as a promised land erased the middle passage narrative of slaves who were brought to the United States against their will, and the stories of migrant laborers the state had newly colonized, and of immigrants who felt their conditions had worsened. (215)

Much of Divakaruni's writing portrays the United States as a safe haven and a promised land for her immigrant characters. In her stories the United States is repeatedly anointed with such classic mythical terms as the promised land, the land beyond the seven seas, and the fairy kingdom. Clear binaries are also constructed between the United States and India, with the United States being endowed with most of the positive and redeeming qualities and India being portrayed as the backward and the evil in need of redemption. The heroine immigrants of her narratives, who are able to find passage from India to the United States, are designated as the lucky ones from a primitive society who receive the benefactions of the advanced society of the promised land.

During the British colonization of India, the official British propaganda, the accounts of British historians, travel writing, Orientalist scholarship, missionary accounts, literature, popular press, theater, and even advertisements repeatedly constructed the kind of Manichean binaries that we can find in Divakaruni's writing. Promoting the superiority of the British and undermining the Indian was the colonizer's most potent tool for chipping away the identity of the colonized. In a book originally published in 1961 with research partially funded by the multinational Shell Oil Company, an American scholar George D. Bearce presents accounts of the reforms brought forth in India by the British colonial administrators. With opinion tinged by his own western imperialist attitudes, Bearce writes: "In the evolution of India to an independent state, both Munro and Elphinstone expected Indians to acquire political and moral qualities like those of the West" (140). Then, moving on to the times of the "great" reformers Bentinck, Metcalfe, and Macaulay, administrative and legislative discourses are saturated with the rhetoric of progress and reform, brought forth by a superior civilization's influence (hegemony) over an inferior one.[10]

Beyond the official discourse machines and the missionary goals of religious conversion, a big part of British popular literature and culture also wanted, by turns, to recast the Indian in European terms and denigrate the Indian. In a study on representations of Indians in Britain, Shompa Lahiri surveys dramas, novels, and press coverage that served these two goals. Shompa Lahiri's research presents us with numerous accounts of stereotypical representations of western educated Indians as "ridiculous babus, monstrous hybrids, discontented villainous nationalists, or disillusioned individuals" to neutralize any "perceived threat" from the English educated Indian who was made to be a poor, ineffectual travesty of the true English gentleman (82-110). Benita Parry, in her research on British accounts of India from 1880-1930, presents us with many acutely prejudiced, often wildly fantastic and disturbing renditions of Indian people and customs as weird, depraved, and primitive, in the British novels on India, some written by people who had lived and worked in India, and some written by those who had never been to India, but desired to participate in a ritual of undermining the colonized Other (3).

When Chitra Divakaruni re-creates the binaries of British colonialist literature in her immigrant literature, the colonialist writer reincarnates through this supposedly decolonized immigrant writer. This kind of writer is not empowered by the condition of cultural hybridity, as envisioned by Homi Bhabha; but, as Aijaz Ahmad would explain, she is afflicted by an excess of belonging as a result of not belonging anywhere in particular, and yet, is very much bonded to the demands of the dominant centre of power, chosen as the immigration destination. In her writing, a once colonized nation is portrayed as its colonial masters and their descendants would want to see it; colonialist thoughts and processes are perpetuated by showing that the people of a once colonized country can find redemption only under the influence of some other "superior" civilization. Both the old colonizers and the new imperialists are characterized as superiors and saviours. The tracks of Euro-American injustices and hegemony are covered up with ease, while their humanitarian glories are demonstrated in comparison with the perceived lack of those glories in the discarded homeland.

NOTES

1. In "US Imperialism: Global Domination without Colonies," Donald Pease writes that the white settlers in the United States collaborated in Britain's "colonial domination of indigenous populations" and continued those practices through policies of racial discrimination even after its cessation from Britain. According to Pease, in the 20th and 21st centuries, the US has established itself as the military, economic, and cultural superpower of the world, using different versions of imperialist tactics used by European empires of the earlier century. Some examples of these imperialist tactics are the acquisition of territorial and informal colonies in South America and Asia, supremacy in the arms race, domination of global energy resources, and cultural and ideological hegemony.
2. For interpretations of Bharati Mukherjee's work focusing on her treatment of the themes of dislocation and identity transformations, see the following texts: "The Aesthetics of Dislocation: Writing the Hybrid Lives of South Asian Americans" by Ketu Katrak, "Looting American Culture: Bharati Mukherjee's Immigrant Narratives" by Jennifer Drake, "Refashioning the Self: Immigrant Women in Bharati Mukherjee's New World" by Arvinda Sant-Wade and Karen Radell, and "'Re-inventing Ourselves a Million Times': Narrative, Desire, Identity, and Bharati Mukherjee's *Jasmine*" by Timothy F. Ruppel.
3. My research on Divakaruni has led me only to book reviews, biographical accounts, and interviews. So the only dialogues that I could generate with other critics of Divakaruni are between those reviewers of her books and myself.
4. Jan Mohammed qtd. in Aschroft, Griffiths, and Tiffin, *Key Concepts* 133-35.
5. For a discussion about Manichean allegory in Mukherjee's *Jasmine*, see the article "'Re-inventing Ourselves a Million Times': Narrative, Desire, Identity, and Bharati Mukherjee's *Jasmine*." In this article, Ruppel remarks that Mukherjee's depiction of India and the Sikh community in *Jasmine* is reliant on Manichean allegory, and hence the novel is not a fully "realized postcolonial text."
6. Here, I list a few examples of feminist figures in Indian history and culture from whom Divakaruni could have sought feminist inspiration. In Hindu religious mythology, the goddesses Kali and Durga are influential icons seen as manifestations of power, preservers of good, and destroyers of evil. As early as the year 1236, Muslim princess Razia Sultana of the Turk dynasty battled against male contenders for the throne of Delhi, and established herself as a just and popular ruler, until her assassination in 1241 by one of her brothers in pursuit of the throne. In 1858, Lakshmi Bai or the Rani (queen) of Jhansi (1830-

1858) led a fierce military resistance to British colonial forces that wanted to annex the independent Indian state of Jhansi on the pretext that the king of Jhansi left no male heir. Bankim Chandra Chatterjee's (1838-1894) novel *Devi Choudhurani* (1884) presents a pseudo-historical treatment of the story of a woman named Devi Choudhurani who transforms herself from a zamindar's (landlord's) bride captured by dacoits into a leader of the dacoits and eventually a freedom fighter aiding rebellions against British colonial rule. To create an association through which all Indian women could promote their own causes, feminist and nationalist Sarala Devi Chaudhurani (not related to Chatterjee's Devi Choudhurani) founded Bharat Stree Mahamandal in 1910. Rokeya Sakhawat Hossain (1880-1932) was a feminist writer and activist who strongly advocated equal rights for women through her writings and social activism. Among her feminist writings are a utopian novel *Sultana's Dream* (1905) and stories about the impact of purdah, *The Secluded Ones* (1928). Historian Bharati Ray has combined the inspirational lives of Chaudhurani and Hossain in *Early Feminists of Colonial India: Sarala Devi Chaudhurani and Rokeya Sakhawat Hossain*. Rabindranath Tagore (1861-1941) has written many novels, stories, and plays foregrounding strong women characters, whose thoughts and aspirations may be characterized as feminist. Kumu from the novel *Yogayog* (1929), Labonyo from the novel *Shesher Kabita* (1929), and Mrinal from the short story "Strir Patra" (1914) are just three of many such characters created by Tagore.

7. Zed Books is a United Kingdom based publishing co-operative that avows to publish books on "international and Third World issues" and asserts that "making a positive difference in the real world of both social action and intellectual ideas is what motivates [them] to persevere as an independent publishing house committed to contributing to a deeper understanding of the issues, conditions of life, oppressive structures and dominant ideologies which confront ordinary people and to drawing attention to the human struggles and innovative ideas that hold out some hope for an improvement in the human condition." To read more about Zed Books, visit their website at <http://www.zedbooks.demon.co.uk/>.

8. Beautifully written, with elements of social criticism, adventure story, and sentimental novel blended together, *Sister of My Heart* may remind a Bengali reader of the novels of Sarat Chandra Chattopadhyaya, the popular Bengali novelist whose criticisms of child marriages, caste discriminations, and injustices to women were interwoven with fascinating tales of love and adventure. Even with such writers as Bankim Chandra Chatterjee and Rabindranath Tagore among his close predecessors, Sarat Chandra Chattopadhyaya (1876-

1938) could claim the position of the most popular Bengali novelist of his time. His novels became such a staple of Bengali culture that any literate Bengali is sure to have read, at least, a few of them. Many of his novels have been translated into other Indian languages such as Hindi, Marathi, Gujarati, and Malayalam, and several of them have been turned into films by various filmmakers of India and Bangladesh. His novel *Devdas* (Chattopadhyaya 1: 583-643), published in 1917, has generated nine films in India, with its latest 2002 Hindi version becoming a major blockbuster.

Chattopadhyaya's novels could deliver social criticism through engaging stories and poignant characterizations. His writing eloquently portrays women's sacrifices, sufferings, and strengths as they struggle to maintain their self respect in a society plagued by gender and caste discriminations. Divakaruni is a native of West Bengal, and therefore, certainly familiar with Chattopadhyaya's works. Like Chattopadhyaya, Divakaruni attempts to draw readers' attention to social injustices against women through the art of sensitive storytelling. Like the women of Chattopadhyaya's novels, Divakaruni's heroines are endowed with sensitivity, strength, and a resilience that enables them to survive through endless trials. *Sister of My Heart* even uses a plot device of hidden identity, similar to what Chattopadhyaya used in the first part of his four-part novel *Srikanta* (1917, 1918, 1927, and 1933). In *Srikanta* (Chattopadhyaya 1: 1-351) a Hindu Brahmin woman, Annada, elopes with a rootless snake-charmer named Shahji, bringing society's condemnation on herself. But it is unknown to everyone else that Shahji is really her husband who went in hiding after murdering Annada's sister. Shahji hides his true identity in the guise of a snake-charmer to escape punishment for murder. Similarly, in *Sister of My Heart*, Singhji works as a chauffeur in the house where his wife and daughter live. But he uses the guises of his burnt face and assumed Sikh persona to hide his true identity, because he is too embarrassed to reveal himself after inadvertently leading his benefactor to his death. Such dark secrets and their revelations add elements of mystery and melodrama to *Srikanta* as well as *Sister of My Heart*. But Divakaruni does not consciously reveal Chattopadhyaya as a source of feminist or narrative inspiration; instead her novel's characters discuss Woolf, Hardy, Dickens, and Dante, with Woolf declared as the primary inspiration as a pioneering western feminist.

9. The doctrine of exceptionalism represents the United States of America as unique and different from Europe and claims that the white European settlers who settled in America did not reproduce the European structures of monarchy, feudalism and colonialism. Instead the foundations of this country are based supposedly on egalitarian and inclusive principles. In an introductory essay to *A Companion to*

Post-colonial Studies, Henry Schwarz (9) explains how the doctrine of exceptionalism pervades U.S. academic traditions and "creates the imaginary divide between postcolonial and other ethnic studies in the United States." So the very common interests and multiple intersections of ethnic and postcolonial studies are often denied in the American universities.

10. The idea that British society was far superior to Indian society and had the responsibility of reforming the inferior Indian society was common among 19th century colonial administrators. The "philosophical legislator" (Bearce 159) Macaulay's now infamous "Minute on Indian Education" is a well-known example of this high-handed ideology. An excerpt from the minute displays how Macaulay takes it upon himself and the Orientalists to be the judges of the low worth of Indian literary efforts and historical knowledge: "I am quite ready to take the Oriental learning at the valuation of the Orientalists themselves. I have never found one among them who could deny that a single shelf of a good European library was worth the whole native literature of India and Arabia [...]. But when we pass from works of imagination to works in which facts are recorded, and general principles investigated, the superiority of the Europeans becomes absolutely immeasurable. It is, I believe, no exaggeration to say, that all the historical information which has been collected from all the books written in the Sanskrit language is less valuable than what may be found in the most paltry abridgements used at preparatory schools in England" (349).

WORKS CITED

Ahmad, Aijaz. *In Theory: Classes, Nations, Literatures*. London: Verso, 1992.

Alexander, Meena. *Fault Lines: A Memoir*. New York: Feminist P at CUNY, 1993.

——. *The Shock of Arrival: Reflections on Postcolonial Experience*. Boston: South End, 1996.

Ashcroft, Bill, Gareth Griffiths, and Helen Tiffin. *The Empire Writes Back: Theory and Practice in Post-Colonial Literatures*. London: Routledge, 1989.

——. *Key Concepts in Post-Colonial Studies*. London: Routledge, 1998.

Bearce, George D. *British Attitudes Towards India 1784-1858*. 1961. Westport: Greenwood, 1982.

Bhabha, Homi K. *The Location of Culture*. London: Routledge, 1994.

Chatterjee, Bankim Chandra. *Devi Choudhurani*. 1884. *Bankim Rachanaboli*. Calcutta: Tuli-Kalam, 1986. N. pag.

Chattopadhyaya, Sarat Chandra. *Srikanta*. Sharat Rachanaboli. Vol. 1. Calcutta: Dey's, 1993. 1-351. [1917-1933]

——. *Devdas*. *Sharat Rachanaboli*. Vol. 1. Calcutta: Dey's, 1993. 583-643. [1917]

Devdas. Dir. Sanjay Leela Bhansali. Perf. Shah Rukh Khan, Aishwarya Rai, and Madhuri Dixit. Mega Bollywood, 2002.

Divakaruni Banerjee, Chitra. *Arranged Marriage*. New York: Anchor-Doubleday, 1995.

——. *Black Candle—Poems about Women from India, Pakistan, and Bangladesh*. Corvallis: Calyx, 1991.

——. *Sister of My Heart*. London: Black Swan-Doubleday, 1999.

Drake, Jennifer. "Looting American Culture: Bharati Mukherjee's Immigrant Narratives." *Contemporary Literature* 40.1 (1999): 60-84.

Grewal, Gurleen. "Indian-American Literature." *New Immigrant Literatures in the United States: A Sourcebook to Our Multicultural Literary Heritage*. Ed. Alpana Sharma Kippling. Westport: Greenwood, 1996.

Hossain, Rokeya Sakhawat. *Sultana's Dream: A Feminist Utopia and Selections from the Secluded Ones*. Ed. and trans. Roushan Jahan. New York: Feminist P, 1988. [1905; 1928]

Katrak, Ketu. "The Aesthetics of Dislocation: Writing the Hybrid Lives of South Asian Americans." *Women's Review of Books* 19.5 (2002): 5-6.

Kernochan, Rose. Rev. of *Arranged Marriage*, by Chitra Banerjee Divakaruni. *The New York Times Book Review* 16 Jul. 1995: 20.

Lahiri, Shompa. *Indians in Britain: Anglo-Indian Encounters, Race and Identity, 1880-1930*. London: Frank Cass, 2000.

Macaulay, T.B. "Minute on Indian Education." 2 Feb. 1835. *Speeches by Lord Macaulay with His Minute on Indian Education*. London: Oxford University Press, 1935.

Mohanty, Chandra Talpade. "Under Western Eyes: Feminist Scholarship and Colonial Discourses." Williams and Chrisman 196-220.

Mukherjee, Bharati. *Jasmine*. New York: Grove, 1989.

Muller, Gilbert H. *New Strangers in Paradise: The Immigrant Experience and Contemporary American Fiction*. Lexington: University of Kentucky Press, 1999.

Nazareth, Peter. "World Literature in Review: India." *World Literature Today* 73.4 (1999): 819-20.

Parry, Benita. *Delusions and Discoveries: Studies on India in the British Imagination 1880-1930*. Berkeley: UCLA P, 1972.

Pease, Donald E. "US Imperialism: Global Dominance without Colonies." Schwarz and Ray 203-20.

Ray, Bharati. *Early Feminists of Colonial India: Sarala Devi Chaudhurani and Rokeya Sakhawat Hossain*. New Delhi: Oxford University Press, 2002.

Ruppel, Timothy F. "'Re-inventing Ourselves a Million Times': Narrative, Desire, Identity, and Bharati Mukherjee's *Jasmine*." *College Literature* 22.1 (1995): 181-91.

Said, Edward W. *Orientalism*. 1978. New York: Vintage, 1979.

Sant-Wade, Arvinda and Karen Radell. "Refashioning the Self: Immigrant Women in Bharati Mukherjee's New World." *Studies in Short Fiction* 29.1 (1992): 11-17.

Schwarz, Henry. "Mission Impossible: Introducing Post-colonial Studies in the US Academy." *A Companion to Post-colonial Studies*. Ed. Henry Schwarz and Sangeeta Ray. Oxford: Blackwell, 2000. 1-20.

Tagore, Rabindranath. *Shesher Kabita*. 1929. *Rabindranather Upanyaas Samagra*. Dhaka: Naoroze, 1990. 1045-1105.

——. "Strir Patra." 1924. *Galpaguchcha*. Dhaka: Naoroze, 1990. 448-56.

——. *Yogayog*. 1929. *Rabindranather Upanyaas Samagra*. 449-566.

Williams, Patrick and Laura Chrisman, eds. *Colonial Discourse and Post-Colonial Theory*. New York: Columbia University Press, 1994.

5

"The Old Rules Aren't Always Right": An Analysis of Four Short Stories by Chitra Banerjee Divakaruni

Felicity Hand

> Life for women in diasporic situations can be doubly painful—struggling with the material and spiritual insecurities of exile, with the demands of family and work, and with the claims of old and new patriarchies. (Clifford 314)
>
> The dichotomy of "Indian" versus "American" thus becomes a gendered and sexualized contrast. (Maira 47)

Until relatively recently, studies on the South Asian diaspora[1] tended to focus on the male experience of uprooting, migration and relocation and extrapolate it to cover the experience of all migrants, regardless of their gender. Political or research attention levelled at the South Asian community[2] rarely discussed women with the result that the general public tended to perceive them in stereotypes: docile, subservient, bound by tradition. Since the 1990s, however, a great deal of new research has contributed to highlighting the female experience of migration in addition to which several authors, themselves NRIs (Non-Resident Indians) have contributed with their creative writing to making certain ethnic experiences public knowledge.

In an article published in *Cultural Studies* in 1992, anthropologist Keya Ganguly focused on the experiences of migration of a group of professional middle-class Indians who had migrated to the United States in the late 1960s and early 1970s. Her research proved the enormous difference between the memories of the past and the appraisal of the present of the men and women of her study. Migration was, in general terms, a liberation and improvement in status for the men, while the women tended to regard the past with nostalgia and the present American experience as an alienating one. For the first generation of migrants, life in the new country may frequently turn out to be one fraught with misunderstandings, discrimination and the day-to-day business of recreating one's culture in an unwelcoming atmosphere. The second generation migrants or those who were taken abroad at a young age have no difficulty in adapting to the host culture but they are obliged to navigate between two traditions, an unenviable position, which can cause distress and feelings of guilt or disloyalty. In this article I would like to focus on four of Chitra Banerjee Divakaruni's short stories from her collection *Arranged Marriage* (1997), which provide a literary representation of women's experience of displacement. The stories deal with a number of issues relating to the experience of South Asian female migrants. Divakaruni analyzes the tensions and constraints that women of Indian origin are subjected to in the diasporic context. However, she does not fall back on the stock character of the helpless Indian woman immigrant, at a loss in a foreign society and lacking the most basic linguistic skills. Divakaruni's protagonists are educated women, frequently either studying or doing dissertations, perfectly at ease with life in America, albeit still connected to Indian codes of conduct and belief systems.

Before I deal with the stories in detail, I will say a few words about the South Asian diaspora in America as it serves as the sociocultural context in which Divakaruni weaves her stories. Until the mid-nineteen sixties, most of the Indians in the United States were Sikh farmers from the Punjab who settled mostly in rural parts of California, answering the call for agricultural labourers. Strict immigration legislation implemented after 1923 together with the United States

Supreme Court decision that East Indians were not eligible for citizenship because they were not "free white people" drastically reduced the entry of Indians in similar circumstances. Apart from small numbers of Indian students fleeing British colonialism, South Asians would not become a sizeable community in the United States until after the Immigration Act of 1965 which removed the race factor from the right to entry and which showed a clear preference for educated and professional people. A steady stream of doctors, engineers, professors and technicians have migrated to the United States from the Indian subcontinent with the result that by the end of the twentieth century there were over one million people of Indian origin in the United States (Rayaprol 2001). In the United States Indians have come to be regarded as a model minority, exemplifying high educational status and strong financial success. In this way the Indian community in America has gained in self-esteem and confidence, and can be seen to have progressed socially and economically from the early twentieth century farm workers. This is not to obviate the racism that still permeates America and that the community itself rejects other so-called "ethnic" groups such as African Americans. The desire and need to fit into U.S. mainstream society and the inevitable culture conflicts when choices must be made between American and traditional Indian values are only some of the pitfalls facing the diasporic subject.

The U.S. media invented the label of "model minority" for Indians and Asian peoples in general in order to justify the exclusion of these communities from social welfare programmes. Thanks to this media myth, it was assumed that Indians were exempt from social problems such as unemployment, poverty, racism, delinquency and familial conflict. Although it may seem to be counterproductive, especially in the case of working-class South Asians, this myth has been internalized by the community themselves. Curiously enough, the burden of living up to the stereotype of model minority has become a priority amongst Indians, who were already anxious to hide any hint of internal diversity. Thus the appearance of a monolithic community is maintained in public and even in private within the sanctity of the home. Calls for cultural purity mean that the usual contradictions and divergences, part and parcel of any lived culture, including those labelled as "traditional" such as the Indian, are hidden from the prying eyes of mainstream America in the United States in the name of unity and coherence.[3] The burden of preserving this image of a coherent, united community, faithful to its ancestral customs and traditions is, to a large extent, placed on the shoulders of the women. The site for preservation of India, its culture and its tradition is the family. The domestic space, domain of the woman, is where Indianness is affirmed. The Indian woman is expected to be responsible for maintaining this Indian home in the diaspora by remaining true to her Indian womanhood. Very often, in the diaspora context, being "true" to one's Indian womanhood means glorifying Hindu mores and codes of conduct and becoming even more conservative than one's counterpart in the subcontinent.[4] This phenomenon is not just confined to Indians in the United States, as it is a common reaction among the various diasporic communities around the globe. Therefore immigrants become frozen in an India of the past and their attempts to preserve their culture translate into rigidly holding on to the values that were prevalent at the time of their departure, ignorant of the fact that Indian society has moved on. As Vijay Mishra points out,

> diasporas construct homelands in ways that are very different from people of the homelands themselves. For an Indian in the diaspora, for instance, India is a very different kind of homeland than for the Indian national. (424)

In British filmmaker Gurinder Chadha's film *Bhaji on the Beach* (1994), this phenomenon is comically portrayed through the characters of saree-clad Pushpa, Bina and Asha, who are aghast at the westernised clothes worn by Rekha, recently arrived from Bombay. They stubbornly cling to an idea of "home," despite the fact that they have lived in Britain for more than twenty years and view British society as decadent and alien. This apparent refusal to accept the norms of the host culture is connected with the myth of return. The belief that one day they will return to India allows them to cope with a society that is often overtly hostile to foreign looks, sounds and even smells. The ladies are not so politely asked to put away their bhajis as only "English food" can be consumed on the premises of a cafeteria.

One of these Indian migrants was the writer Chitra Banerjee Divakaruni, who emigrated to the United States in 1976 at the age of nineteen. To date, Divakaruni has published three volumes of poetry, three novels, two books for children as well as two collections of short stories, *Arranged Marriage*, published in 1997, and more recently *The Unknown Errors of Our Lives* in 2001. *Arranged Marriage* is a collection of eleven short stories which deal with conflicts arising out of love. The short story "Affair" highlights the double dislocation of the migrant, middle-class Indian woman who, in most instances, is primarily a housewife. "The Word Love," on the other hand, analyses the different conceptions of love in India and the United States. "Doors" suggests that cross-cultural marriages, even between an American-raised Indian and an Indian brought up in the subcontinent, are often doomed to fail. "Ultrasound" contrasts and contextualises Indian patriarchy and American feminism.[5]

"Affair" traces the awakening of Abha, a middle-class, Indian housewife living in the United States to her own individuality. The discovery that her best friend is having an affair makes her rethink her own marriage. Despite her initial suspicions, her friend's lover does not turn out to be her own husband, but instead of feeling relief, the effect of this knowledge is to speed up her understanding of her relationship with him. She finally takes the decision to leave him and live her own life with the possibility of economic independence after she is offered a well-paid job compiling an Indian cookbook.

The story opens up with a highly domestic scene in which the female protagonist, Abha, is busy preparing dinner. Her husband, Ashok, casually and slyly informs her that her best friend and confidante, Meena, is having an affair. Abha's world suddenly collapses all around her, shocked as she is by the news of her friend's extra-marital liaison and by the latter's failure to confide first in her instead of in a man. Abha finds relief in her domain, the kitchen, where she feels "sane and in control" (A 233). Meena's action, not so much the actual affair but the divulging of the secret to Ashok, is a grievous blow to Abha's understanding of Indian female solidarity. Maintaining social networks and family connections is of vital importance to Indian women migrants. Through this network they manage to preserve a certain degree of influence within the home and in society at large. In the diasporic context many women find themselves alone and lacking the support system they had grown up with in India and which provided emotional and psychological sustenance. Thus Meena has deliberately distanced herself from her Indian upbringing, first by refusing to accommodate herself to her husband, Srikant, and secondly by denying the female members of her community the opportunity to criticise and lament her decision.

Divakaruni uses Meena as a foil for Abha in order to contrast and comment on two possible adaptations for women in the migrant's world. Meena has totally reconstructed her identity, she has no hang-ups about preserving family honour, she has completely shaken off the chains of patriarchy. Even in moments of despair, when contemplating suicide as the only outlet to her unhappy marriage, she knew that her friend would accuse her of being "so melodramatic, so Californian" (A 267). Meena takes pride in her appearance, she wants to be admired and have all the men gathered around her "like bemused moths" (A 245). Abha, on the other hand, bears the burden of being Indian in a foreign context having assumed the public role that is assigned to women. Women are made responsible for community morals and the good name of the family and, by extension, the community. All this is closely linked to the concept of family pride or *izzat*. This notion of honour clearly lies with the women who are assigned the role of bearers of traditions and culture as well as transmitters to the next generation (see Hand, "Shaking Off"). The logical consequence of this is that the conduct of immigrant and second generation women is monitored closely and any transgressors are branded as "westernized" or worse, "traitors" to their culture. Throughout the story Abha's thoughts, rendered in italics, first constitute a running commentary on Meena's affair and then gradually develop into a soul-searching analysis of her own marriage.

> *But what kind of man would be worth giving up your principles for? What kind of man would be more important than being a good wife?* (A 237)
>
> *We're spiraling toward hate. And hopelessness. That's not what I want for the rest of my life. Or yours.* (A 271)

Indian women in the United States seem to have to make the choice between being properly South Asian or being a feminist as these are perceived as being mutually exclusive categories. Paradoxically, some Indian scholars argue that Westernization actually denies variability in women's roles as, according to the West, Indian women must be either traditional or progressive, whereas the reality may be a healthy mixture of the two (Dasgupta 11-12). Having taken the decision to leave her husband for another man, Meena appears to have chosen American individualism over loyalty to her cultural traditions. She is, however, still occasionally tormented by doubts as she explains to Abha:

> Sometimes I still feel so guilty. I think of what my parents will say, and Srikant's mother, when they find out. *Selfish*, they'll call me. *Immoral*. A *bad woman*. I have to keep telling myself I'm not that. It's not wrong to want to be happy, is it? To want more out of life than fulfilling duties you took on before you knew what they truly meant? (A 270: emphases original)

Social relations rather than individual behaviour are the hallmark of Indian people and as identity is constructed in family terms, it follows that there is little space for discussion of individual sexuality. Sexuality is an individual practice, which if not legitimized by marriage, can be construed to be destructive to the family. So not only is it not openly talked about but it is definitely relegated to the privacy of the home. As Abha reasons, "Sex for me was a matter between married people, carried out in the silent privacy of their bedroom and resulting, hopefully, in babies" (A 234).

For her, duty and love are incompatible. She shies away from any public demonstration of affection, "too traditional to even touch hands" (A 238). Meena, however, has no qualms about indulging in free physical contact as she kisses both Abha and Ashok on the cheek, "not something Indians did as a rule" (A 246).

Abha's slow realization that her marriage to Ashok is empty runs parallel with her gradual sexual awakening and the understanding of her own selfhood,

> Had I been wrong all this time, when I refused to let him turn the lights on as we made love, when I lay stiff and submissive under his thrusts until he was done with it? When I escaped thankfully to the bathroom to wash myself as soon as he moved off me? (A 243-44)
>
> Had I ever really been myself? I didn't think so. All my energy had been taken up in being a good daughter. A good friend. And of course a good wife. (A 269)

Benedict Anderson states that because the family has always been regarded as the "domain of disinterested love and solidarity" and because one does not freely choose the family one is to be born into, it is "interestless" so for that reason it, like the nation, "can ask for sacrifices" (131). The Indian family has traditionally asked women to forfeit their own ambitions and desires for the sake of family unity. Any challenge to the family or, by extension to the Indian community, is seen as a betrayal of national cultural values as the site for preservation of India, its culture, and its tradition is precisely the family. Seen in this light, the decision of both Meena and Abha to terminate their unsuccessful marriages is a direct attack on the institution of arranged marriage and a challenge to parental authority. Matching horoscopes and hasty bride-viewing are not always conducive to lifelong relationships. As Abha herself realises, "*The old rules aren't always right. Not here, not even in India*" (A 270).

Divakaruni's story "The Word Love" confronts two opposing, but at the same time, complementary understandings of the concept of love. The young woman protagonist of the story, who remains nameless throughout her confession, is wrought with guilt for not daring to tell her mother in Calcutta that she is living with an American. The choice of the second person narrative confessional mode is highly appropriate for Divakaruni to transmit the woman's growing doubts and anguish to the reader. She is tormented by the deception that her circumstances in America have forced her into. Much as she would like to tell her mother that she has simply fallen in love with a foreigner and has moved in with him, she knows she cannot, she is conscious that her mother, widowed when her only child was a mere two years old and devoted to bringing her up ever since, would never understand her daughter's apparent rejection of customs and traditions. The woman is torn between divided loyalties and her American partner Rex is unable to comprehend her silence. For him, their relationship was the logical step for them to take. At first he is almost offended that she cannot bring herself to tell her mother that she has found a man she wants to share her life with, later he dismisses her distress with a simple remedy. If she cannot tell her mother about him as it would upset her, the best solution for her is to keep their relationship a secret. What Rex fails to grasp is that it is precisely the deceit more than the relationship itself what is tormenting the woman. Rex's apparent indifference to her plight triggers off a series of mind wrenching thoughts about the nature of their relationship. The awareness that they hail from utterly different backgrounds and have totally dissimilar conceptions of the world only appears when she feels her culture to be questioned or even ridiculed.

> "So don't tell her," he said, "that you're living in sin. With a foreigner, no less. Someone whose favorite food is sacred cow steak and Budweiser. Who pops a pill now and then when he gets depressed. The shock'll probably do her in." You hate it when he talks like that, biting off the ends of words and spitting them out. (WL 59)

Two different attitudes to sexuality and love, Western and Indian, are held up to scrutiny in this story. While reducing concepts to essentialisms always results in oversimplification, it is reasonable to posit that erotic love has long been privileged in Western discourses while other forms of love, in particular the familiar, is regarded as outside the erotic or romantic relationship (Dwyer 2000). Sexual desire, following Foucault, forms an essential part of love, as the key to personal or individual satisfaction and, to a certain extent, to self-knowledge.

While the sexual urge is universal and therefore not culturally specific, the relationship between sexual desire and love can be seen to vary according to different cultures. The nature of sexual love is an intimate and private phenomenon, requiring no outside intervention, for example from the family, and designed to gratify the couple, whether heterosexual or homosexual, themselves. Other forms of love, such as love of one's parents, siblings, relatives, are relegated to a subordinate position in the West and do not constitute a form of self-definition as sexual and/or erotic love does. In Indian families sexuality in adolescence is not only suppressed and repressed but even feared as potentially dangerous.

> Rarely does a mother discuss the mystery and seriousness of sexual awakening with her daughter. Sex education is left to nature and precocious peers. It is a taboo which has been handed down for generations [...]. Sexuality is approached indirectly through symbolic and metaphoric language rather than as a human behaviour needing open discussion, understanding and acceptance. These repressions are justified with the unspoken agreement that such a potentially dangerous awakening of body and psyche must be controlled and deferred until after marriage. (Roy 103)

As women have the responsibility to preserve the family honour, by extension, they have been assigned guardianship of community honour as well. Thus the connection made between sexuality and love in the Indian context is not the pursuit of individual self-satisfaction as it may be construed in the Western world but rather one that is intricately entwined with the duties and responsibilities of the family. Thus the conscience of the young woman in "The Word Love" gradually leaks into her, textually represented by italics, challenging her confidence in her decision because her relationship with Rex is based on physical attraction, sexual passion, and the lure of the forbidden fruit.

> *How did you get yourself into this mess*, or perhaps *why*, so you leap in with that magic word. *Love*, you tell yourself, *lovelovelove.*
>
> You try to shut out the whispery voice that lives behind the ache in your eyes, the one that started when you said yes [I will move in with you] and he kissed you, hard. (WL 59)

When whole families are together in the diaspora context, the daughter, who lives most of her life within the American culture, has little choice but to remain in confusion even when she feels more at home with her American identity. The power of internalised ideals, what a "good Indian girl" should and should not do, constantly make her public life a painful struggle. It is still difficult for an American-born daughter or young woman living in the United States to defy her parents' wishes in career choices and marriage. She is constantly alert to the mantra "what will others say?" It is interesting that young women do not feel guilty about having relationships with boys that their parents may not approve of because of the inherent immorality of such a relationship, but rather because they are being disobedient to their parents. It is the disloyalty to their parents that may disturb them not to a set of outdated moral codes (see DasGupta and Dasgupta).

To a lesser extent, this is also true of the young woman who is away from immediate parental control, as is the case of the troubled young woman in "The Word Love" who feels she has to make a choice between pleasure or duty. She becomes so tired and worn with the deceit and pretence that when the mother phones from Calcutta unexpectedly early one morning, she blurts out her secret. The mother's response is silent but swift:

> All through the next month you try to reach her. You call. The *ayah* answers. She sounds frightened when she hears your voice. *Memsaab* has told her not to speak to you, or else she'll lose her job.
>
> "She had the lawyer over yesterday to change her will. What did you do, Missybaba, that was so bad?"
>
> You hear your mother in the background. "Who are you talking to, Ayah? What? How can it be my daughter? I don't *have* a daughter. Hang up right now." (WL 65, emphases original)

Her mother's rigidity only strengthens the young woman's feelings of guilt. She becomes frantic about the loss of contact with her mother, and perhaps by extension, with her Indianness. What Rex sees as an obsession, she views as a rupture within her own self. Ironically, her disclosure to her mother of her relationship with an American ends in her being left by both of her loves, Rex and her own mother. The choice between emotional dependence and cultural loyalty has led to the realization that there exists a third choice—personal liberation:

> And a word comes to you out of the opening sky. The word *love*. You see that you had never understood it before. It is like rain, and when you life your face to it, like rain it washes away inessentials, leaving you hollow, clean, ready to begin. (WL 71, emphasis original)

The wisdom and experience of parents is proved by the ending of the story "Doors." Preeti's mother has foreseen that a marriage between a young woman raised in the individualistic society of the United States and a young man born and brought up in India will not work out. She is not blind to the differing expectations that each will bring to the relationship and can anticipate that her future son-in-law will one day yearn for his wife to be "obedient and adjusting and forgiving" in accordance with what she calls his "prehistoric values" (D 184). Likewise, Deepak's friends question his choice of marriage partner as ABCDs (American-Born-Confused-Desis) are notorious for being independent, self-confident and assertive. Heedless of these well-intentioned warnings, Preeti and Deepak embark on what they see as a lifelong relationship, stronger than a traditional, arranged marriage, confident that their love will conquer all. It is when the first obstacle arrives in the shape of Deepak's friend, Raj, that cracks start appearing in what had been up to then a perfect marriage.

Raj becomes a long-term houseguest, which in itself would have disturbed the peace and tranquillity of Preeti, a self-confessed private person, but Raj's presence brings out the Indianness in Deepak that has lain dormant since he has lived in America with Preeti, "this exotic creature—Indian and yet not Indian" (D 189). Not only does he acquire a long-lost taste for Bollywood films, but his accent becomes significantly more Indian and his duty as host leads him to allow Raj's welfare to take precedence over his wife's. Deepak and Preeti discover early on in their marriage that they have diametrically opposing concepts of space. Preeti is an only child, unaccustomed to sharing space and emotions with siblings. Her clear-cut conception of individual space is a totally westernised understanding of the need for privacy and closed doors. It is a complete reversal of Deepak's Indian upbringing within the boundary-less atmosphere of an extended family, where "they had constantly spilled into each other's rooms, doors always left open for chance remarks and jokes" (D 189).

Space is not only culturally but also gender constructed. In India women enjoy the company and support of other women in what is understood to be the women's part of the house. In traditional households where *purdah* was observed, the *zenana* or *andar-mahal* (women's quarters) was the domain of the female members of the family, and a space where they could abandon the strictures imposed on them by the patriarchal order. Women's personal problems, sexual or otherwise, could be openly discussed in a relaxed atmosphere, out of sight of the menfolk. The enormous psychological support that such a shared space can afford women cannot be underestimated and has to be seen as an empowering tool for Indian women. Indian women's identities are often articulated through this female network of interdependence as opposed to the Western feminist idea of individual selfhood. In Preeti's case this private female space has been irretrievably lost in the migration process. So strongly has she embraced her American persona that she clings desperately to her private space and shuts out any outside threat to her sanctuary, even her husband. Her almost obsessive door locking could represent her subconscious attempt to shut out any traces of Indianness that may still remain. What for Preeti is an individual right that must be respected, for Deepak is a rejection of the open, caring family ethos he was brought up in and an attitude bordering on the offensive:

> "Even family members sometimes need time and space away from each other. In my family no one ever intruded [...]."
>
> "Well, maybe they should have," Deepak interrupted in a hard tone that made Preeti stare at him. "Maybe then you'd be a little more flexible now." (D 198)

Preeti's outburst at Raj when he enters her bedroom uninvited to tell her some good news forces her to rethink her situation in the house. She has become Raj's *bhaviji* rather than Deepak's wife. The latter's male bonding with his friend has relegated her to a highly un-American secondary position, where her duty to her guest must override any inconvenience suffered because of extra chores or distaste at Raj's irritating habits. When Preeti announces she is moving in with her friend Cathy in the hope that this temporary separation will help them both to straighten things out, Deepak's reaction proved her mother to be right when she warned her that the couple might one day show signs of cultural incompatibility,

> "It's never too late to stop yourself from ruining your life," her mother said. "What do you really know about how Indian men think? About what they expect from their women?" (D 184)
>
> "You can't leave. What would people say? Besides, you're my wife. You belong in my home." (D 200)

Losing face, having people gossip, fearing his *izzat* to be jeopardized, are situations that cannot be tolerated in Deepak's world. His rigidity in keeping up a public image of marital bliss despite the cleavage that has opened up between them parallels Preeti's lack of understanding of Indian cultural norms. The final click of the guest room door, where Deepak has moved his belongings, signals the end of the honeymoon for the "perfectly matched couple" (D 187).

In "Ultrasound" Chitra Banerjee Divakaruni draws attention to one of the scourges of contemporary India: female infanticide. In recent years the sex ratio had been declining rather alarmingly in favour of male infants and clinics which offered sex determination diagnoses were springing up all over the country. The connection between these two events was obvious to the government as the Pre-Natal Diagnostic Techniques (PNDT) Act was passed in 1994, which banned the use of these techniques for the purpose of determining the sex of the foetus. Despite the act, hundreds of female foetuses were still being aborted after ultrasound detection, which led the Supreme Court in May 2001 to call on the Centre and State governments to implement the law more strictly. Discovery of a female foetus had led many parents to seek an abortion owing to the inferior social status still afforded women in Indian society. Girls, moreover, are seen as a heavy financial burden for parents who feel obliged by custom to provide a dowry, which in many cases, far exceeds their income. In Divakaruni's story, which, it should be noted, was written soon after the PNDT Act was passed, an abortion is desired merely to ensure that the eldest child of a wealthy, respectable, Brahmin family is not female. Far from being an economic necessity, tradition demands that the Bhattacharjee household close ranks and insist on Arundhati, the eldest daughter-in-law, terminating her pregnancy.

Arundhati's plight is contrasted with the liberal atmosphere of her cousin, Anjali's marriage in California. Both cousins had had a traditional arranged marriage but fate took Anjali to San Jose with her husband, Sunil, who, despite the fact that his salary is modest, has encouraged his wife to continue her studies. Arundhati's husband, Ramesh works for Indian Railways and is frequently absent from the home leaving his young wife to cope with his mother and younger brothers.

Differences apart, both girls share a similarly unromantic view of marriage. As Anju muses: "Our husbands are kind and dependable and take good care of us. In the Indian culture, that is the same as love" (U 213). However, the lifestyles and expectations of the two cousins have little in common. Anju looks forward to graduation and sharing parenthood with Sunil, while Arundhati's world evolves around domestic chores and motherhood is an obligation that she must fulfil. Her role is to be accommodating, self-effacing, serving, kind and chaste and failure to comply with these approved standards can end up in anything ranging from mild disapproval to callous rejection.

After five years of marriage and visits to holy shrines, Arundhati finally becomes pregnant but her initial happiness is shattered when the news that the child she is carrying is a girl is not greeted with the same joy by her in-laws. Her options are limited as public opinion would brand her as a bad woman. She would not be seen to have abandoned her husband's home, they would have thrown her out for transgressing the norms of accepted Indian wifely behaviour. Anju is horrified both by her cousin's dilemma and by the indifference shown by Arundhati's and her own mother and Sunil. Her sense of justice and gender equality is grievously insulted first when she learns that her cousin has had to undergo a gynaecological examination to check she was fertile and later when she discovers the abortion plan.

> My mother, who is usually an outspoken woman, was strangely silent. Then she'd said, "That's how they do things here, Anju. Have you forgotten?"
>
> "Why is it always taken to be the woman's fault?" I fumed to Sunil when he came home that night. "If I were Runu, I'd just pack my bags and leave!"
>
> I'd expected him to be shocked and angry, like myself. Sympathetic. But he merely shrugged and said, "It's a man's world in India. Runu's in-laws are a lot better than some others I could name. And anyway, where would Runu go if she left?" (U 218)

> "Did you tell her [Arundhati's mother] they're determined to make you go through with the abortion?"
>
> "I did. She thinks it's the lesser of the two evils." (U 225)
>
> "That's easy for you to say from here. Runu's the one who'll have to face [the social stigma] everyday. Even if money isn't a problem, what kind of life will it be for her? She certainly won't have the chance to remarry. She'll be alone with her daughter the rest of her life, a social pariah, someone the neighbors point a finger at every time she walks down the street." (U 227)

Patriarchy definitely bears a large share of the responsibility for the low status that women have in India, but that argument shifts the emotional responsibility to only one half of humanity. Middle class women, such as the characters of the story, also are to blame for their lack of group worth and constant deference to male approval. Real female consciousness can only start working if women themselves begin to take responsibility for their own fate and demand their rightful position in the family.

Anju believes that her advice to Runu to leave the Bhattacharjee household and fight for her baby is the only solution that her cousin can take if she is to preserve her dignity and integrity. Anju believes she can offer Runu a new life in the United States with her daughter. One hopes that the Indian community she will try to join will not ostracize her for failing to conform to the rules. It should be remembered that ethnic communities often tend to define themselves with reference to an idealized home, a frozen, almost fossilized version of the country they have left behind. In this romanticized idea of the nation, religious, linguistic and regional specificities are subsumed under a kind of pan-Indian identity which is articulated and presented to the mainstream host society. Thus ethnic associations that set themselves up as spokespeople of the diasporic community promote the idea of one Indian culture, one set of Indian beliefs, one Indian lifestyle and so forth. As outlined above, such monolithic constructs of Indianness force a fixed code of conduct on women, who are cast in the role of the transmitters of the eternal spirit of India. Consequently, anyone who threatens to transgress the unwritten rules of Indian womanhood is branded as a betrayer of all those sacred values: culture, tradition, the family, the Indian community itself.

The examples chosen for this analysis conform to Khushwant Singh's definition of the short story: a piece of creative writing that has a sense of unity, a distinct beginning, middle and end, "a ring of truth," "a message to convey" and a "sting in its tail" (quoted in Naik 118). The unity derives from the compactness of the stories. "The Word Love" focuses on the theme of filial guilt, "Doors" on the cultural construction of space, "Ultrasound" on the dichotomy Indian or feminist and "Affair" on public female roles. Distinct beginnings, middles and ends are clearly distinguishable in all four narratives. Chitra Banerjee Divakaruni sets the scene, poses the questions, proceeds to develop the situation and neatly, although not necessarily conclusively, brings the tale to an end. In "The Word Love" the story ends with the break up of the unnamed narrator's relationship with the American Rex, in part caused by the strain of her anxiety over her mother's outright disowning of her. "Affair" leads up to the separation of Ashok and Abha, an ill-suited couple, and hints at a possible future relationship between Abha and Srikant, Meena's rejected husband. The denouement of "Doors" heralds the irreparable chasm that has been opened between Preeti and her husband made visible through the prolonged visit of Deepak's friend, Raj. The end of the story is the beginning of a marriage that will be one in name only. "Ultrasound" concludes with Arundhati's flight from her husband's family and points to the start of a new life away from the constraints of a traditional Indian household and the tyranny of patriarchal traditions that deny women any agency. All four stories have a grounding in social realism. They are credible and respond to the sociocultural context of South Asian immigrants in the United States. Likewise, Chitra Banerjee Divakaruni transmits a particular message to her readers. First and foremost, she shows the South Asian community to be heterogeneous with its internal divisions, far from the monolithic construct the United States media and in part the Indian community itself would like to portray. Secondly, she uses her stories as a means to empower women, to encourage them to be themselves. She shows how personal choice is the birth right of all humans, men and women, Indians or Americans and that traditions can frequently encumber more than inspire.

To a greater or lesser extent, Divakaruni's female protagonists in these four stories from *Arranged Marriage* all have to overcome a deeply-rooted sense of guilt. Despite their education, acquired independence, and increasing self-confidence, they are not completely free from nagging doubts of cultural transgression. Although the stories are, to a certain extent, subversive by cutting at the roots of the prevalent order and organizing principle of the Indian family and community, the sting in the tail is perhaps the women's awareness that the old rules are not always right but their trace is permanently etched in their consciousness.

NOTES

1. I do not wish to go into the appropriateness of the term "diaspora" when discussing South Asians, who in many cases have migrated for reasons of economic security and improvement rather than due to political or religious persecution, but suffice it to say that I have chosen to use it because the term is a convenient one and frequently resorted to in postcolonial discourse. For further discussion see Clifford (1994) and Srinivasan (2001).
2. I am using the term "South Asian" as a convenient shorthand for people from the Indian subcontinent, which is sometimes less confusing than the term "Indian" when discussing the American context.
3. It should be noted that the myth of the NRIs in America as a monolithic success story has been taken up by neoliberals in India. The former BJP government, eager for investments from non-resident Indians happily grouped together all Indian citizens living abroad even referring to them as a unified diasporic entity regardless of country of residence and socio-economic class (Rayaprol 2001).
4. It is a curious phenomenon that migrant communities in the diaspora aim to recreate a monolithic culture which simply does not exist in the homeland. In this respect, and following from the previous note, it is worth remembering that the more fanatical branches of the recently

ousted BJP government had tried to emphasize a uniform Hindu culture in India.

5. Henceforth, quotations from these short stories will be cited with the abbreviations A, WL, D and U, followed by the page numbers.

WORKS CITED

Anderson, Benedict. *Imagined Communities.* 1983. London: Verso, 1987.

Clifford, James. "Diasporas." *Cultural Anthropology* 9.3 (1994): 302-38.

DasGupta, Sayantani and Shamita Das Dasgupta, "Sex, Lies, and Women's Lives. An Intergenerational Dialogue." *A Patchwork Shawl: Chronicles of South Asian Women in America.* Ed. Shamita Das Dasgupta. New Brunswick: Rutgers University Press, 2002. 111-28.

Dasgupta, Shamita Das, ed. Introduction. *A Patchwork Shawl: Chronicles of South Asian Women in America.* New Brunswick: Rutgers University Press, 2002. 11-12.

Dasgupta, Shamita Das, ed. *A Patchwork Shawl: Chronicles of South Asian Women in America.* New Brunswick: Rutgers University Press, 2002.

Divakaruni, Chitra Banerjee. *Arranged Marriage.* London: Black Swan, 1997.

Dwyer, Rachel. *All You Want Is Money, All You Need Is Love: Sex and Romance in Modern India.* London: Cassell, 2000.

Hand, Felicity. "Shaking Off *Sharam*: The Double Burden of British Asian Women." *On Writing (and) Race in Contemporary Britain.* Ed. Fernando Galván and Mercedes Bengoechea. Madrid: Universidad de Alcalá, Servicio de Publicaciones, 1999.

Ganguly, Keya. "Migrant Identities: Personal Memory and the Construction of Selfhood." *Cultural Studies* 6.1 (Jan. 1992): 27-50.

Maira, Sunaina. "Identity Dub: the Paradoxes of an Indian American Youth Subculture (New York Mix)." *Cultural Anthropology* 14.1 (1999): 29-60.

Mishra, Vijay. "The Diasporic Imaginary: Theorizing the Indian Diaspora." *Textual Practice* 10.3 (1996): 421-47.

Naik, M.K. and Shyamala A. Narayan. *Indian English Literature 1980-2000: A Critical Survey.* Delhi: Pencraft, 2001.

Paranjape, Makarand, ed. *In Diaspora. Theories, Histories, Texts.* New Delhi: Indialog Publications, 2001.

Rayaprol, Aparna. "'Can You Talk Indian?' Shifting Notions of Community and Identity in the Indian Diaspora." *Community and Identities. Contemporary Discourses on Culture and Politics in India.* Ed. Surinder S. Jodhka. New Delhi: Sage, 2001. 163-90.

Roy, Manisha. "Mothers and Daughters in Indian-American Families. A Failed Communication." Ed. Shamita Das Dasgupta. New Brunswick: Rutgers University Press, 2002. 97-110.

Srinivasan, Shiva Kumar. "Diaspora and Its Discontents." *In Diaspora. Theories, Histories, Texts*. Ed. Makarand Paranjape. New Delhi: Indialog, 2001. 52-67.

Vijayasree, C. "Survival as an Ethic: South Asian Immigrant Women's Writing." *In Diaspora. Theories, Histories, Texts*. Ed. Makarand Paranjape. New Delhi: Indialog, 2001. 130-40.

6

Looking Through the Glass House: Diasporic Women Writers of Bengali Heritage[1]

Antonia Navarro Tejero

In this article, I will focus on the two levels at which Indian women's self-definition is restricted in the South Asian diaspora. India is a multicultural nation, with thousand of different languages, communities and traditions that cross regional borders. In order to try not to generalise, we have chosen two collections of short stories by US women writers of Bengali heritage: a second generation, Jhumpa Lahiri's *Interpreter of Maladies* (1999) and a first generation of diasporans, Chitra Banerjee Divakaruni's *Arranged Marriage* (1995).

Both authors focus their short stories on themes that encompass characters who must find ways of reconciling themselves to their shifting and evolving identities that are the result of their migratory experience. Additionally, I will reflect upon the particular challenges and contradictions in their female Indian experiences and their positions regarding 'home.'

Bearing this complex interweaving of cultural forms in mind, I will discuss how both authors challenge or not the existing models for unidimensional categories within the United States, by referring back to their countries of origin—India, and more specifically West Bengal—by invoking frames of reference alien to the Anglo-American cultural landscape, and by depicting characters in continual transition.

However, Lahiri and Divakaruni use different techniques when examining their native culture, and when dealing with the tensions produced by being between the original and adopted homelands, and between rootlessness and a desire for stability. I will then analyse both collections of short stories following the idea that western criticism, both non-feminist and feminist, artificially constructed two entities, that of the (liberated white female) colonizer and the (oppressed Third World) colonized. I will finally argue that if on the one hand, Lahiri's stories are a celebration of human beings with their virtues and defects, Divakaruni's stories seem to reconstruct the colonial binaries of East versus West.

Characters in the Mirror

Each one of Lahiri's stories deal with the human condition, and though her central characters are not always women, each story is skilfully told from a feminine perspective that goes beyond stereotypes, as female characters are depicted as victims or not, or both under different circumstances. The characters' voices break the barriers between the imposed dichotomy East/West. Lahiri balances the one-dimensional portrayal of women by introducing multiple, cross-cultural narratives of women's lives and women's alternative strategies to some of the most complex issues facing the current globalised world. It has been argued that women in particular suffer the collective horror of a double oppression. However, Lahiri does not follow a gross oversimplification.

To summarise her stories, we find a young couple avoiding each other after her miscarriage in "A Temporary Matter;" the horrors of Partition with a satiric wink to history lessons in the US schools, in "When Mr. Pirzada Came to Dine;" an American family of Indian descent travelling to their parents' country as tourists in "Interpreter of Maladies;" the bad treatment of a watchwoman in "A Real Durwan;" an interracial sexual relationship outside marriage in "Sexy;" Mrs. Sen's interactions with the American boy she was baby sitting in "Mrs. Sen's;" the Christian idols a just married Hindu couple finds in their home in "This Blessed House;" the sad story of a sick woman whose cure was the delivery of her child in "The Treatment of Bibi Haldar;" and the adjusting process of an arranged marriage couple in "The Third and Final Continent."

On the other hand, Divakaruni's stories deal with the horrors of Indian marriages as opposed to the liberal attitudes found in the United States. The non-Indian women are depicted as independent, whereas Indian women are depicted as victims, and if liberal, they are considered westernized. Divakaruni, thus, focuses exclusively on Indian women as victims of domestic violence with preconceptions of how the changing times are affecting the Indian institution of arranged marriage. In her stories, the characters live in a time-warp and are stereotypical, which is reminiscent of the kind of colonial writing.

In "Meeting Mrinal," it is implied that in India divorce is impossible whereas in the United States it is a socially acceptable option. The female character considers suicide, but she does not as her son fills the gap left by her oppressive husband. In "Clothes," Sunita's clothes symbolise her deeply felt belief that the United States will be a happy paradise in which she will experience the freedom to work and live in a way that would have been impossible in her native India. But as her husband is murdered, she is confronted with the stereotypical in-laws expectations of an Indian widow.[2]

In "The Ultrasound" Anju, who is in the United States, rescues her friend Runu from her unhappy marriage in India as her in-laws try to force her into aborting the baby girl. Essentially, what Divakaruni is proposing is that women must abandon India in order to retain some power over their destinies due to their marginalised place in Indian society. Anjali seeks freedom as the American dream. Anju embodies the Brahminical ideal of wife and mother at the same time that she believes in the idyllic American life.

In "The Word Love," the protagonist takes for granted that her mother would not accept her relationship with her American boyfriend. Her sense of self as a good Indian girl and an adult woman in the United States appears as conflict, implying that she is torn between her deep-rooted Indian morals and the American acceptance of unmarried couples cohabiting. Unsurprisingly, Divakaruni resolves the conflict by making her female protagonist reject what she believes is the Indian norm. This character's cut off from her mother is symbolic as through her, the protagonist is also disowned by India.

In "A Perfect Life," the protagonist Meera, a sophisticated professional, rejects Indian men as a symbol of rebelling against Indian tradition, and in order to de-colonise her Indian body, she dates Richard as when she is with him, she feels "true America" (73), contrasting later American men's attitudes towards motherhood with Indian men's, another stereotype made of one single instance. So Meera goes from one side of the Indian/American binary structure to the other, applying a static oversimplified characteristic to it: Americans are liberal but do not care for their children, whereas Indians are traditional good parents.

In "Silver Pavements, Golden Roofs," Jayati is a university student who is shocked both by the fact that she faces racism in the street and her uncle's savage abuse of Aunt Pratima who is enclosed in her home and beaten. In "Affair," Abha struggles with the weight of being the perfect 'Indian' wife in contrast with Meena, who has a marketing job to whom Abha says: "You're starting to sound like an American" (236), and even thinks Meena is having an affair just because she takes care of her looks, is a terrible cook, a good dancer, and melodramatic in the "*Californian*" way (267, emphasis original).

In "Doors" Deepak is going to marry Preeti, an ABCD "American-Born-Confused-*Desis*" (185). His friends discourage him by saying "[s]he's been here so long it's almost like she was born in this country." And you know how these "'American' women are, always bossing you, always thinking about themselves" (185), while another friend adds "I'd go for an arranged marriage from back home any day, a pretty young girl from my parents' village, not too educated, brought up to treat a man right and not talk back" (185). In this case,

American privacy appears as opposite to the suffocating Indian communality. So, even when they are both living in the United States, she is considered westernised to the extreme of leaving him until his friend Raj left their house.

Divakaruni seems to provide a one-dimensional reading of Indian relationships, that of the woman oppressed by male traditions, stereotyping Indian men, and seeking freedom in the United States as their saviour. Her protagonists are determined to reject Indian men, as if all Indian men were oppressive to their wives, and they are left in precarious positions (they are self-absorbed, insensitive, wife-abusers, servant-rapists, etc.). Her stories are stereotypical as they depict a one-sided portrait of Indian malehood, and bring out the practical problems of isolation and lack of financial independence for women in their marriages. This is maybe because Divakaruni got inspiration from the help group she co-founded and volunteered at (Maitri, a Bay Area hotline for South Asian abused women). On the other hand, Lahiri's male characters are round who manipulate and are manipulated depending on the individualised case, and never because of their identity as Indian.

Divakaruni has claimed several times in interviews that the diaspora has changed the lives of Indians, and that women are concerned about their identity and the question of being Indian as a space they are negotiating and an identity they are reinventing constantly. But it seems to me that the proposed hybrid immigrant woman is that who, by re-evaluating her homeland's culture, rejects tradition to adapt to the new conventions found in the United States, no matter if those conventions are even more misogynist than those in India, like the case of James Bond movies, which her female characters love.

Opposite Encounters

Jhumpa Lahiri, unlike Chitra Divakaruni, does not portray in her stories Indian and American values and customs in an opposite encounter. On the contrary, Lahiri presents the complexities of characters (some of them exclusively set in

India, others who travel to India, apart from those whose stories unfold in the United States), rather than simplified monolithic characters, who glorify the 'land of freedom' where opportunities fulfil their dreams.

Lahiri talks about the human condition of being an immigrant, the human tragedy of abuse, but never implies that Indian women are always victims and need to be saved from the oppressions they live within Indian traditions. Lahiri writes with sensibility about her family's ethnic heritage and the lives of South Asian immigrants in the United States. She is an interpreter of conflicts between humans, sometimes between immigrants and natives, some other times among natives, or immigrants only. So from my point of view, Lahiri transcends narrow nationalism and evokes universality.

According to M.W. Cox, either the narrators or the main characters in every story by Lahiri act as interpreters, as cultural or linguistic bridges, between Indian culture and the culture of the United States. He asserts that the stories, and more concretely "Mrs. Sen," serve to de-familiarise both worlds and thus these are stories without simple interpretations (120-21). Some stories are sad, others make the readers enjoy the characters' happiness, but they do not emphasise domestic intergenerational or gender hierarchies.

In Divakaruni's short stories we find the ambivalent feeling of nostalgia for the homeland left behind and at the same time a kind of relief for having escaped from the barriers that her native country poses on women, as it is the case of many other diasporic authors. Divakaruni emigrated to the United States when she was young without really having lived in India as an adult and having submitted to its oppression. As a consequence, her glass house analysis of culture has a reductionist element that simplifies the culture to its two-dimensional stereotypes.

For the critic Vijayasree, the diasporic writer has three alternatives: keeping her/his culture and remaining in the eternal position of the Other; seeking for assimilation; or staying in-between the two cultures with an ambivalent feeling. Let me first react to the last option proposed by Vijayasree with an excerpt from Gloria Anzaldúa's *This Bridge Called My Back*:

> What am I? [...] They would chop me up into little fragments and tag each piece with a label. You say my name is ambivalence? Think of me as Shiva, a many armed and legged body with one foot on brown soil, one on white, one in straight society, one in the gay world, the man's world, the women's, one limb in the literary world, another in the working class, the social, and the occult worlds [...]. Who, me confused? Ambivalent? Not so. Only your labels split me. (205)[3]

The idea of an immigrant writer being between two cultures and having to negotiate and make choices implies that both cultures (East and West) appear as opposites with tensions provoked between the supposedly "traditional" old country and the "liberal" new one. This would be, thus, a construction of a dichotomised view of the world that would inevitably lead to the creation of stereotypes.

Postcolonial feminist criticism includes an analysis of how women are represented in colonial and postcolonial literature, which challenges assumptions and stereotypes about women in both literature and society. Though both colonialism and patriarchy have been closely entwined historically, an end to formal empire has not meant an end to the oppression of women in the former colonies. Postcolonial feminists point out the ways in which women continue to be stereotyped and marginalised, ironically sometimes by postcolonial authors who might claim to be challenging a culture of oppression, which is the case of Divakaruni's *Arranged Marriage*.

Third World critics could claim postmodernism, with its de-centering strategies, as an ally. Sara Suleri's disarticulation of the Third World woman and denaturalisation of the category of woman is a gesture in keeping with post-modern disavowal of essentialist productions of meaning (1989: 20). According to Jahan, this is bonded to the demands of the dominant centre of power, as the colonisers describe the colonised during the (neo)colonisation process. This idea of stereotyping Indian women and men is related to the problematic concept 'postcolonial women,' about which Sara Suleri said that—

> it inevitably leads to the simplicities that underlie unthinking celebrations of oppression, elevating the racially female voice into a metaphor for 'the good.' Such metaphoricity cannot exactly be called essentialist, but it certainly functions as an impediment to a reading that attempts to look beyond obvious questions of good and evil. (1992: 758-59)

While Sunder argues that "the construction of women in terms of recognizable roles, images, models, and labels occurs in discourse in response to specific social imperatives even where it may be offered in terms of the universal and abstract rhetoric of 'woman' or 'women' (or the 'Indian woman,' as the case may be)" (1993: 129), Mohanty points out that western criticism, both non-feminist and feminist, artificially constructs two entities: the colonizer and the colonized. Its political implications would be that it allows the colonized only a language permitted, or indeed constructed, by the colonizer. She attacks the principles at work in Western feminist criticism about the Third World, being the first one the assumption that Third World women are an identical group regardless of place or ethnicity, and the uncritical use of particular methodologies involved in the first assumption. The third principle is the politics, which both these frames of analysis create. This involves the self-representation of western women in literature or other disciplines as modern women with some degree of control over their bodies and sexualities and western feminists 're-presentation' of women in the Third World as domestic or uneducated victims (1985: 337).

We find in Divakaruni, what Mohanty in her essay "Cartographies of Struggle: Third World Women and the Politics of Feminism," has called western women literature, as she represents Indian women as victims in every of her short stories. "Third Word feminists" have been claiming a voice of their own at the same time that have challenged white Western feminists in their formation of stereotypes. Through women-centered narratives authors highlight women's perception of the world that surrounds them as well as their own concerns.

Since Toru Dutt's times, Indian women authors in English are re-constructing female identity. Immigration has added a new connotation to the formation of the Indian identity, that of feelings of dislocation, among others. But for a western audience, unaware of the complexities of the Indian culture, the putting together of stories focused on the dichotomy Indian female victim versus American liberalized woman tremendously damages the de-colonization project.

Lahiri also talks about the lives of women in male centered communities, but the scope of her narrative is wider than Divakaruni's. With Lahiri example, we can argue that biology is not determinant, and that a writer who was born in India and has lived most of her life there can write about Indian women in an one-dimensional, partial way, and an American writer with Indian heritage can be more sensitive, with an exquisite representation of individual Indian lives with all its variations, and its dignity. Issues of authenticity related to essentialism can be dismantled.

We could go further and state that in a United States panorama, Divakaruni's stories are in a way selectively exotic. The dichotomy western liberated woman/Indian oppressed victim described above recalls us of George W. Bush's good/evil Machiavellian discourse. His father's description of international relations as "the New World order" quotes Hitler's regime of "New Order" in the quincentenary of European imperialism to locate hegemony in the New World.[4] This 'new world' trope is used by Divakaruni as it foregrounds the experience of immigration.

Alexander and Mohanty use the example of Hindus and Muslims, which we can apply to Divakaruni's short stories when describing women's roles in the community. They warn against the danger of considering all women to be structured as an oppressed group and be affected by the patriarchal system, without being aware of class and cultural conditions, as if they existed outside history (1997: 204). Actually, Indian women who stay at their home country had published fiction in which they have moved away from the self-sacrificing female characters in favor of more conflicted ones, realizing the diversity of women in India rather than limiting the depiction of female characters according to a manipulated traditional Hindu ideal.[5]

As Bharati Mukherjee started doing in the 80s, when postcolonial theory emerged out of the shadow of European theories of post-structuralism and post-modernism, Divakaruni celebrates immigration as a liberating agent. In her awarded *The Middleman and Other Stories*, Mukherjee insistently focuses on issues of migration from an American perspective (it is important to notice that Mukherjee claims herself to be an American writer, and not Asian-American).[6] Now, these diasporic women authors are part of the American 'multicultural canon,' as they easily portray their adoptive country as a mythical paradise for women. Husne Jahan radically asserts that "the problems, pains, and erasures brought about by immigration are downplayed in Divakaruni's work, while the celebrations of the promises of immigration are emphasised to the point where some aspects of her work strongly promote neo-Orientalist and neo-imperialist projects" (151-52).

Looking through Particular Windows

Then, the questions could be if these writers are competent authorities to be interpreters of a culture of which they are outsiders. This question may lead us to issues of essentialism, which we will not analyse here. However, in these two collections of short stories we clearly find different ways of approaching a culture, albeit partially through their particular windows. Viswanathan, as many other critics, argues that the distance between the authors and their homeland seems to afford them the safety to critically examine their native culture, as it can "embolden writers to criticise or satirise in a way that would be trickier to pull off if they were still living in the community under examination" (41).

This means that the "immigrant" writer—first or second generations—have a more sharpened double perspective of their home left behind and the theme of displacement is more visible as they are self-conscious. The popular South Asian writer Salman Rushdie asserts that the writer who is "out-of-country and even out-of-language" (1991: 12) experiences the loss of what she/he thought of as home when a child in an intensified form. On the other hand, the Indian critic Rosemary George suggests that the diaspora is not connected to place or space, but rather to transportable objects that connote home (171).

Longing for homes left behind may be intense for first-generation immigrants who seek a community to belong to. When we talk about the diaspora, we need to keep in mind the political parameters of time, community and nation, as analysed by Mohanty, who questions if home is a geographical space, a historical space, or an emotional sensory space. In her revised article of the so much influential "Under Western Eyes," Mohanty shifts her focus to "'under and inside' the hegemonic spaces of the One-Third World" (2002: 516), as the fact that people of and from the Third World live not only under Western eyes but also within them necessitates recrafting the project of decolonization.

Immigrant writers who are fluent in English have the advantage of being able to translate their experiences and/or family memories into something a Western reader would understand. In their collections of short stories, Divakaruni and Lahiri become interpreters or intermediaries who write short stories, but at the same time translate cultural issues thanks to their double disjunctive perspective, that of an Indian and at the same time as an American, as Bruce King argued. The result is a cultural text, according to Bhabha, a hybrid object. Both collections of short stories provide multiple examples of such hybrid identity formation. These are stories about experiences in the world left behind and the one newly adopted, and the bridge that puts them together. Through this back and forth movement the authors draw attention to hitherto ignored cultural and material resources that can be sources of strength for a minority population. However, I would like to agree with the late critic Edward Said, who asserted that neither culture "is single and pure, all are hybrid, heterogeneous, extraordinarily differentiated, and unmonolithic" (1994: xxv).

As a Conclusion

I hope to have clarified how both Divakaruni and Lahiri are trying to look back at their cultural backgrounds with different perspectives. As Divakaruni fails to de-colonise her past, Lahiri succeeds in the way that she no longer identifies the relationship between self and place, negative and positive, even when some of her characters feel dislocation at some point resulting from their migration experience. Finally, it is not surprising to notice that *Arranged Marriage* ends with a glossary for Bengali and Hindi terms, something non-existent in Lahiri's collection of short stories.

Let me finish this essay by posing a simple question: what would a western reader, without knowledge of India, think about Indian women and men after reading the stories in *Arranged Marriage*, and what idea would she/he get from Indian culture after reading Lahiri's collection? I do not mean to say that there is not domestic violence in India, or that prescriptive Brahminism does not impose hard norms on women and men. Evidently, there is much to change in the Indian society regarding gender violence, as in any other society in this world where we find a misogynist ideology.[7]

We can argue that these stereotypes about Indians belong to colonial times, when the Empire described them as wild creatures living in a uncivilised land in need of development. We will finally state that *Arranged Marriage* is aimed at a western audience as it primarily engages with western feminist theory of liberating the poor "Third World" victim. This contrasts with the idea that every woman in India is seen as being capable of an entire range of qualities and manifestations. The collective unconscious is full of positive feminine images, such as the feminine principle that rules the universe, *shakti*, and powerful goddesses. Indian history has seen women in power positions, and many professional women of today, who demand not to be one or the other, that is, the one-dimensional creature forever rebelling or forever submissive, as dichotomies are not mutually exclusive qualities in India, but colonial constructions.

Finally, Divakaruni seems to imply in her collection of short stories that Indian women are being colonised by her Indian men. At the same time, she seems to imply that immigrant Indian men subjugate their women in a desperate need to control their new world. This is a dangerous project, as we take the risk of oversimplifying a millenary culture. On the other hand, Lahiri's collection of short stories is a great instance of recuperating the family's history without falling into the denigration of blaming an ancient culture. Lahiri has perfectly shown among other things the fears, frustrations and successes of Indians, being they immigrants or not, NRIs, second generations, and whatever their social condition may be.

NOTES

1. I own much of the ideas generated here to the conversations maintained with Bijoy Sagar over the last six years. I would like to thank him for the discussions and comments about authenticity and the commercialization of the exotic in the diasporic Indian context, which have much influenced this project.
2. As Sunder points out, the perception that Hindu women were victims was the basis for the establishment of *sati* (self-immolation of a widow in her husband's pyre) as a women's issue. It provoked an implicit comparison of their devalued social position with the freedom and privileges of British women—thus offering further proof of the superiority of British civilization (1993: 46).
3. See Mary Kaldor's *New and Old Wars: Organised Violence in a Global Era* (1999) for a closer examination on 'labeling.' She argues that labels are mobilized for political purposes, as they offer a new sense of security in a context where the political and economic certainties have disappeared.
4. For a complete insight on the etymology, see William Safire (1978), 459.
5. See Vasudha Narayanan's interesting article about the manipulation of the female role in Hinduism by Brahmins employed by the British colonizers.

6. In Ketu H. Katrak's words: "Mukherjee embraces being 'American,' not Indian and American, not hyphenated. Further, she wants to be recognized as 'an American writer' in the tradition of American writers" (5). Katrak compares this statement with the case of Meena Alexander, who links her present and past history as a South Asian American to that of other ethnic groups in the United States.
7. For example, we would not say that the culture of the United States is misogynist, even when three million women are physically abused by their husband or boyfriend per year in the United States according to The Commonwealth Fund, Health Concerns Across a Woman's Lifespan: 1998 Survey of Women's Health, May 1999.

WORKS CITED

Alexander, M. Jacqui and Chandra Talpade Mohanty, eds. *Feminist Genealogies, Colonial Legacies, Democratic Futures.* New York: Routledge, 1997.

Anzaldúa, Gloria and Cherrie Moraga, eds. *This Bridge Called My Back: Writings by Radical Women of Color.* Watertown MA: Persephone, 1983.

Bhabha, Homi K. *The Location of Culture.* London: Routledge, 1994.

Cox, Michael W. "Interpreters of Cultural Difference: The Use of Children in Jhumpa Lahiri's Short Fiction." *South Asian Review* 24.2 (2003): 120-32.

Divakaruni, Chitra Banerjee. *Arranged Marriage.* London: Black Swan, 1997.

George, Rosemary Marangoly. *The Politics of Home: Postcolonial Relocations and Twentieth-Century Fiction.* Cambridge: Cambridge University Press, 1996.

Jahan, Husne. "Colonial Woes in Post-Colonial Writing: Chitra Divakaruni's Immigrant Narratives." *South Asian Review* 24.2 (2003): 149-69.

Kaldor, Mary. *New and Old Wars: Organized Violence in a Global Era.* Cambridge: Polity Press, 1999.

Katrak, Ketu H. "The Aesthetics of Dislocation: Writing the Hybrid Lives of South Asian Americans." *The Women's Review of Books* 19.5 (Feb. 2002): 5-6.

King, Bruce. "The Commonwealth Writer in Exile." *From Commonwealth to Post-Colonial.* Ed. Anna Rutherford. Coventry, U.K.: Dangaroo P, 1992. 39-43.

Lahiri, Jhumpa. *Interpreter of Maladies.* New York: Houghton Mifflin, 1999.

Mohanty, Chandra Talpade. "Under Western Eyes: Feminist Scholarship and Colonial Discourses." *Boundary* 12.3-13.1 (Spring/Fall 1985): 333-59.

——. "Cartographies of Struggle: Third World Women and the Politics of Feminism." *Third World Women and the Politics of Feminism.* Ed. C.T. Mohanty, Ann Russo and Lourdes Torres. Bloomington: Indiana University Press, 1991. 1-47.

——. "'Under Western Eyes' Revisited: Feminist Solidarity through Anticapitalist Struggles." *Signs: Journal of Women in Culture and Society* 28.2 (2002): 499-535.

Mukherjee, Bharati. *The Middleman and Other Stories.* Grove, 1988.

Narayanan, Vasudha. "Brimming with *Bhakti*, Embodiments of *Shakti:* Devotees, Deities, Performers, Reformers, and Other Women of Power in the Hindu Tradition." *Feminism and World Religions.* Ed. Arvind Sharma and Katherine K. Young. New York: State University of New York Press, 1999. 25-77.

Rushdie, Salman. *Imaginary Homelands: Essays and Criticism 1981-1991.* London: Granta Books, 1991.

Safire, William. *Safire's Political Dictionary.* New York: Random House, 1978.

Said, Edward. *Culture and Imperialism.* New York: Vintage, 1994.

Suleri, Sara. *Meatless Days.* Chicago: University of Chicago Press, 1989.

——. "Woman Skin Deep: Feminism and the Postcolonial Condition." *Critical Inquiry* 18 (Summer 1992): 756-69.

Sunder Rajan, Rajeswari. *Real and Imagined Women: Gender, Culture and Postcolonialism.* London: Routledge, 1993.

Vijayasree, C. "The Politics and Poetics of Expatriation: The Indian Version(s)" *Interrogating Post-Colonialism: Theory, Text and Context.* Ed. Harish Trivedi and Meenakshi Mukherjee. Shimla: Indian Institute of Advanced Study, 1996.

Viswanathan, Gauri. *Masks of Conquest: Literary Study and British Rule in India.* New York: Columbia University Press, 1989.

7

The Spectral Art of Storytelling: Disease, Displacement and Death in Jhumpa Lahiri's *Interpreter of Maladies*

Puspa Damai

In his reflections on the stories of Nikolai Leskov, Walter Benjamin comes very close to announcing the demise of the art of storytelling, which for him also implies the end of human ability to communicate experiences. Talking about stories, if one can still do so after Benjamin, however, is not to get ready for the requiem to the lost art of storytelling, for he conjures its ending not as an event of total cessation, but as a pathological process that is at once infinitely open-ended and intimately, immediately or even incurably present. In other words, Benjamin conceives of the art of storytelling as a relentless and agonizing journey towards its own death without ever attaining the state of complete surcease.

The uncanny art of storytelling therefore is a familiar element of estrangement that we can observe only at the moments it vanishes away. Benjamin illustrates its motility towards muteness not only by referring to the conversion of oral tradition of storytelling into the print culture of the novel, but also by recalling the returnees from the First World War, who came home from the battlefield too quiet and too traumatized to communicate their experiences of the war (Benjamin 84). The return of the aphasic warriors from the battlefield only concatenates with the surfacing of the malaise that Benjamin relates to the rise of the novel. On the one hand, therefore, storytelling is dying into the rise of the novel; on the other hand these symptoms like information-orientedness, reproducibility, and disembodiedness of the novelistic discourse *vis-à-vis* the tradition of the story guided by the communicability of human experience and "epic wisdom" keep it from gasping its last thereby rendering it frighteningly spectral.

The attenuating force of the stories perpetually getting dissociated and deflected from its itinerary "from mouth to mouth," is made resonant with two traditional figures of storytelling: one "who has come from a far," and the other who has always "stayed at home" (84). Once Benjamin hits upon this "aporetic" moment in the art of storytelling, a moment that conceives it as an art traversing not only the borders of times and geographies, but also the moment that thinks this art right at the limits of life and death, he immediately relapses into "corporealizing" or even "unionizing" its contradictory forces by introducing the figures of the resident tiller of the soil and the trading seaman as archetypical storytellers.

Following the cue from Benjamin that the one who comes from afar is also the one who is afflicted with the art of storytelling, this essay will dwell on the relationship of illness, "coming from afar,"[1] and storytelling. It will also ask if we can grant a recognizable face and a name to the one that appears as symptom (as opposed to Benjamin's description of the arrival of the tradesman from afar with wealth and stories). If storytelling prefers going from mouth to mouth, or put differently, from one body to the other in communicating nothing less than the "experience," can we perceive it as a single body (of writing)? And if one allows it an ailing and trailing body of an invalid at times assailed by the forces of techno-induced reproduction of the modern novelistic discourse that further infects its integrity, how is one supposed to draw the boundaries of its body? How is one even to conceptualize the porous body of storytelling stretched across different times and locations? What is the nature of the locus at which the motility of this art and its careers, the displaced that include, without limiting themselves to, the aphasic returnees of the wars, the seafarers, the migrants, the homeless and the uncanny[2] beings? If the intertwined pairs of stories and disease, death and disappearance, silence and symptomatic "compearance," only reflect the geographies and times storytelling has traversed, what are we to make of the burgeoning writings on illness that confine to individuals' mental and physical hygiene?

Keeping these questions in mind and by drawing upon the insightful explorations into the complex art of storytelling and its relation to illness and death by writers like Benjamin, Virginia Woolf and others, this essay attempts to read Jhumpa Lahiri's Pulitzer winning debut, *Interpreter of Maladies*, by stressing upon the themes of illness, death, and spectrality in relation to the "displaced" figures not only of the migrants, but also of those wretched creatures who, unlike Fanon's verdict that they are condemned into immobility (Fanon 51), are relentlessly in search of healing for their inexpressible maladies.

Lahiri's narrative grace and stylistic elegance conceal a world of maladies inhabited by haunted and possessed beings. Almost all the stories deal with some maladies and the sufferers' attempts at healing. Not only the title story, "Interpreter of Maladies," but almost all stories deal to a great extent with the "interpretation" of maladies, which in turn takes us to the limit of language and narration. Contrary to Susan Sontag's beliefs in *Against Interpretation* that 'interpretation" is violation (10), which continue in her monograph on the metaphoricity of illness, where she equates totalitarianisms of various types with the political use of cancer-metaphor (Sontag, *Illness* 82-84), Lahiri carries malady as metaphor to its limit, so that she could better grasp the interdependent nature of illness, language and healing.

If Sontag seems to be even against naming the disease in front of the ill (Sontag, *Illness* 85), in the title story for instance, it is the "name" of the illness Mina is looking for from the interpreter, since her malady is not fully known even to herself. If the title story expresses the incomprehensibility and incommunicability of the malady even to the ill herself and the strategy of interpretation as the sole method of healing, "A Temporary Matter" stages a game to just "say something" (Lahiri 12), so that through other inadvertent narratives the couple, Shoba and Shukumar, could come up with the event of their child's death and understand the tragedy better and possibly overcome it by putting it in language. Boori Ma of "A Real Durwan," and her pathogenic stories about her affluent past, Mrs. Sen's unbridled passion for fish in "Mrs. Sen's," Twinkle's mad pursuit of effigies and busts in "This Blessed House," the hysteric Bibi of "The Treatment of Bibi Haldar," and the morbid and macabre world of "The Third and Final Continent" are some of the striking examples of Lahiri's fascination with illness.

This reading would have been impossible, if there had not already been rigorous polemical studies, like Gilbert and Gubar's among many others, that explored the uncanny bond between women and disease. In *The Mad Woman in the Attic*, for instance, Gilbert and Gubar argue that a "cult of female invalidism," inextricably present in British and American societies throughout history, required women to "act in ways which would cause them to become ill" (54). On the one hand therefore these writers detect the cancerous presence of the infectious prescriptions from patriarchy in "literary" women's anxieties of authorship and locate the cause of female disease in "too much storytelling" (55). Kapasi's interpretation of Mina's malaise as "guilt" or common and vulgar secret in "Interpreter of Maladies" (Lahiri 66) can be cited as an example of the stakes of using patriarchal language to "name" women's illness. On the other hand however, they stress upon exorcising the sentence that bred infection, and they pursue the "madwoman" in the nineteenth century literature and posit her not only as the replica of the "author's double" (Gilbert and Gubar 78), but also as the only healing available to the fragmented self of the women writers, thereby confining themselves to the realm of (hallucinogenic) "images," rage, and madness.

This ironic moment of healing and exorcising that eventually ends up in conjuring (as if through infection) the figure of the madwoman never passes unnoticed by other feminists. Shoshana Felman, for instance, sees through this ruse and argues that far from being a form of contestation, "mental illness" is "a request for help, a manifestation both of cultural impotence and of political castration" (8). If for Elaine Showalter "Bertha Mason [remains] a paradigmatic figure" (68), Lahiri's unforgettable characters like Bibi Haldar, her version of the hysteric woman in the attic, engage the issues of disease and displacement and seizures and sexuality differently, for they seem to pass between and beyond two models of illness based either on the mental diseases, as we have seen in Gilbert and Gubar or exclusively on physiology, as in Virginia Woolf, another important writer on illness.

If Gilbert and Gubar locate illness at the moment when women attempt to speak only to get infected by patriarchal language, thereby necessitating the figuration of an ambivalent creature of the madwoman in their expression, Woolf bemoans the general silence about the subject of illness. For her illness has not yet become the common subject in literature as are battles, love and jealousy. In that case, she ruminates, influenza would be the hero of the novels, typhoid would be the protagonist in epic poems, odes would be devoted to pneumonia and lyrics to tooth-ache (10). Woolf's ideal epic of illness therefore depicts body as a warrior against the onslaught of fever or melancholia and mind as just a slave to the war that the body raises: "To look these things squarely in the face would need the courage of a lion tamer; a robust philosophy; a reason rooted in the bowels of the earth. Short of these, this monster, the body, this miracle, its pain, will soon make us taper into mysticism [...]" (11-12).

Without advancing more theoretical antes here, let us pause with these images of the monster that we come across both in Gilbert and Gubar and also in Woolf. The monster in the former is a psychic projection by the women writers against the monsterization, as it were, of women by patriarchally defined literary tradition. If getting infected with the monster is a mandatory initiation into storytelling, destroying that incorporated monster is a curative ritual of self-immolation required of every women writer. The complexity of the ritual unfolds not only as Gilbert and Gubar state that the mad character is created "only to be destroyed" (78), but also the way in which they treat Bertha as a surrogate victim to be sacrificed for Jane's advancement. Bertha becomes the "sacred"[3] creature, or a *pharmakon*, the venomous figure employed to cure the poison. In other words, conjuring the madwoman becomes complicit with the act of creating the figure of the diseased and the abnormal. Or to be more precise, this psychic projection of the monster assumes the form of perpetration against, as Gayatri Spivak called in her essay, "Three Women's Text and a Critique of Imperialism," this figure of the human/animal frontier" (266). As Spivak has already noticed, this psychological perspective entails the violent exorcism of Creole figures like Bertha that are produced by, to borrow from Spivak again, "the axiomatics of imperialism" (266). What follows from Spivak is a grim realization that taking into account only the psychic aspect of the disease is further exacerbating the disease, let alone coming close to cure.

No wonder, Woolf seems to be aware of this danger as she proposes her "carnal speculations" in the service of the monster that causes miracles. Being ill for her is to land on hitherto "undiscovered countries" (9), where one is beset with unimaginable loneliness that puts the question of sympathy or its effectuality out of question, for "illness is like a virgin forest where even the print of birds' feet are unknown." Being ill for Woolf is the sudden discovery of the foreign in us, or as she herself puts, it is "the uprooting of the ancient oaks in us." But even after this astute realization that illness turns all human "efforts to communicate, to civilize, to share, to cultivate the desert, educate the native" into fruitless illusions (18), she nevertheless falls victim to the virgin forest of the body where lives the beast of the earth. In other words, seen from the perspective of the body, illness might signify, to borrow from one of the few readers of this wonderful essay by Woolf, "a return to absolute materiality, when one is too sick even to think or feel" (Ender 115). And we know that Woolf's absolute materiality, the total body-consciousness as the form of empowerment is as fatal as Gibert and Gubar's monstrous image of rage since it takes us, to cite Judith Butler, to irreducible, unintelligible, and formless "matter of bodies," which needs to be unsettled for "new ways for bodies to matter" (30). One can still go further and argue that insentient monster of the body once again takes us to the borders of animal/human, which we can see happening, if we put aside her desire to recreate her body that "matters," to Bibi Haldar, who, in the wake of her incapacitating illness and her brother's negligence, was not even a woman (Lahiri 163).

As opposed to these readings of illness that borders on human sacredness, being ill is, to say the least, keeping the company of the other. It is to live with the violent intruder[4] that invades the interiors of one's self. It is this sense of rupture and invasion, wounding and division that we find pervading the world of Lahiri's storytelling. Lahiri seems to be rethinking this "reason rooted in the earth," by presenting the cases afflicted with severe loss of body and the patient's desperate attempts at re-incorporation. She seems to be narrating displacement—irreparable severance from body, the body politic, the body of nation and culture—as disease that exposes these "unreal" creatures to the regimes of hygiene and home, and posits them as the unsettling abnormality amidst the economy of cure and corporeality.

"Mrs. Sen's" for instance, narrates the story of a woman haunted by the presence of the intimate but disturbing other. It is about an Indian woman in America, who baby-sits in her own apartment at the fringes of the university in which her husband teaches. As the story unfolds, however, it is the kid who happens to watch and observe all the pranks and practices that Mrs. Sen indulges in including the way things are arranged in the apartment, slippers and shoes, mismatched but neatly arranged furniture, TV and telephone, all draped with cloths, her saris and her reddened scalp, which Eliot, the kid she baby-sits, mistakes for a wound.

There are times in the story, when Mrs. Sen herself disappears into the neat order of the apartment only to re-emerge with her big and beautiful eyes with "thick flaring brows and liquid flourishes" (112) and her shimmering saris with numerous colors and patterns. Otherwise she camouflages among the piles created through her daily rituals of chopping and grating, splitting and slicing. So much so that time and again she gets imprisoned by the mess she collects and produces during the chopping, and from the "catastrophic mess that barricades her," she has to ask Eliot to fetch something from the kitchen (115). One cannot miss the irony when Lahiri compares the blade that Mrs. Sen uses with the prow of a Viking ship (114). Eliot equates this self-imprisoning slashing and cutting to the red parting on her scalp. When Mrs. Sen jumps onto the newspapers with her blade to chop vegetables, the readers cannot miss the resemblance she bears to Boori Ma (the protagonist of another story in the collection to which we will return), who sleeps on the bedding of the newspapers.

The barricaded self, which is visibly invisible acquires more ghostly dimension, when during the interview for baby-sitting, Mrs. Sen explains to Eliot's mother that she is learning how to drive:

> "Yes, I am learning," Mrs. Sen said. "But I am a slow student. At home, you know, we have a driver."
>
> "You mean a chauffeur?"
>
> Mrs. Sen glanced at Mr. Sen, who nodded.
>
> Eliot's mother nodded too, looking around the room. "And that's all [...] in India?"
>
> "Yes," Mrs. Sen replied. The mention of the word seemed to release something in her. She neatened the border of her sari where it rose diagonally across her chest. She, too looked around the room, as if she noticed in the lampshades, in the teapot, in the shadows frozen on the carpet, something the rest of them could not.
>
> "Everything is there." (113)

By declaring that everything is "there," Mrs. Sen not only interrogates the order and neatness of her apartment, which is only a ghostly shadow of its absent "original," but she also foregrounds the specter, the intimate other present as much in herself as it is in the lampshades, teapots and carpets. There are two more ways ghosts enter and exeunt Mrs. Sen's barricaded life: letters and fish. The mere arrival of a letter from "home" is enough to upset the rules in the house. On the day she got one, for instance, she embraced Eliot for the first time, "clasping his face to her sari surrounding him with her odor of mothballs and cumin" (121). As soon as she gets in, she kicks off her slippers this way and that. Once she starts reading the content of her letter, Eliot realizes that Mrs. Sen is no longer present in the room and the apartment is "too small to contain her" (122).

An account of a body and its maladies is not enough to explain Mrs. Sen's bloating self as mere reference to anorexia cannot fully explain her passion for a particular fish and her aversion to the fish from the supermarket. If on the hand "Mrs. Sen's" is a case of the haunted self, it also presents her attempts to escape the prison of the ghostly world around her. Her crazy idea of screaming from her apartment and her desperate attempt to drive to the fish market herself exemplify her desire to escape.

"A Real Durwan" presents another surgical site where Lahiri jabs into the interior of a house and its lodgers, including the protagonist of the story, Boori Ma, who is the sweeper of the stairwell, and the honorary guard of the house. A dweller of odd places of the house, like roof-top and underneath the letterboxes, she infects the tenants not only with her delirious stories of her pre-partition affluence, but also with her mite-consumed two dimensional body and her flagrant non-belonging. Given to improvising the stories of her past that multiply in luxury and comfort each time they are narrated, she at once maintains vigil at the collapsible gate of the her shelter against the idlers and the thieves and exposes the house to the world of her stories. This woman, whose burgeoning narratives could never be verified, is not only homeless, but also "stateless" as she is a deportee from "east Bengal." A person from the place that ceases to (politically) exist except for in her stories, she often finds her present ghosted by the (imaginary) comforts of the past. "A man came," she would wistfully remark, "to pick our dates. Another clipped the hibiscus. Yes, there I tasted life. Here I eat my dinner from a rice pot" (71).

A "bare life" beyond life, therefore, continues to haunt the premises until the day Mr. Chatterjee, who never "strayed from his balcony nor opened a newspaper since Independence," pronounces his verdict that to keep pace with the changing face of the building what it needs is a "real durwan," as if Boori Ma, the vigil she kept were just the make belief like her stories themselves. After the mysterious disappearance of the basin on the stairwell, not only her stories, but also her spectral presence are considered the real threat to the house. One of the residents said, "Boori Ma has endangered the security of this building" (82). Her lies and her ramblings in the locality are considered infectious and her rags, baskets and brooms are thrown out of the building.

Mr. Pirzada of "When Mr. Pirzada Came to Dine" depicts another instance of a displaced and spectral being, who with his state of non-belonging assumes an abnormal dimension. As in "A Real Durwan," in this story as well, we move beyond simple equation of "health, disease and nativism" that Kraut explores in his *Silent Travelers: Germs, Genes, and the "Immigrant Menace"* (2). Mr. Pirzada looks like an Indian, but he is not. He came to a University in the United States on a government grant from Pakistan, but he is not a Pakistani in true sense of the term. The little lady narrator of the story wonders:

> It made no sense to me. Mr. Pirzada and my parents spoke the same language, laughed at the same jokes, looked more or less the same [...]. Nevertheless my father insisted that I understand the difference [...]. He seemed concerned that Mr. Pirzada might take offense if I accidentally referred to him as an Indian [...]. "Mr. Pirzada is a Bengali, but he is a Muslim," my father informed me. "Therefore he lives in East Pakistan, not India." (25-26)

In this story with a particular historical context, the maladies diagnosed are not only the war in Eastern Pakistan, or the blatant absence of world history from the curricula of the schools in the United States, but also the regimes of sameness that always produce otherness in order to persecute it either in the name of religion, language or ethnicity. The beauty of the story seems to be the context in which it is set. Lahiri has the advantage of a double-edged perspective whereby she is able not only to critique the parochial educational system in the United States, but also to critique the political parochialism and its intolerance of difference that led to the civil war in Pakistan. These two fronts Lahiri engages for her critique are connected not only by the television news, but also by the mimicry that the characters are involved in a gesture to overcome the incommunicability between these worlds and time zones. Pirzada arrives, for instance, at Lilia's house and announces himself: "Another refuge, I am afraid on Indian territory" (28), as if to mimic the exodus of the Bengalis precipitated by the war in eastern Pakistan.

Mr. Pirzada always surprises Lilia by his curious ritual with a watch before meals. She takes this to be one of the things which make him different. He takes out a watch from his pocket, winds it and puts it on the coffee table during the dinner. He explains to her that unlike the watch on his wrist, the pocket watch is set to the local time in Dacca, eleven hours ahead. The narrator continues:

> When I saw it that night as he wound it and arranged it on the coffee table, an uneasiness possessed me; life, I realized, was being lived in Dacca first. I imagined Mr. Pirzada's daughter rising from sleep, tying ribbons in their hair, anticipating breakfast, preparing for school. Our meals, our actions, were only a shadow of what had already happened there, a lagging ghost of where Mr. Pirzada really belonged. (30-31)

The global sensorium that the story evokes however is not confined to mere ghostly mimicry. It also suggests propitiatory rituals as if Mr. Pirzada with his watch set to local time in Dacca were keeping track of his lost family; as if his being welcome in Lilia's house were to guarantee food and refuge for his lost children, as if in buying Lilia sweets, he were buying sweets for his own daughters. The wounds and malaise that stretch across different time zones and geographies and the illness that infects several bodies at a time are attended by propitiatory rituals including Lilia's silent prayers for Mr. Pirzada's lost daughters.

If we look deeper into the concluding story, "The Third and Final Continent," we realize that it revolves around the figure of an insane woman, who constitutes the powerful subtext of the narrative, though appearing sparsely and only in apparitions in the story. She continues to haunt the nameless narrator of the story virtually in all continents he happens to go to. Because of this rare but recurring apparition of the insane woman, this story can be said to have borrowed, to quote Benjamin, its "authority from death" (94). The insane woman, who is the mother of the narrator, is not evoked in order to destroy her, nor is she the monster figure of rage. This figure does not either bequeath a "transmissible sequence of images" that Benjamin believes even the poorest wretch in dying possesses (94). Benjamin is right in detecting modern aversion to death as something unhygienic as he remarks that the "thoughts of death," like storytelling have declined to possess human consciousness for centuries (in the West) for people avoid the sight of the dying and death, which once used to be a public process.

A deeper meaning of death than its mere "thought" or its presence as a cultural phenomenon emerges once we look closer at this story, where the transmissible legacy of death that Benjamin upholds changes into a relentless ghosting and apparitions of the dead.

As Derrida reminds us in his *Specters of Marx*, the apparition appears only through re-incorporation. The first time we get the visitation from the insane woman in the otherwise smoothly developing plot of the story with its run-of-the-mill motif of the rags to riches is when the narrator recalls the first five nights he shared with a stranger he married. The wife missed her parents, who agreed to ship their only child overseas fearing that more people might reject her for not looking "fair" enough to be a wife, and she might end up being a spinster; so she wept in bed. The narrator on the other hand lay on his side of the bed, reading his guidebook to America, without doing anything to console her. In between her sobs and the anticipation of his impending journey to the final continent, there emerges the image of his long dead mother, who used to live in the room next to theirs. The apparition is strong enough to permeate through the wall that separates the couple from her room:

> At times I thought of the tiny room on the other side of the wall, which belonged to my mother. Now the room was practically empty; the wooden pallet on which she had once slept was piled with trunks and old bedding. Nearly six years ago, before leaving for London, I had watched her die on that bed, had found her playing with her excrement in her final days. Before we cremated her I had cleaned each of her fingernails with a hairpin, and then, because my brother could not bear it, I had assumed the role of the eldest son, and had touched the flame to her temple, to release her tormented soul to heaven. (181-82)

At that time the narrator did not realize however that the wall that separated him from his wife could be the same wall that at once divided the couple as well as related them to the insane and dead mother in the next room. It takes another apparition of the same woman to make him understand it, which happens months later in a very old woman's house in Boston, where the narrator stays for some weeks.

Mrs. Croft was the first landlady the narrator had in the United States. She was not only old, but had peculiar ideas about etiquette, culture and nationality. The first day the narrator met her, he was baffled when she made him repeat "splendid" every time she mentioned that there was an American flag on the moon, which was to become a refrain in her conversation. After all this old woman, who says she would have anyone with miniskirts arrested, has not forgotten "civilizing with stick" (as Woolf foretold) in spite of her swollen knuckles and weak limbs.

In the meanwhile, the narrator's wife, Mala, joins him in Boston, still a stranger to the man she is married to, who has nothing else but a sense of duty to take care of Mala and to "protect" her (190). What heals the growing estrangement between them and the infectious proprietoriality in him is not what Mrs. Croft says about Mala's being a perfect lady. In fact whatever she says either echoes the conservative time she lived in ("It is improper for a lady and gentleman who are not married to one another to hold private conversation without a chaperone") or the ideology of America's opening of the final frontier ("say Splendid, boy!"). Beyond the body of the nation and its language, it is the apparition of what she does not say that brings Mala and the narrator together, and it also exorcizes the ghost of proprietoriality in him.

The second apparition occurred when Mrs. Croft's daughter Helen mentioned that Mrs. Croft gave piano lessons for forty years to raise her children after her husband's death. The knowledge of Mrs. Croft's struggle mortified him because now he saw in her his own mother, who too was a widow, but she could not overcome her husband's death and got insane:

> That this person was a widow who lived alone mortified me further [than the knowledge that she has already lived over a century] still. It was widowhood that had driven my own mother insane [...]. My mother refused to adjust to life without him; instead she sank into the world of darkness from which neither I, nor my brother, nor concerned relatives, nor psychiatric clinics on Rashbihari Avenue could save her. (187)

The narrator suddenly realizes this unsettling bond of death not only between these widows, one dying and the other already dead, who stand to each other as do illness and cure, but also between Mala and himself. By calling Mrs. Croft's place his "first home in America," and her death "the first death I mourned in America" the narrator symbolically revisits his mother's room, but this time with the cure he found in Mrs. Croft's struggle with her loneliness and invalidity. It is at that moment he discovers the bond that yokes Mala and himself together: the bond of death, as he confesses: "As strange as it seemed, I knew in my heart that one day her death would affect me, and stranger still, mine would affect her" (195). A curious exorcism therefore is at work here, not against the illness and the ghosts he carries across the continents, which has unfortunately become the routine task of the officials at all ports of entries around the world, but an exorcism that stages a séance to open a space so that one can live with the specters.

Lahiri's stories in general and "The Third and Final Continent" in particular imagine a hospitality that shelters these specters from the evil epidemic of what Derrida, towards the end of his brilliant intervention into Marxism, *Specters of Marx*, calls "the life of absolute presence," the one that does not know death and does not want to hear about it (175).

NOTES

1. Since coming from afar in Benjamin is not being even an immigrant, let alone, exile, homeless and displaced person, it is justifiable to hold this category suspect and try to revise it to incorporate modern versions of diasporas.
2. The term uncanny here is used in the sense used by Freud in his powerful and often misinterpreted essay, "Das Unheimlich" meaning unhomely, or the unfamiliar turning suddenly familiar to surprise and shock (Freud 220).
3. Here "sacredness" is used in the sense it is employed by Giorgio Agamben in *Homo Sacer*, where he defines it as a condition to be killed with impunity, or an unconditional capacity to be killed (85), to argue that conjuration of the madwoman is not only a "political castration," but it is also a form of witch hunting ironically prescribed by some feminists themselves.
4. This is an echo of Jean-Luc Nancy's "L'Intrus," where he narrates the heart transplant he underwent a couple of years ago and the subsequent struggle with his new acquisition and the promise and pain it held for him. The idea of the intruding, but the intimate self, which is not only cure but also infection and introjection and incorporation are very resonant, especially at this moment when we are evoking the other that invades and displaces, infects and heals. Towards the end of the essay, Nancy notes:

   > This [a condition of becoming "indissociable from a polymorphous dissociation"] was always, more or less, the life of the infirm and the aged: but, precisely, I am neither one nor the other. What cures

> me is what infects and affects me; what allows me to live causes me to age prematurely. My heart is twenty years younger than I am, and the rest of my body (at least) a dozen years older. [...] I am nothing of what I am supposed to be [...] unless I remain subsumed within the very general condition of the *intrus*, of diverse *intrus* that at any moment can appear in my place in my relations with, or in the representations of, others [*autrui*]. (12)

WORKS CITED

Agamben, Giorgio. *Homo Sacer: Sovereign Power and Bare Life*. Trans. Daniell Helen-Roazen. Stanford: Stanford University Press, 1998.

Benjamin, Walter. *Illuminations*. Trans. Harry Zohn. New York: Schocken Books, 1968.

Butler, Judith. *Bodies that Matter: On the Discursive Limits of Sex*. New York: Routledge, 1993.

Derrida, Jacques. *Specters of Marx: The State of Debt, the Work of Mourning, and the New International*. Trans. Peggy Kamuf. New York: Routledge, 1994.

Ender, Evelyne. "'Speculating Carnally'" or, Some Reflections on the Modernist Body." *The Yale Journal of Criticism* 12.1 (1999): 113-30.

Fanon, Frantz. *The Wretched of the Earth*. Trans. Constance Farrington. New York: Grove P, 1963.

Felman, Shoshana. "Women and Madness: The Critical Phallacy." *Feminisms: An Anthology of Literary Theory and Criticism*. Ed. Robyn R. Warhol and Diane Price Herndl. New Brunswick: Rutgers University Press, 1997. 7-20.

Freud, Sigmund. "The 'Uncanny." *The Standard Edition of the Complete Psychological Works of Sigmund Freud*. Vol. XVII. Trans. James Strachey. London: The Hogarth Press, 1955. 217-56.

Gilbert, Sandra M., and Susan Gubar. *The Mad Woman in the Attic: The Woman Writer and the Nineteenth-Century Literary Imagination*. New Haven: Yale University Press, 1979.

Kraut, Alan M. *Silent Travelers: Germs, Genes, and the "Immigrant Menace*." New York: Basic Books, 1994.

Lahiri, Jhumpa. *Interpreter of Maladies*. Boston: Houghton Mifflin, 1999.

Nancy, Jean-Luc. "L'Intrus." *The New Centennial Review (At the Heart: Of Jean-Luc Nancy)*. 2.3 (2002): 1-14.

Showalter, Elaine. *The Female Malady: Women, Madness, and English Culture, 1830-1980*. New York: Pantheon, 1985.

Sontag, Susan. *Against Interpretation and Other Essays*. New York: Farrar, Straus and Giroux, 1966.

Sontag, Susan. *Illness as Metaphor*. New York: Farrar, Straus and Giroux, 1978.

Spivak, Gayatri Chakravorty. "Three Women's Texts and a Critique of Imperialism." "*Race*," *Writing and Difference*. Ed. Henry Louis Gates, Jr., Chicago: University of Chicago Press, 1985. 262-80.

Woolf, Virginia. *On Being Ill*. London: Hogarth Press, 1930.

8 Hybrid Identities in Jhumpa Lahiri's *Interpreter of Maladies*

Rajeshwar Mittapalli

> To migrate is to experience deep changes and wrenches in the soul, but the migrant is not simply transformed by his act, he also transforms the new world. Migrants might well become mutants, but it is out of such hybridization that newness can emerge.
>
> – Salman Rushdie (BBC "Conversation" series)

Postcolonial theoretical discussion so far has centered mostly round the processes of how the dominant cultures cannibalize the non-dominant ones, whether in the colonial or neo-colonial context. There have been studies aplenty of the ways the non-dominant cultures hybridize with the dominant ones. However, as the United States is basically a migrant nation where the center-periphery polarities and culture cartographies are blurred to some extent, it is not hard to come across instances of hybridity occurring in the reverse direction. The percolation of Indian spirituality into everyday American life through high-profile gurus, the large-scale migration of Indian IT professionals leading to the creation of "Little Indias" within the United States,[1] the increasing popularity of Indian food, films, popular music and, most importantly, the phenomenon of Indian Writing in English, with its high potential for writing back to the center, becoming a rage: all these developments, as well as some strategic American interests, have led recently to the opening of departments of South Asian Literatures and Cultures in about a dozen American universities.

It is against this backdrop that the Indian-American Jhumpa Lahiri's Pulitzer-winning collection of short stories *Interpreter of Maladies* can be viewed as a subtle corrective to North American 'melting pot' cultural politics. It has been said of her immigrant characters that they "live neither here nor there—neither fully comfortable in their skins nor steeped in fear and nostalgia" (Hajari 2001, online), and that they "are not traumatized refugees but are negotiating a path in a country (the United States) that seems to provide opportunities" (Aull 1999, online). Her characters stand in sharp contrast to those of the grand dame of Indian diasporic fiction, Bharati Mukherjee, for whom America constitutes a veritable El Dorado:

> What America offers me is romanticism and hope. I'm coming out of a continent of cynicism and irony and despair in many ways—a traditional society where you are what you are according to the family that you were born into, the caste, the class, the gender, and suddenly I found myself in a country where I can choose to discard that part of my history that I want and invent a whole new history for myself. (Mukherjee 1990)

Mukherjee's characters, specially Dimple of *Wife* and Jasmine of the novel named after the heroine, partake her worldview and overenthusiastically cut bits and pieces of themselves to fit into the definition of assimilated Indians in America. They are formula figures who have escaped from the allegedly oppressive environment of their country of origin and landed on the American shores, sometimes illegally, to find 'happiness' and often a white husband, giving in the process their host nation a chance to pat itself on being 'progressive.'

Unlike Bharati Mukherjee (and her women protagonists), Lahiri inhabits a "perplexing bicultural universe" (Lahiri 2000, online) and, being located at the intersection of Indian and western cultures, she can "see things in a way that not everyone around" (Patel 1999, online) her can, and knows also how to put these worlds in perspective through fiction which is the "foreign land" of her "choosing," a place where she strives "to convey and preserve the meaningful" (Lahiri 1999, 96)[2] from both the Indian and western perspectives. Her stories have a "subtext of ambiguity toward modern American life" (Millar 1999, online) and are written "from a perspective that is between cultures" (Aull 1999, online). Lahiri thus brings the ideal frame of mind to use hybridity as a counter narrative strategy to demonstrate how not just the East hybridizes with the West, but how the West too hybridizes with the East.

Unlike Mukherjee again, Lahiri displays a more mature and complex understanding of the political compulsions of the Indian diaspora in the United States. She never loses sight of the fact that Indians hail from a culture that has withstood innumerable onslaughts on it for well over a thousand years. Any other similarly situated culture would have been completely wiped out given the sustained coercive methods the then rulers employed. It is a time-tested and highly codified culture. Lahiri herself says: "There's a legacy and tradition there [in India] that we just don't have here [in America]. The ink hasn't dried yet on our lives here" (Patel 1999, online). And yet Indians are not averse to hybridizing with other cultures as long as their core beliefs and practices are not threatened. During the eight hundred years of Muslim rule and then two hundred years of the British Raj there was much cultural commingling, which, however, had no bearing on the core belief systems and cultural practices of the Hindus.

The argument of my paper therefore is that the diasporans of Jhumpa Lahiri being mostly a cerebral lot—researchers, investment bankers, university professors, and MIT graduates—live out their hybridity as part of a strategy: to survive in an alien land, to make sense of an alien culture and where possible to redefine their own and the adoptive culture in opposition to each other. However, there seems to be a vast difference in terms of the experience of hybridity between one generation of Lahiri's Indian diasporic characters and another. I will go into these differences in course of my discussion of some of the stories. It should be noted, however, that Lahiri's stories "don't have grand passions and tumultuous relationships, or dramatic plots" (Chacko [1999], online). She "eschews showiness in favor of simplicity, delicacy and sustained understatement" (Ram 1999, online). It is therefore not right to look for dramatic instances of hybridity, one way or the other.

Meet Mrs. Sen of "Mrs. Sen's" who has recently migrated to the United States with her husband, a math professor. She greatly misses India, not for sentimental reasons alone but for the lack of real material comforts which are taken so much for granted in India. She feels literally like a fish out of water, having to make enormous efforts each time she wishes to buy whole fish. In fact the whole story is a bitter complaint against the sterility and unfriendliness of American life, bringing up the question why in the first place Indians migrate to the United States these days. In terms of material comforts, for those who can afford them, modern India compares well with the United States and in addition services like that of a chauffeur are very cheap. It is only for the sake of money then that skilled Indian workers migrate to the United States and not necessarily in search of a great life, nor is it because of a professed admiration for the western culture. Mrs. Sen therefore complains to the mother of Eliot, the eleven-year-old American boy whom she baby-sits, "Everything is there" back home in Calcutta including a chauffeur, plenty of seafood at every street corner and every other imaginable comfort. In the United States she is not only emotionally alienated but also deprived of material comforts. She tells Eliot, "'send pictures,' they [her relatives in Calcutta] write. 'Send pictures of your new life.' What pictures can I send? [...]. 'They think I live the life of a queen, Eliot. [...] 'They think I press buttons and the house is clean. They think I live in a palace'" (IM 125).

Left in the care of the kindly Mrs. Sen, Eliot learns to admire Indian lifestyle and culture. At their very first meeting Mrs. Sen impresses him with her warmth and pleasant bearing.

Her company several hours a day is an education in Indian culture for Eliot. On the spontaneity with which Indians socialize she tells him: "At home [...] just raise your voice a bit, or express grief or joy of any kind, and one whole neighborhood and half of another has come to share the news, to help with arrangements" (IM 116). Eliot is an intelligent boy. He immediately recalls how he and his mother were not even invited by their only neighbours on Labour Day when they had thrown a party.

Mrs. Sen explains to Eliot the durability of Indian marriage through the symbolic gesture of wearing crushed vermilion powder in the part of her hair: "I must wear the powder everyday [...] for the rest of the days that I am married," she tells him, "[...] like a wedding ring. Only with *no fear of losing* it in the dishwater" (IM 117, emphasis added). In contrast, Eliot notes, his mother has already separated and she often spends her nights with her male colleagues.

The second story which I would like to discuss in the context of hybridity occurring in the reverse direction is the provocatively-titled "Sexy." It is the story of a young Caucasian woman, Miranda, whose name itself contains the name of the mystic devotee-cum-lover of Lord Krishna, Mira. She meets Devajit Mitra, a handsome married Bengali investment banker, at a departmental store and falls headlong in love with him. Their affair is facilitated by the absence of Dev's wife who is away in Calcutta. Miranda's association with Dev sets forth a cultural transformation in her. She grows to admire everything Indian. This is a surprise even to her, since as a child she had experienced intense dislike for the neighbourhood Indian family, the Dixits, and their culture. The Dixits liked to display the picture of the fierce goddess Kali at the bottom of their staircase. The picture gave the nine-year-old Miranda such a fright that she was scared for months of walking on that side of the street on her way to and back from school. She would even "hold her breath until she reached the next lawn, just as she did when the school bus passed a cemetery" (IM 96). She is ashamed of it now. The mystery and romance of India fascinate her. When Dev makes love to her she imagines "deserts and elephants, and marble pavilions floating on lakes beneath a full moon" (IM 96). This admiration translates into her desire to experience things Indian. She therefore visits an Indian restaurant in Central Square and orders tandoori chicken. She learns the Bengali script and even to spell the Indian part of her name, Mira. When Dev tells her, on her request, that his wife looks like the Bombay actress Madhuri Dixit, she sets out to find out what the actress looks like. From the videos displayed in an Indian grocery she understands that Madhuri Dixit, and indeed many Indian women, are beautiful. This is a reversal of the western media's representation of South Asian women as being exotic or erotic. Still the affair fizzles out because Miranda does not want to devalue the beauty of the experience by ruining the marital happiness of an Indian woman.

With the second-generation immigrants, however, the articulation of hybrid identities becomes problematic. Second-generation diasporic Indians seem to lose some of their will-power to resist assimilation. A dramatic depiction of this form of hybridity occurs in the story "This Blessed House." In this story assimilation and resistance are played out on the mental planes of a newly married Indian couple, the husband being a recent immigrant and the wife a second-generation immigrant. They discover in their newly bought home a number of kitsch Christian artefacts left behind by the previous occupants: a porcelain effigy of Christ, a 3-D postcard of St. Francis done in four colours, a plastic snow-filled dome containing a miniature Nativity scene, a larger-than-life-size watercolour poster of Christ weeping translucent tears, and so on. Twinkle, the wife, "who normally displayed good taste" (IM 138), is charmed by them while her husband Sanjeev finds it acutely embarrassing and irksome to have them prominently displayed in his house. "We're not Christian," (IM 137) he repeatedly tells her, "[a]ll the neighbors will see. They'll think that we're insane" (IM 146). But her fascination only intensifies with each new discovery. Clearly, Christian cultural values are deeply embedded in her mind due to sustained exposure to them within the school system and outside. Unlike Sanjeev she was born and raised in the United States, and like the girl protagonist Lilia in another story, "When Mr. Pirzada Came to Dine," she must have grown up imbibing the dominant religious discourses of America. That it is not an innocent curiosity on the part of Twinkle is brought home by the fact that she sheds bitter tears when Sanjeev threatens to take the freshly discovered statue of Virgin Mary to the dump. The war of nerves continues, often bringing the couple to serious disagreements, but finally a makeshift peace is arrived at ironically with the discovery of a silver bust of Christ, the prince of peace.

As a reviewer has rightly pointed out Lahiri is "not out to convert Hindus here, nor is she indulging in sarcasm at the expense of sincere belief" (Crain 1999, online). What is being dramatized is the clash between assimilation and resistance finally finding its compromise in hybridity. It dawns on Sanjeev that he has to live with the objects signifying an alien faith and culture right in his house for Twinkle's sake, for the sake of survival in an alien land by appearing to accept its values but actually resisting them.

Moving a little down the generation lane we meet Shukumar and Shobha of the opening story "A Temporary Matter." These two are apparently Americanized second-generation Bengali immigrants in the US who are projected as having been alienated from each other in the aftermath of a stillbirth, but are actually influenced by the American social environment which treats marriage itself as a temporary matter. During a succession of power cuts in the evenings they play the game of confessing to each other hitherto jealously guarded secrets. The pretence of a game is abandoned toward the end with Shobha declaring her intention to walk out on him and Shukumar revealing that their stillborn baby was a boy. Once the mystery is unveiled, and knowledge having dawned on them, they tacitly make peace and weep together "for the things they now knew" (IM 20). This development has been interpreted as striking a "Christian chord: the act of weeping after 'knowledge' ranges all the way from the Bible to Boney M." (Khair 2000). However, unlike in the Biblical story the dawn of knowledge does not result here in mutual recrimination and loss, but in reconciliation and a strengthening of emotional bonds, exemplifying in the process the enduring quality of Indian marriage. Marriage for the Hindus is not only a sacred institution but also an immutable one. The western cultural influence which has brought the Shobha-Shukumar marriage to the point of dissolution exposes itself to be weak.

But the characters that appeal to us most compellingly, as we have seen earlier on, are the first-generation immigrants who, like Lahiri's own parents, think that they are first and forever Indian. They are not passive beings allowing others to define them but self-confident individuals, often constituting the cream of Indian society, who have come to America (and in what appears to be a reversal of the colonial situation) to 'conquer' and take over, forging hybrid identities along the way, for it is in hybridity that the hope for survival lies, not just for Indian-Americans but for the whole of mankind. Essentialist ideologies have always proved to be counterproductive and led to tensions and civil strife. In this information age, the era of globalization, it is no longer possible to maintain pure cultural essences, and in multiracial and multicultural societies like America it is neither desirable nor possible. The question is one of the ratio of cultural exchange. Peoples with well-established and well codified cultural traditions tend to give more than what they take, and that is what seems to happen in some stories of Jhumpa Lahiri's *Interpreter of Maladies*.

NOTES

1. According to the statistics released by the US Population Bureau there are currently 1.6 million (0.6% of the US population) Indians living in America. During the nineties alone Indian population recorded a phenomenal 105.87 per cent growth, the largest among all Asian immigrant groups.
2. All further parenthetical references to this edition are marked with IM.

WORKS CITED

Aull, Felice. Review of *Interpreter of Maladies* by Jhumpa Lahiri. Nov. 5 (1999). Available at the Literature, Arts and Medicine Database web site: <endeavor.med.nyu.edu/lit-med/lit-med-db/webdocs/webdescrips/lahiri1563-des-.html>. (5 Nov. 2005)

Chacko, Susan. Review of *Interpreter of Maladies* by Jhumpa Lahiri [1999]. Available at the South Asian Women's NETwork web site: <www.sawnet.org/books/reviews.php?Interpreter+of+Maladies>. (5 Nov. 2005)

Crain, Caleb. "Subcontinental Drift: *Interpreter of Maladies: Stories* by Jhumpa Lahiri." *New York Times*, July 11 (1999). Available at the *New York Times* web site: <www.nytimes.com/books/99/07/11/reviews/990711.11craint.html>. (5 Nov. 2005)

Hajari, Nisid. "The Promising Land: Indian-American Jhumpa Lahiri's heralded debut only partly lives up to its advance hype." *Time* 154.10, Sep. 13 (1999) Available at the *Time* web site: <www.time.com/time/asia/magazine/99/0913/books.html>. (5 Nov. 2005)

Khair, Tabish. "Knowledge of Loss, the Loss of Knowledge: Jhumpa Lahiri, Shashi Deshpande, Mahasweta Devi." Paper presented at an international conference on English Fiction from the Indian Subcontinent and the South Asian Diaspora, held at Copenhagen University, Denmark, 6–7, Nov. 2000. Published in the Copenhagen University's official journal *Angles* (Summer 2001).

Lahiri, Jhumpa. "To Heaven Without Dying: Where does authorial freedom end and identity politics begin?" *FEED Books Issue*, July 24 (2000). Partially available as "Translato ergo sum" at the *Himâl Southasian* web site: <www.himalmag.com/oct2000/voices.html>. (5 Nov. 2005)

Millar, Jared. Review of *Interpreter of Maladies* by Jhumpa Lahiri. Scrawl Electronic Magazine (1999). Available at: <home.att.net/~perimeter/bookmaladies.htm>. (5 Nov. 2005)

Mukherjee, Bharati. "Conquering America with Bharati Mukherjee: World of Ideas Interview with Bill Moyers." Public Broadcasting System. Alexandria, Va.: PBS Video, 1990.

Patel, Vibhuti. "Maladies of Belonging: An interview with Jhumpa Lahiri." *Newsweek International*, Sep. 20 (1999). Available at the South Asian Women's NETwork web site: <www.sawnet.org/books/writing/patel_lahiri.html>. (5 Nov. 2005)

Ram, Susan. "Chronicle of the Cultural Interface: *Interpreter of Maladies* by Jhumpa Lahiri." *Frontline* 16.21, Oct. 9 (1999). Available at <www.flonnet.com/fl1621/16210700.htm>. (5 Nov. 2005)

Rushdie, Salman. BBC "Conversation" series [videorecording] (n.d.).

9

The Nostalgic Note in their Flute: A Reading of Arundhati Roy and Jhumpa Lahiri

Nandini Sahu

Critical attention that has been paid to the young Indian writers in the last two decades calls for a critical inquiry. This article offers a re-reading of the literary output of Arundhati Roy and Jhumpa Lahiri that has added tremendously to the tradition of the Indian literary scene through the intensity and the narrative technique which they both demonstrate in their creative pursuits. In this article, I will analyze how literature is a global gateway or a meeting point of world's traditions through encounter of cultures and existential rediscovery.

In the post-colonial era, new Indian writers have succeeded in drawing the world attention with their methods of characterization. Jhumpa Lahiri, Manju Kapur, Arundhati Roy, Gita Mehta, Shashi Tharoor, Pankaj Mishra, Rajkamal Jha, Githa Hariharan, Amit Choudhury, Manil Suri, Mark Tully, Anita Nair, David Davidhar, Radhika Jha, Preeti Singh, Makrand Paranjape, Mrinal Pande among others have all written works that can be termed as literature of encounter and synthesis—both culturally and linguistically. The world's literary creativity is enhanced by a significant enrichment of the narrative in the hands of writers like Arundhati Roy and Jhumpa Lahiri. These writers employ their cultural, ethnic as well as familial past as their recurring theme. The literature of exile, particularly the literature where recollection acts as a mode of redemption, is not peculiar to modern India, but so important is the past to both Lahiri and Roy that a consciousness of it colours their insistent preoccupation with living. Memory plays a vigorous, creative role in their writings and a preoccupation with their personal past leads in the long run to a search for cultural roots.

Roy and Lahiri do not write from the position of a distant observer, rather their writings reflect the perspective of someone between a paradisiacal past and a tormenting present. The oppressiveness of the present reality and the temporal time are the facts to accept here and now. Life is viewed as a nostalgic recollection through the eyes of sensitive, vulnerable and observant characters. The writers' efforts to bring out a meeting point for the past and the present has been intensified by their nostalgic representation of characterization. The dichotomy with which both these writers present the present existence is resulted by the aesthetic dilemma, which they perceive due to their nostalgic experience. In the context of the contemporary milieu, the lack of unity of being with the self is reinforced by the lack of unity of the past and the present, which is focused throughout. In my analysis of Roy's novel *The God of Small Things* and Jhumpa Lahiri's collection of stories *Interpreter of Maladies*, I will look at the ways in which their characters live in two worlds, one within and one without, and the past keeps intruding into the present.

Memory and *The God of Small Things*

In the case of Arundhati Roy's *The God of Small Things*, a major concern is the necessity to regain identity through language as a creative mode. Through the story of the twins Rahel and Estha, Roy's text overtly discusses the passage from alienation to an awareness of a sense of discovering the world and its values, roots. The knowledge of the world gives one a knowledge of herself. In *The God of Small Things*, Estha's early euphoric adolescence works as a stepping stone towards his maturity. Rahel's unrestrained enthusiasm of everything around gives her a broad vision to narrate the picture gallery of life as a whole. Rahel, a character of 31 years, "a viable diable age" is in a self-introspective mood crossing the border from youth to maturity. Though her stance is detached and controlled, it is all the while infused with emotion. She recalls the years of mistakes they have committed, the years they have been deeply wronged, have been "more sinned against then sinning." In the process, self-delusion overtakes her, she gets distanced from her present self while evoking the moments of their past.

A sense of loss, non-fulfilment, apparent failure, a desire for the oblivion, and a love for the small things—which, in fact, convey big things—occur repeatedly in the novel. *The God of Small Things* is a story about love, death, lies and law. It is the universal tale of love and tragedy. Through it Roy pictures a child's view of the adult world, a tragic world of the feudal Christians, a barbarian Communist who wipes his armpits with his terylene shirt, and a few sentimental untouchables. Two main interlocking streams in the story are the erotic and cross-caste love-story between the Paravan Velutha and the Syrian Christian Ammu, and the insight into the complicacy of Keralan politics.

Roy uses flash-back technique for the narrative, memory serving as the source of narration. The characters are life-like, becoming almost alive in each one of us, yet they are allegorical, sometimes more like attributes rather than individuals. Baby Kochamma stands for the inferiority complex and jealousy, Ammu for suppressed desire and hurt pride, Rahel and Estha for curiosity and unbounded love, Chacko for affectedness, Pappachi for male-chauvinism, Mammachi for inner blindness of a woman. About this deep concern for humanity in the novel, Roy says: "My work is not an academic, sociological study of untouchability but a human story that springs from love for human beings and a close contact with what happens to them" (*Indian Express* 11). Rahel, the narrator, is sometimes a stranger, sometimes an observer and yet some other times she is the performer. She expresses herself in the language of generic human emotion with its inevitable commitment to images, symbols, allegory, repetition, fluidity of language, and the tension between the intense experience and its verbalization.

The narrative evolves around early memories of Rahel that are suddenly activated years later when the siblings meet once again. The memories of trivial things of childhood reveal how childhood impression years later add new meanings to adult experience. Roy's thematic strategy seems to be a suitable one for a writer of her situation, who writes about her characters caringly. Roy loves her characters and that is why they seem so lifelike. When film producers proposed her for making a movie of the story, she said: "It may sound silly, but I could not bear the idea of seeing actors play Eshta, Rahel, Velutha [...] it would kill me. I love them too much. I always will" (Ram 17).

The familial memories Roy employs are more of human interest at large, prone to social plane speaking of the higher values of life and complex human situation. The small memories of Rahel create a masterpiece of moving psychological fiction. Though the "Little Man" Estha had always thought that "anything might happen to anyone, so it's better to be prepared" (118), he himself was never prepared for that anything in his life. Sophie Mol's funeral, the memory of her 'child sized,' 'satin-lined,' 'brass handled Shined' coffin, her go-go bag, yellow bellbottoms that made Rahel feel inferior, Baby Kochamma's expensive funeral saree, are haunting, picturesque experiences. Other memories—the 'porket-munny' of children, their learning of pronunciation to impress Sophie, Kochamma's make up, K.N.M. Pillai's sister's rendering of the poem "Lochinvar," Ammu and Baba's pushing the children to each other like billiard balls, the pseudo-Latin comment "Et Tu, Kochu Mariye" to the house maid, incidents in the Abhilash Talkies bathroom, the Orangedrink Lemondrink man episode—all these add a comic side to the otherwise tragic storyline. But the underlying deep tragedy, mysterious like the Meenachal river speaks volumes of the deceptive simplicity of the novel. Through nostalgia the present is arranged in a (supposedly) correct order and the memories convey deep emotions.

Roy's tone gets satirical whenever she discusses the politics of contemporary Kerala. Comrade E.M.S. Namboodiripad is referred to as "Kerala's Mao Tse-Tung," who "broke the egg, but burnt the omelette" (281). Similarly comrade K.N.M. Pillai is portrayed as an opportunist who pretends to forget the past and his role in Velutha's murder.

Observing life from all directions, blending the past, present and the future in the single thread of life, Roy makes the storyline timeless. Her concern is with memory and the way it establishes or falsifies relationships in a challenging world. She is neither a nostalgic traditionalist nor an advocate of modernization, but the product of both. Her novel reflects a personality conscious of change and aware of memories, which form her inner self. For her, past is a time before Fall, she can be viewed as a writer on cultural cross-roads.

Interpreter of Maladies

Following the publication of three of her stories in the *New Yorker* in 1998, Jhumpa Lahiri's reputation was established among both critics and readers alike. When a collection of her short stories, *Interpreter of Maladies*, was released in 1999, it received a flurry of reviews. In an interview with Vibhuti Patel, Lahiri commented on her first career progression from scholar to Pulitzer prize winner, saying: "Its all been a surprise—getting an agent, an editor, a book contract—it was all so fast. I feel extraordinary gratitude and amazement. Writers need time, some money and a little encouragement. This book has given me just the right amount of all three" (Patel 80).

In her stories, Jhumpa Lahiri is concerned with the consciousness of the need for regaining roots in the tradition of India and a rueful nostalgia towards it. Her quest for identity is a consciousness towards exile, the dynamic force working to bring about this quest is a point of active engagement between two cultures—Indian and Western. The collection is a 'confessional piece,' speaking of the pattern of hope and disenchantment arising from the predicament of the writer placed between two traditions, neither of which she can wholly accept or renounce. Like with many other expatriates, it sounds as if the Western culture forms (a part of) Lahiri's intellectual and rational make up whereas Indian culture of her emotional make up. Professor R.K. Kaul writes about her: "The author has narrative skill, which captures the reader's attention immediately. [...] Whether the setting is in Bengal or in the US, she creates a probable world where human relations are all that matter" (Kaul 3). Lahiri writes about how the English culture produces disenchantment in the minds of the expatriate Indians, and how they find themselves crushed under the burden of alienation and rootlessness. There is a sense of loss of identify with their own culture, therefore the need for roots.

There is an aesthetic continuum in Lahiri's writing. The stories present the writer's intercontinental journey during which she gets herself accustomed to different cultures—by her stay abroad and regular trips to India during every summer. The realization that is dawned on her is about the possibility of affirming the identity of her Indian self. It seems that for Lahiri, East is the symbol of intellectual alertness and west is of emotional poverty. An identification of herself with either one is a frustrating experience, the artistic self is at war with the collective consciousness of both. Her stories seem to attempt to bring meaning to the present by reassessing the past and by giving shape to the accumulated experience of the characters' past prior to the period of westernization.

With every detail of the experiences of both first and second generation of Indian immigrants, the topics of Lahiri's stories range from emotional struggles of love to immigrants battling in a new world. The stories draw upon the racial past of India, Indian cultural heritage, the topics of communication, relationships. She can herself be interpreted as one kind of an interpreter of maladies of people "[w]ho think in a way they can't fully express" (Patel 80). About her Indian past, she spoke to Rediff.com: "India is the place where my parents are from, a place I visited frequently for extended time and formed relationship with people and with my relatives and felt a tie over time even though it was a sort of parenthesis in my life to be there" ("Jhumpa" online). Lahiri's writings are scattered with details of traditional Indian names, food, flavour, and wardrobe giving shape to her stories. In her representation,

Indian culture is inherently present without exaggeration. Even if the characters belong to different ages, nationalities, and religions, they demonstrate the universality of real life experience.

In the story "Mrs. Sen's," an eleven-year-old boy in an American college town watches his baby sitter Mrs. Sen with her eccentricities, from chopping vegetable with a "blade curved like the prow of a Viking ship" to applying a fresh streak of crushed vermilion to the parting of her hair with the head of a thumbtack while recollecting the life she reluctantly left behind in Calcutta (114). Lahiri manages to portray so well the confusion and despair a young Indian wife feels so far from home. Her anxiety for letters from her kith and kin in her motherland, her Indian dishes, fish curry, family members' voice on the tape recorder during her farewell and many other things reflect the pathos of an expatriate Indian. In "A Temporary Matter" the characters live with the memory of their lost love, and during the power failures, they remember India, Shobha's granny's house, where during such power failures each has to say something like a joke, a story and a little poem. This leads towards a confession game, and a catastrophe.

"When Mr. Pirzada Came to Dine," then, is an emotional story with flashbacks of Pakistan's civil war and the partition, its history, and geography. Lilia's mother recollects her past in India during the Independence: the crisis, the power failures, the light of kerosene lamps, the pressures, the English tutors, the constant examinations, and facts secure about her daughters life in the US. Still Lilia would never choose to distance herself from her roots, store her chocolates in her grandmother's sandalwood box, the only memento of a grandmother she had never known. The predominant tone of the story is nostalgia, with Mr. Pirzada's memory of his wife and seven daughters living in Dacca. Ultimately, after Mr. Pirzada's departure, Lilia could realize "what it meant to miss someone who was so many miles and hours away, just as he had missed his wife and daughter for so many months" (42).

The title story "Interpreter of Maladies" deals with the ethnic past of India with a vivid description of the Sun Temple at Konark, and the confession of Mrs. Das about her past to Mr. Kapasi, the interpreter of maladies. In "A Real Durwan" for the protagonist Boori Ma, the memory of her royal youth is the only source of remaining alive in her old age (she "[e]xaggerates her past at elaborate lengths and heights" 73) whereas the story "Sexy" is about identity crisis with Dev as an expatriate Bengali boy and Miranda as someone born and bred in the US. Dev talks to her nostalgically about the Taj as "[t]he everlasting monument to love," speaks of the Indian significance of her name Mira, and Goddess Kali, Indian food, Indian spices are mentioned all over. Finally, "The Third and Final Continent" is a touchingly transparent story as it tells about the protagonist's past with his landlady, Mrs. Croft.

There is an ardor of empathy in the stories where Lahiri displays a steadfast curiosity about human behavior and a healthy respect for its mystery. She makes the readers share the characters' tragedies, their nostalgic experiences. She does not point out the loss of their cultural identity directly, her characters seem to be relieved when they adjust to the new world and regret at the separation from their original culture. Indian food, spices, flavors act as a talisman in the stories, a reassuring bit of the homeland to brood over. Lahiri does not filter life through the single, steady voice of a young satirist, instead she writes about Indian American experience from many angles in the indelible, lifelike stories that cling to memory as a source of living, she herself being the interpreter of human maladies.

In her perception the journey of the Indian becomes an aesthetic continuum reading the Indian landscape as a foreigner would read it. The characters look back to India satirically celebrating their freedom or asserting their biculturalism, look skeptically and wryly on their new homeland as outsiders with a feeling of something being lost, a sense of longing, a loss that often comes with the life of an immigrant. She confesses to Elizabeth Farnsworth in an interview:

> I think that, in part, it's a reflection of what I observed my parents experiencing and their friends, their circle of fellow Indian immigrant friends. It's also, in part, drawn from my own experiences and a sense of [...] loss from my parents that was so palpable all the time while I was growing up, the sense of what my parents had sacrificed in moving to the US." (Farnsworth online)

The characters' ability to accommodate and absorb the other culture without losing the consciousness of being Indian marks the major concern of Lahiri. She pictures how life abroad is exciting, a bit absurd, and often lonely.

Through Lahiri's stories, we learn bits and pieces about Indian life in diaspora and how Indians fit into their lives in America. In the title story, an Indian family from New Jersey who are every bit 'ugly Americans' hire an old fashioned Indian guide Mr. Kapasi who knows nine languages. The dual theme—love and duty—in the story emphasises on the word interpreter. Mr. Kapasi wants to get to the heart of the matter. Lahiri is at her best in getting to the heart of any matter through the themes of love, fidelity, tradition and alienation. In a conversation with Arun Aguiar, she talks about the creation of one of her Indian characters, Bibi Haldar, who stemmed

> from going there and observing people. For that story I took as my subject a young woman whom I got to know over the course of a couple of visits [...]. She lived in the same building as my aunt and uncle [...]. I learnt from my aunt that she had some epileptic like disease. (Aguiar online)

Furthermore, when asked about the reaction of the Indian readers to her stories, she said:

> When I read for a predominantly Indian audience, there are more questions that are based on issues of identity and representation. That also happened in England last week. Some Indians will come up and say that a story reminded them of something very specific to their experience. (Aguiar online)

Nostalgic Note of Exile

"There is something to be said for exile," writes the poet R. Parthasarathy in the second part of his poem "Exile": "you learn roots are deep" (Parthasarathy 75). The illustration of this conviction may be best found in the writings of Jhumpa Lahiri. In spite of the slightly ironic tone employed throughout her descriptions, the final impression is that of an obsession with and an admiration of Indian traditional culture. Arundhati Roy and Jhumpa Lahiri prove it wrong that a language a writer uses (here English) must mean everything to her. There is a feeling of buoyancy for the language in their writing and they are comfortable with it even if they have alien experiences with life. Even if there is discomfort, it is purely intellectual. The use of private experiences, especially the inner world of memories and the continuities with the past, can be seen on the basis of their writing. They are not attempts to intellectualize and make moral choices, their writings are a retrospective photoflash.

Along with these intimate portrayals, their vocabulary is touchingly Indian. The Indian phrases and syntactical patterns transplanted in the English milieu in their writings add a new flavour to the English idiom itself. Their writings convey a whole range of feelings: from the ecstasy of transcendence of emotions to the drugged mindless trance of passion, from the feeling of being cleansed by love and sex to the poignant bitter sweet memories of love and loss, their flutes play the nostalgic note from their heart and intellect. In the writings of both Roy and Lahiri, the protagonists' search for the symbols of collective past and the attempts to resensitise their sensibility through their communion with past, with heritage, is obvious.

WORKS CITED

Aguiar, Arun. "Interview with Jhumpa Lahiri." pifmagazine.com (1999). Available at <www.pifmagazine.com/SID/598/>. (Sep. 9, 2005)

Farnsworth, Elizabeth. "Pulitzer Prize Winner-Fiction." pbs.org/newshour April 12, 2000. Available at <www.pbs.org/newshour/gergen/jan-june00/lahiri_4-12.html>. (9 Sep. 2005)

Indian Express 18 Oct. 1997: 11.

"Jhumpa Lahiri wins Pulitzer." Available at <www.rediff.com/news/2000/apr/11jhumpa.htm>. (9 Sep. 2005)

Kaul, R.K. "Twinkling Interpretations of Bengali Characters." *Indian Book Chronicle* 25.7 (July 2000): 3.

Lahiri, Jhumpa. *Interpreter of Maladies*. New Delhi: Harper Collins, 1999.

Patel, Vibhuti. "The Maladies of Belonging." Interview with Jhumpa Lahiri. *Newsweek* Sep. 20 (1999): 80. Available at <www.sawnet.org/books/writing/patel_lahiri.html>. (9 Sep. 2005)

Parthasarathy, R. "Exile." *Ten Twentieth Century Indian Poets*. Ed. R. Parthasarathy. Delhi: Oxford UP, 1976. 75.

Ram, N. "Scimitars in the Sun." Interview with Arundhati Roy. *Frontline* 19 Jan. 2001: 17. Available at <www.flonnet.com/fl1801/18010040.htm>. (9 Sep. 2005)

Roy, Arundhati. *The God of Small Things*. New Delhi: India Ink, 1997.

10

A Paradigm Shift in the Representation of Violence in Partition Short Stories by Women: Political Irony in Shauna Singh Baldwin's "Family Ties"

Beerendra Pandey

During the bloody partition of India in 1947, which had taken on the proportions of a war, at least one hundred thousand women are said to have been abducted and raped by all the three parties involved—Muslims, Hindus and Sikhs. The representation of the gendered violence, which remains effaced in the history textbooks of both India and Pakistan, receives a central treatment in partition fiction by women writers, especially the survivors. Ian Talbot stresses that historians can get clue about "this neglected aspect of the reality of partition" from the creative writings of the women survivors (235). These writings

> drive home the point that in times of external war or civil war, it is women who are inevitably singled out for particularly humiliating treatment—molestation, rape, abduction or forcible marriage—and it is they who have to suffer for the imposed ignominy. Women's bodies are considered by Indian men, Hindu, Muslim or Sikh, as the repository of men's honour. 'Power rape,' the raping of women to demonstrate and defeat rival men in patriarchal societies, is quite common in many parts of India, as indeed in many other areas of the world. The rape of a woman is akin to the rape of the community to which she belongs. (Ray 14)

The feminist reconstruction of partition violence has received central attention in the revisionist historiography of 1947 by women writers such as Ritu Menon, Veena Das and Urvashi Butalia who focus on the double subordination of women through abduction and recovery, rape and murder. The revisionist feminist history, in the words of Mrinal Pande, "has developed a third subaltern eye, that glosses over accepted social mores and eminent personalities of the day, for the working-class women's version of what history and society look like from a woman's point of view" (120). The spotlight falls on investigating how far the gendered identity is subordinated to the needs of the religious or the ethic community, and what this means for a concept such as secondary citizenship. Honour—whether family or national—turns out to be the major factor in the subordination of women to the status of secondary citizenship.

The stories, "A Leaf in the Storm" by Lalithambika Antharajanam and "Family Ties" by Shauna Singh Baldwin, which deal with the theme of abduction and recovery, dramatize the elliptical and discontinuous subjectivities of women victims—the subjectivities which make "visible the imagination of the nation as a *masculine* nation," the women of which have only secondary citizenship (Das 205, emphasis added). The stories by the partition generation women writers such as Lalithambika Antharajanam, Amrita Pritam and Jamila Hashmi also underscore the irrationality of the violence on women. One of the ways whereby these writers underline the absurdity of the gendered violence is by highlighting the rationality of the battered victims in choosing to live with their abductors because of the demand of motherhood—a demand that remains within the realm of patriarchy—in the texts by Antharajanam, Pritam and Hashmi. Unlike these partition generation women writers, the granddaughter of partition, Shauna Singh Baldwin, does not deploy the trope of motherhood in "Family Ties;" instead she interrogates the patriarchal nature of the Indian society by placing at the center the silenced subaltern subjectivity of a ten/eleven-year female child in a manner that helps her avoid marginalizing women—a limitation obtaining in "A

Leaf in the Storm" because of the narrative closure obtained through the tropes of continuity and motherhood. The present essay argues that the irony available through the narrative perspective of a female child narrator in "Family Ties" equips the subaltern narrator with a much-needed critical perspective that underwrites a feminist agenda which marks a paradigm shift in the representation of gendered violence in partition short stories by women writers.

In "A Leaf in the Storm," written in 1948, the central issue with which the narrative grapples, relates to the quandary that an expectant woman has—the dilemma between abortion and delivery. Jyoti, a relatively assertive, educated young girl arrives pregnant and despondent in a refugee camp, having been betrayed, abducted and raped in her migration across the border. She happens to be one among the many victims of mass rape. Mass rape, as Robert Hayden points out, "is a tool used to partition permanently an already conscious heterogeneous population at the time when territory in which these people(s) live is being divided physically" (31). Mass rape is directed at making the victims hate the rapists so that the minority community thinks it in their own interest to migrate permanently. After having migrated to India, Jyoti has to live with the memory of an earlier life lost and the despair of ever recovering it. The nascent life, conceived in the mass rape, tortures her as she watches births and deaths in the camp. As the narrative puts it, she is besieged by the despondency arising from the shattering of her long-cherished desire "to free the bonded, those who were enslaved by convention" (142). She vacillates between terminating the pregnancy and persisting with it. Finally, almost despite herself, she chooses life, "swoop[ing] the child up into her arms, "caressing it gently" and letting "her life-blood flow [...] like fresh milk" (145).

Jyoti's aggressive motherhood, however, constitutes the climactic irony in the text, for she enslaves herself by finally succumbing to the convention of continuity and motherhood at a time when the Indian State, in clear violation of the Gandhian principle of non-violence, had not only allowed but also financed "mass abortion" (Butalia 128). The State's authorization, as Urvashi Butalia points out, had twin goals: of minimizing the number of children born of mixed union, a constant reminder of the violation of woman, of Mother India and of maintaining the purity of the violated women who otherwise would be easily taken as polluted in the society. For the State, however, these women remained as pure as Sita after the abduction by Ravana (Butalia 127-28). Jyoti's decision to go for delivery after a considerable bit of dillydallying that tantalizes with the possibility of a consciousness at odds with the codes of continuity and motherhood turns out to be a strategy of mother politics at the time of conflict—a ploy to make the male-perpetrated violence on women look irrational and monstrous. Identification as mother at the end of the narrative helps Jyoti to enlist generous feelings of care and love that powerfully contradict violence—whether perpetrated by the people or done in collusion with the State. Interestingly, the closure of "A Leaf in the Storm," wherein Jyoti is shown walking towards the camp with the child, is informed by an aura of beatific motherhood when the stars beaming from heaven, have "resolved a complicated puzzle" for her (145). But the affirmation of motherhood skirts dangerously close to the patriarchal definitions of women's role and is seen in the text as being co-opted by the dominant nationalism propagating that very ideology. History is twisted here in order to maintain an idealistic vision of Gandhi's position—the Gandhian conviction that it is only in acts of well-doing, even as the world goes mad, that humanism resides. All that Lalithambika Antharajanam can do in the nationalist framework is to express her rage at the disruption of the order of humanity, of the private space of women and to re-establish the continuity of the order, shared by the writer and the reader of her time, in which the familiar code of women's motherhood and compassion prevails. The narrative closure, which shows appropriation of the discontinuous feminine subjectivity by Gandhian nationalist project, defuses the conflicts implicit in these subaltern experiences. Jyoti's dithering, which encapsulates the possibility of a consciousness that threatens to veer away from the codes of continuity and motherhood, is finally "absorbed into the projects of the narrative and become emblematic of national spaces" (Tharu 79).

Shauna Singh Baldwin's "Family Ties," written in 1996, unlike Lalithambika Antharajanam's "A Leaf in the Storm," heightens the subaltern subjectivity of a ten/eleven-year-old female child narrator who mobilizes political irony to radically map the micropolitics of power relations between men and women *vis-à-vis* partition violence. Baldwin's main purpose in using political irony in "Family Ties" is to enable the marginalized, to quote the words of Linda Hutcheon, "be heard by the center, and yet keep [...] critical distance and thus unbalance and undermine" the patriarchal discourses (31). In line with her goal of provocative decentering of the masculinist discourse, Baldwin, unlike Antharajanam, makes no attempt to neutralize the subaltern subjectivity: here is a woman speaking about women with no transaction between the speaker and listener.

The story, which takes place in 1971 at the time of Indo-Pakistan war that partitioned Pakistan in two nation states—Pakistan and Bangladesh, creates a world in which women can be truly important only as *Alakshmi*, as a stain on family pride, as an impediment to prosperity, to be disposed of as casually and thoughtlessly as wringing a chicken's neck; where the daughter even for the mother is a burden. Through the mother's attitude to the narrator-daughter, "Family Ties" shows that patriarchy is at its strongest when women themselves participate in it, colluding in notions of honour that privilege male control over sexuality, and over their lives and desires.

It is in such a world that the child narrator learns about her father's 1947 partition experience from a distance, with the imperfect understanding that all of us born after 1950 must share. As she learns, the central question that haunts her is: "If I had a Muslim baby, would I have the courage to drown it?" (32). She is speaking of her father's sister Chandini Kaur, who was abducted and raped by Muslims during the partition. Of course, the sister is dead to the family for allowing this dishonour to come to the family. After her recovery, she has begged to come home but the family will not accept her with a Muslim child. Later, with the child drowned to death by the mother herself, she is still not accepted because of the shame she has brought on brother's family and community. Through the plight of Chandini Kaur, Baldwin reminds us that a woman's modesty signifies the masculinity of her community. The hapless woman becomes the symbol of violence as the shame and subjection of her community is represented in her. Chandini Kaur's condition makes her, to quote one of the informants of Ritu Menon and Kamla Bhasin, a permanent refugee: "Abducted as Hindus, converted and married as Muslims, recovered as Hindus but required to relinquish their children because they were born of Muslim fathers, and disowned as 'impure' and ineligible for membership within their erstwhile family and community, their identities were in a continual state of construction and reconstruction, making them, as one woman said to us, 'permanent refugees'" (16).

The narrator-girl's own fate is no different from that of her aunt, Chandini Kaur as the fear of the Muslims abducting Hindu and Sikh girls grips the city in the wake of the Indo-Pakistan war of 1971. Her brother credibly and dispassionately threatens to kill her after the advice from his father to do so. During a pistol shooting demonstration at which she is present but curiously absent from consideration, the father makes her brother fire the gun and tells him that it is his duty to kill his sister with the pistol if the Muslims come to kidnap her. Her brother vows that he will do so. The scene, which recalls the so-called martyrdom of Sikh women at Thoa Khalsa during the Rawalpindi massacre of March 1947—an incident likened in the Indian media of the time to "the extreme 'sacrifice' of Rajput women who undertook mass immolation when they lost their husbands in war," receives a critique at Baldwin's hands (Butalia 165). The narrator-girl lets tears come as she wonders about her brother's vow and her family, where even intra-familial love does not matter as much as does the question of honour—honour of the family in protecting its women from the patriarchal violence of the enemy community.

The narrator-girl's pondering exposes the aura of sacrifice built around a pure and simple act of gendered violence. There is no free will where masculinist notions of honour and shame have been so deeply internalized. Ritu Menon and Kamla Bhasin comment with regard to the intra-familial violence thus:

> Overriding all these was a violence that was horrifying in its intensity, and one which knew no boundaries; for many women, it was not only 'miscreants,' 'outsiders' or 'marauding mobs' that they needed to fear—husbands, fathers, brothers and even sons, could turn killers. That terrible stunning violence and then the silencing pall that descended like a shroud around it have always hovered at the edges of history [...]. (3)

Baldwin's political irony not only cancels out the legitimatization of the intra-familial violence as martyrdom in the Sikh community discourses on partition but it also discloses patriarchy's attempt "to keep women within their *aukat*, their ordained boundary, which is one that defines them as non-violent. Their actions are thus relocated into the comfortably symbolic realm of sacrifice—for the community, victimhood and even non-violence" (Butalia 171). The valorization of Thoa Khalsa incident, which Baldwin subjects to political irony, continues to be lionized even today through an annual remembrance service in the Delhi gurudwara by a small community of survivors from that village. However, other kinds of violence—abduction and rape—continue to be consigned to be oblivion in the community discourses on partition.

For Baldwin, the selective memory of a particular instance of partition violence to the amnesia of the unspeakable in the community discourses parallels textbooks' privileging of the non-violent campaign for independence at the cost of the absence of partition violence. The story of modern India, unlike the narrator-girl's history textbook's staple of Gandhi's quit India movement and Nehru's trust with destiny, is not just of the attainment of independence but also a gendered narrative of displacement, dispossession and family realignment.

Towards the end of the story, the veil of silence that the narrator-girl's family has put up around the existence of Chandini Kaur and the madness of the violence that has passed down from one generation to the other—from the father to the son—parallels official India's amnesia of the madness of the gendered partition violence. Yet right at the end of "Family Ties," the memory of Chandini Kaur refuses to disappear in oblivion: "Above us, luminescent and reproachful, a woman-face moon dangles like a pendant on the breast of the dissipating day" (36).

Political irony in Shauna Singh Baldwin's "Family Ties, apart from revealing dominant historiographies of partition as a chronotope—in the sense of keeping their ability to contain certain elements while effacing others—functions as what Paola Bacchetta calls "critical-intersubjective-feminist-historiography" (570). "Family Ties" and "A Leaf in the Storm" have different implications for the historiography of partition. If Baldwin's story reflects a truly subaltern kind of feminist writing that picks holes in the bourgeoisie nationalist patriarchy as it narrates the gendered partition violence, the focus on the discontinuous female subjectivity in "A Leaf in the Storm" remains limited by the narrative decision that Lalithambika Antharajanam makes in keeping with the codes of continuity and motherhood—tropes which remain the realm of patriarchy. If the subaltern voice in Antharajanam's story continues to marginalize women, the subalternist irony in Baldwin's story brings to the fore a contemporary feminist perception of the gendered partition violence that reorders partition history with a contemporary feminist ethics in mind and with a much more radical possibility of socio-political enablement than the women writers of the partition generation.

WORKS CITED

Bacchetta, Paola. "Reinterrogating Partition Violence: Voices of Women, Children/Dalits in India's Partition." *Feminist Studies* 26.3 (Fall 2000): 567-85.

Baldwin, Shauna Singh. "Family Ties." *English Lessons and Other Stories*. Fredericton: Goose Lane, 1996. 21-36.

Butalia, Urvashi. *The Other Side of Silence*. Durham: Duke University Press, 2000.

Lalithambika Antharajanam. "A Leaf in the Storm." Trans. Narayan Chandran. *Stories About the Partition of India*. Vol. 1. Ed. Alok Bhalla. New Delhi: Indus, 1994. 137-45.

Das, Veena. "The Act of Witnessing: Violence, Poisonous Knowledge, and Subjectivity." *Violence and Subjectivity*. Ed. Veena Das et al. Berkeley: University of California Press, 2000. 205-24.

Hashmi, Jamila. "Exile." Trans. Alok Bhalla. *Stories About the Partition of India*. Vol. 1. Ed. Alok Bhalla. New Delhi: Indus, 1994. 39-53.

Hayden, Robert. "Rape and Rape Avoidance in Ethno-National Conflicts: Sexual Violence in Liminalized States." *American Anthropologist* 102.1 (March 2000): 27-41.

Hutcheon, Linda. *The Edge of Irony: The Theory and Politics of Irony*. London: Routledge, 1996.

Menon, Ritu and Kamla Bhasin. "Abducted Women, the State and Questions of Honour: Three Perspectives on the Recovery Operation in Post-Partition India," *Embodied Violence: Communalizing Women's Sexuality in South Asia*. Ed. Kumari Jayawardena and Malathi de Alwis. London: Zed Books, 1996. 1-31.

Pande, Mrinal. "1947: The Great Migration." *Pangs of Partition*. Vol. II. Ed. S. Settar and Indira Baptista Gupta. New Delhi: Manohar, 2002. 117-23.

Pritam, Amrita. *The Skeleton and Other Writings*. Trans. Khushwant Singh. Bombay: Jaico, 1964.

Ray, Bharati. "Women and Partition: Some Questions." *From Independence Towards Freedom: India Women Since 1947*. Ed. Bharati Roy and Aparna Basu. New Delhi: Oxford University Press, 1999. 1-18.

Talbot, Ian. "Literature and Human Drama of the 1947 Partition." *Region and Partition: Bengal, Punjab and the Partition of the Subcontinent*. Ed. Ian Talbot and Gurharpal Singh. Karachi: Oxford University Press, 1999. 228-68.

Tharu, Susie. "Rendering Account of the Nation: Partition Narratives and Other Genres of the Passive Revolution." *The Oxford Literary Review* 16.1-2 (1994): 61-145.

11

Tradition and Modernity as Played out in Anjana Appachana's "Her Mother"

Rebecca Sultana

Anjana Appachana's short story "Her Mother"[1] strikes a poignant note as a mother interweaves through the writing of a letter to her daughter the pain she had concealed for years only to discover the one that her daughter was going through. The daughter is studying abroad and the mother, in the course of her writing, comes to know the principle behind her daughter's increasing alienation with her. Through the multiple themes of female bonding, or, on the other hand, the lack of such attachment, societal pressure to conform, and mother-daughter relationships are revealed in the suffering and silence so implicit in gender politics.

The story gives voice to an ordinary woman by showing in very simple ways all the turbulence of passion and pain, happiness and sorrow, guilt and anger, which is normally assumed to belong only to the extraordinary. Such rendering makes all this consequential by giving voice to the mother's nameless longings and resentments, desires and frustrations, thus legitimizing the agonies rooted so deep in her life. These agonies seem to arise out of trivial issues, but have their cause in deeper ones. The burning emotions do not hide the fact that she is a loving albeit a conservative and protective mother.

That both the mother and daughter are nameless in the story is significant. They represent the iconic nurturing mother and the younger rebellious daughter as they play out their conflicting roles. In the story that evolves from the mother's reminisces and writings it becomes clear that the two women are from two different schools of thought. The daughter is a modern Indian woman, educated, independent, and at times head strong. On the other hand, the mother is a traditional Indian wife and mother, looking after her younger daughter and husband. The daughter might appear to be the one at an advantage with her freedom and higher education, especially as we come to know of the mother's pent up resentment. But in the process as the mother gradually disintegrates the daughter's armor of modern day feminism the story itself becomes a microcosm of the accusatory politics among the different waves of feminism itself.

The mother is figured, at first sight, in a stereotyped way of the traditional Indian wife. Such representation is not different from what feminist criticism proposes to revert. Writing about the "images of women" approach of feminist criticism, Josephine Donovan claims that female characters lack authenticity if they are not portrayed as complex and unique individuals. Although "women have in all historical periods been seats of consciousness and moral agents" (212), they are too often represented in literature as the Other—a subordinate class of objects "of interest only insofar as they serve or detract from the goals of the male protagonist" (212). Too often women are merely stereotypes that allow the male protagonist to define his own role and fulfil his own selfhood. In response to this misrepresentation of women in literature, feminist criticism has necessarily often become a negative one, revisiting stereotyped images of women. By exposing the often subtle portrayal of woman as Other and by celebrating truly authentic female characters, feminist criticism functions as a liberating moral criticism.

The daughter purports to have the "moral" vision through which she judges her own mother. Yet to her the mother symbolizes the one end of the endemic Manichean dualism, especially in the western feminist world-view, where women are used as "vehicle[s] for the male's growth in self-awareness," while themselves lacking insight (214). The stereotypes of women in literature are judged to be either positive or negative: either spiritual (good) or material (evil) with both resulting in inauthenticity. In Appachana's story the mother becomes the epitome of the spiritual with all its connotations—ideal, inspirational and good, within the context of the Indian social system. In becoming the ideal wife and mother, the mother then serves the "good woman" stereotypes—"the patient wife, the mother/martyr, and the lady" (Donavan 214).

To the daughter, then, the mother represents everything that modern feminism claims to deconstruct in the stereotyped images of women. To her, as to feminist critics, authentic female characters are self-defined; they are not only conscious of themselves but also "capable of self-determined action" (212). Yet, the daughter refuses the mother a similar selfhood, while looking up to her father as the example of modernity, freedom and understanding.

The mother herself plays into the archetypal stereotypes of the good vs. bad woman by believing that one's personal values should not be in disagreement with societal ones. As an example of such principles she explains to her daughter about the compromises that she had made to fit in within the societal standards. The mother also reinforces her place within this category while she contrasts a "liberated" woman whom she situates in the other divide to be used as a moral lesson for her daughter. Pointing out the heavy toll of being liberated she retorts, "And talking of women's rights, some women take it too far." She looks askance at Mrs. Parekh who is "having a torrid affair with a married man" (Appachana 86).

We get further instances of the mother's reconciliatory nature as she voluntarily assumes the family's responsibility, so that her husband may have the luxury of "solitude" or the space in which to brood while her own thoughts jumped to and fro and up and down and in and out as she dusted, cooked, cleaned, arranged cupboards, polished the brass, put buttons on shirts and falls on saris, as she sympathized with her neighbour's problems and scolded the dhobi for not putting enough starch on the saris, as she reprimanded the milkman for watering the milk and lit the kerosene stove because the gas had finished, as she took the dry clothes from the clothes line and couldn't press them because the electricity had failed and realized that the cake in the oven would now never rise. (183)

The mother is the one who sustains the household because she chooses to and because she knows that if she does not, nobody else would. Conditioned to uphold ideals of domestic rituals this is a difficult tradition from which to extricate oneself. She desires a well-maintained household, yearns for better lives for her both daughters and comfort for her husband. But in the process she finds herself objectified into the family's caregiver status whose only purpose is to provide sustenance. She remains no longer a person with agency but someone who is denied the power to take charge or to act according to her will. She is overlooked, ignored and reduced to insignificance.

Yet, as we learn more about her, we trace out a rebellious spirit that has managed to survive within the confines of her nurturing self as wife and mother. Traces of consciousness emerge that would promptly re-signify her, especially in her daughter's eyes, out of the dual spectrum of the Good/Evil divide. As her letter progresses, more is revealed about a woman who voluntarily gives up her prerogatives so that others might have theirs. She is a woman who "once dreamt of love and a large home, silk and saris and sapphires" (183). As she took on the responsibilities of her own as well as her husband's extended family she found love but "the rest she did not."

Throughout the writing of the letter, until she stumbles into her daughter's secret, the mother is a repository of wisdom and morals as she provides her daughter with guidelines of proper etiquette and a healthy lifestyle that she hopes would keep her secure in an alien land. As the truth dawns on her about the probability of an unacceptable relationship within the family and the impending repercussions of such an alliance, the mother is never judgmental. Understanding the fallibility of the human heart and the pain that it can cause the mother is at once stunned yet lovingly sympathetic.

In her theories of moral reasoning and development, Harvard psychologist Carol Gilligan sets forth the idea that women make decisions according to a criteria of ethics of care and that men make decisions according to an ethic of rights. From her interviews with women making momentous decisions in their lives, Gilligan concluded that these women were thinking more about the caring thing to do rather than the thing the rules allowed. Gilligan's book emerges as a complaint against the male centered personality psychology of Sigmund Freud and Erick Erickson, and the male centered developmental psychology of Lawrence Kohlberg. Her complaint is that since men have dominated the discussion of moral theory, women's perspective is often not taken seriously, and is considered to be less developed and sophisticated.

As a student of Kohlberg's, Gilligan was influenced by his approach to understanding moral reasoning. But she disagreed with her mentor's assessment of the content of the moral system within which people developed and deviated much from the current trend in psychological trends. To put it simply, Freud thought women's moral sense was stunted because they stayed attached to their mothers. Erickson thought the tasks of development were separation from the mother and the family suggesting that if women did not succeed in this scale, then they were obviously deficient. Gilligan's reply was to assert that women were not inferior in their personal or moral development, but that they were different. They developed in a way that focused on connections among people (rather than separation) and with an ethic of care for those people (rather than an ethic of justice).

In light of Gilligan's research, the mother in Appachana's story assumes the role not of a deviant but rather as a protective nurturer. The daughter, blinded by the achievements of the modern women, misreads her mother's actions as subservient, rather than self-sacrificial, obedient rather than assertive and being entirely devoid of a selfhood rather than being a person in her own right. The daughter who sees herself as the liberated modern young woman, ironically, adopts the stereotypes perpetuated by male writers for a docile woman as the ideal model for her mother and faults her for fitting within the category. As the daughter views her mother in this light, she plays into the dominant male discourses by seeing her mother as an object with no opportunity for her growth, wisdom and moral resolution. What she becomes guilty of is not undertaking an ideological probe behind her mother's ideological assumptions. In spite of her feminist stance the daughter's perspective is molded by male oriented indoctrination.

What neither the father nor the daughters realize, however, is the feeling of victimization that the mother keeps hidden away. For a woman given such lowly status by both the daughters and the husband, the mother reveals surprising insights as she enumerates how often she has abandoned her wants so that others can have theirs. The daughters have grown up strong and independent who nevertheless adore their father blindly enough to see no flaw in his treatment of their own mother. The mother writes to her daughter, "With all your talk about women's rights [...] you refuse to see that your father has given me none" (186). While the father is "enraptured by other women who stand up for themselves" similar attitude from his wife would tantamount to betrayal (189). That she is molded by her circumstances is also made clear to her daughter, "If I am a nag, it is because he's made me one" (186). When she writes that "a daughter will always regard her parents' home as her only home, unlike sons who attach themselves to their wives," she not only suggests that men are not capable of providing similar care for their wives but also indicates that women remain as care givers even though they might not receive the same from their male partners.

The mother's account highlights the societal flaws which force women to adapt and to compromise and the societal situations of previous generations, which lead to the continuations of such norms. For example, herself marrying for love she nevertheless advises her daughter about the sagacity of an arranged marriage, "In an arranged marriage you will not be disillusioned because you will not have any illusions to begin with" (188).

As the mother ponders about her daughter's secretive ways, both past and present, the "omniscience of motherhood" that she thought she had lost gives her enough insight to piece together the past events and find her answers. When the daughter is undergoing pain, it is the mother who discerns the secret. Ultimately, the two must depend on each other once again for support and friendship.

In order to develop a more woman oriented discourse and to deconstruct the "images of women" approach of feminism, Elaine Showalter proposes that "In contrast to this angry or loving fixation on male literature, the programme of gynocritics is to construct a female framework for the analysis of women's literature, to develop new models based on the study of female experience, rather than to adapt male models and theories" (217). Armed with similar criteria, the daughter has to renegotiate with her mother if some connection is to be expected. It is more crucial for the daughter to forge such a connection than for the husband as the success of such a negotiation can depend on the mutual cooperation between women.

As women take on multiple roles in the work force as well as in the academia, they are doing so within a male tradition, which demands that women be "rational, marginal and grateful" (Showalter 219). In the face of such demands women need to develop their own lexicon of interpreting other women through "a new way of reading that can integrate our intelligence and our experience, our reason and our suffering, our skepticism and our vision" (Showalter 219). Just as gynocritics "begins at the point when we free ourselves from the linear absolutes of male literary history, stop trying to fit women between the lines of the male literary history, and focus instead on the nearly visible world of female culture" (217), the daughter has to break away from her ingrained ideologies regarding women.

Unlike many of her contemporary Indian short fiction writers, however, Appachana's focus is on the domestic rather than the political landscape of modern Indian life. Listening and giving voice to women's stories has been identified as her predominant literary project. Reviewers describe Appachana's fiction as realist, although her inclusion of cinematic, melodramatic elements has also been noted. Appachana uses women's sexuality and relationships—within families and with friends—as her major subjects. Her ability to capture the rhythms of everyday speech has been praised by reviewers and critics. Appachana succeeds in drawing us deep into a complex vision of compromised happiness and withered dreams. At the same time, she convincingly portrays the strains on women in modern India—confined by their extended families, diminished and betrayed by the men they look to for security. Ultimately, in this story, the reader is compelled, through the mother's writing, to lean in close and truly hear her voice—and, in the process, discover how similar both the daughter's and her mother's lives are.

NOTE

1. The story first appeared in *The O. Henry Festival Stories* (Greensboro, NC: Transverse Press, 1987). It is also included in Appachana's short story collection *Incantation and Other Stories* (New Brunswick, NJ: Rutgers University Press, 1992).

WORKS CITED

Appachana, Anjana. "Her Mother." *The Inner Courtyard: Stories by Indian Women*. Ed. Lakshmi Holmström. New Delhi: Rupa, 1991. 180-94.

Donovan, Josephine. "Beyond the Net: Feminist Criticism as a Moral Criticism." *Twentieth Century Literary Theory: A Reader*. Ed. K.M. Newton. New York: St. Martin's, 1997.

Gilligan, Carol. *In a Different Voice: Psychological Theory and Women's Development*. Cambridge, Mass.: Harvard University Press, 1982.

Showalter, Elaine. "Towards a Feminist Poetics." *Twentieth Century Literary Theory: A Reader*. Ed. K.M. Newton. New York: St. Martin's, 1997. 216-20.

12

Cultural Perspectivism in Bharati Mukherjee's Short Stories

Andrew Hammond

Bharati Mukherjee is one of the best-known writers of short stories to emerge from the Indian diaspora. An author also of novels and non-fiction, she has produced a string of popular and critically well-received works over the last thirty years, from her first novel, *The Tiger's Daughter* (1971), through such volumes as *Jasmine* (1989) and *The Holder of the World* (1993), to her recent *Desirable Daughters* (2002). The power of her writing is due in no small measure to the sense of lived experience, of events grounded in autobiography, that pervades her fictional world. Mukherjee was born into a Bengali Brahmin family in 1940, the elite caste of Hindu society, and received a prestigious education, partly in Western European schools where she was taught through the medium of English. From the 1960s, after enrolling on a writing course in the University of Iowa, she has resided in Canada and the United States. Here, her life as an Indian woman in a frequently intolerant environment has produced a very different social positioning to that of her upbringing, exposing her to sexism and racial prejudice,[1] and to the uprootedness that is the common lot of the migrant. Yet it was this experience that inspired an engaged, oppositional thematics which quickly established her oeuvre at the forefront of contemporary "postcolonial" literature, not to mention of American letters more broadly. Focusing on the lives of characters migrating to North America, Mukherjee has produced some of our most powerful meditations on cultural displacement, on the pleasures and regrets of exile, and on what Elleke Boehmer terms "the exuberant clash of immigrant cultures" (240).

Of particular concern in her writing is the location and exploration of the contingent, fluid forms of identity that are the inevitable concomitant of geographical displacement. It is with acute insight that Mukherjee probes the processes of transculturation, the tragedies, misunderstandings and comedies that define the "contact zone,"[2] and the disruptive effect that migrancy can have on the individual. In this, her work is closely aligned to psychoanalytic strains of postcolonial theory, particularly that of Homi Bhabha, with his elaboration of hybrid culture and the "in-betweenness" of exilic experience. In *The Location of Culture* (1994), Bhabha challenges the essentialised notion of pure cultures that underpins racial and national discourse, arguing for the heterogeneity of all ethnic formations and for a recognition of the porousness and interdependency of all cultural groups. It is the responsibility of the intellectual, he writes, "to think beyond narratives of originary and initial subjectivities" and to "authorize [the] cultural hybridities" necessary for "the displacement of all sites of discrimination and domination" (1, 2, 112). For Bhabha, hybridity is not only a crucial recognition for a culture as a whole, but also for the individual, whose identity is similarly viewed as multifarious and lacking in any stable core. In considering the hybrid nature of the self, many critics have pointed to the representative status of the exile, who inhabits—as refugee, asylum seeker or economic migrant—that interstitial space between "pure" cultures (what Bhabha termed the "Third Space of enunciation" [37]) where cultural loyalty breaks down and a multiplicity of influence begins. For Edward Said, famously, this positioning of oneself on the "boundary" can lead to revelation. "Exiles cross borders," he declares, and in so doing "break barriers of thought and experience," exchanging "dogma and orthodoxy" for a "plurality of vision [that] gives rise to an awareness of simultaneous dimensions" ("Reflections on Exile" 170, 171). Displacement is not only an alienating and impoverishing ordeal, therefore, but also a strategy of personal transformation, where the act of crossing thresholds between cultures, between home and abroad, between metropolitan and pre-modern, upsets entrenched identifications.[3]

Mukherjee's work is, as Leela Gandhi argues, "explicit in its commitment to hybridity," and to developing an understanding of the migrant's "in-between space of cultural ambivalence" (153). This is evident in her two collections of short stories, *Darkness* (1985) and *The Middleman* (1988), the latter a winner of the National Book Critic Circle Award for Fiction. Influenced by Bernard Malamud's tales of Jewish immigrants, and written in a burst of creativity in the mid-1980s, the two volumes focus strongly on the heterogeneous nature of self and society, both in the former colonies and in the new imperial centres. Those stories set in the States, for example, where transculturation has become more intense and urgent than ever before, give a vivid portrait of migratory patterns during the decade of composition. Benedict Anderson has recorded that during the 1980s, some 740,000 immigrants were entering the United States annually, 80 per cent of which came from the Third World, almost 10 million in the decade as a whole (321), and it is this contingent, heaving, fractured world that forms the backdrop and subject of her two collections, with characters drawn from a plethora of source cultures (Sri Lanka, Ghana, India, Nigeria, Algeria, El Salvador, Italy, Poland, to name but a few). At the same time, Mukherjee is keen to explore how, in this environment, the processes of hybridisation effect the selfhood. The opening passage of "The Middleman," for example, which introduces the volume of the same name, foretells the ethnic diversity that defines the rest of the collection. The story is narrated by a professional gunman working for an arms smuggling operation somewhere in the Central American jungle. "My name is Alfie Judah, of the once-illustrious Smyrna, Aleppo, Baghdad [...] Judahs," he tells us, and, looking around him, announces: "I've seen worse. I've seen Baghdad, Bombay, Queens—and now this mouldering spread deep in Mayan country. Aztecs, Toltecs, mestizos, even some bashful whites with German accents. All that and a lot of Texans. I'll learn the ropes" (3). The passage is a typical celebration of ethnic diversity. For this Iraqi Jew, currently resident in the United States, there is little to fear from the physical/demographic jungle he faces, with its melange of Europeans, Middle Easterners and indigenes (the mestizos themselves a syncretic mix of Amerindian and Spanish ancestry). Judah's story is also typical for Mukherjee's choice of the first-person narrative to explore the minutiae of cultural subjectivity. The short stories are often told through disparate narrators, men and women of divergent ethnicities and nationalities who are themselves hybrid products of alien, hostile cultures, and whose perspectives are consequently as caught up in the processes of negotiation, anxiety, violence and transformation as those whose lives they narrate.

Mukherjee's perspectivism is the specific feature of her exploration of hybridity that I wish to focus upon in this essay. The short stories are fascinating for their epistemological examination of the range of subjectivities that are brought to bear on the cross-cultural encounter. Their complexity is evidenced by the sheer heterogeneity of forces influencing the perspectives of the characters, the cultural encounter refracted through a tortuous negotiation of tradition, modernity, nationhood and class, as well as the more evident identifications with "ethnicity, postcoloniality, gender and migrancy" (Nelson x). While acknowledging this diversity, however, Mukherjee's stories delve deeper into cultural perspectivism and find, beneath the variables of class, gender and ethnicity, that the perception of self and other is restricted to a limited number of rigid models which transcend background and which unite apparently disparate characters. On the one hand, she locates three models grouped around essentialisation. Here, as the host society feels itself threatened by immigration, and as migrants feel their uprootedness as a shattering of identity that necessitates a search for stability, the two parties resort to one of three binaristic modes of perception; specifically, to racism, to the assimilation of dominant ideology or to a retention of traditional loyalties. On the other hand, there is the hybrid model, with an acceptance of diversity and a resolution of conflict via the recognition of duality within self and other. It is in the latter that Mukherjee naturally finds hope for "[t]he confused world of the immigrant" ("The Tenant," *Middleman* 106) although it is the former that often win out. A study of cultural perspectivism in the stories reveals that while hybridity is Mukherjee's ideal, it is an ideal achieved with extreme difficulty, and one constantly under threat from the forces of essentialisation. With a focus on the stories in *The Middleman*, but also making reference to those of *Darkness*, I shall be examining the four models of perception in order to gauge exactly how optimistic Mukherjee is about the achievement of hybrid awareness.

The first perspective, that of racism, is a common strand in the two volumes, particularly in the North American stories. The act of forgetting the immigrant roots of such societies, the denigratory essentialisation of non-Western cultures, and the harmful effects that exclusion and intolerance can have on the migrant, are powerful concerns for Mukherjee. As Gail Low argues, the notion that her fiction emphasises the "exuberance of immigration" ("Preface," *Darkness* 3)—the writer's own suggestion, which critics have taken up—is misleading, the stories often exploring "alienation and madness in ways that paint a dystopic view of America" (Low 115).[4] An example is found towards the opening of "A Wife's Story." In this first-person narration, the wife of an Indian businessman, a woman of fine breeding ("My manners are exquisite, my feelings are delicate" [*Middleman* 27]), tells of her life in the States after she receives a scholarship for doctoral study there. For the most part, Panna Bhatt's experience is of profound liberation. In contrast to India, a world not only of poverty and social turmoil, but also—for women—of arranged marriage, deference and a lack of sustained education, America represents unlimited freedom, as symbolised by the opportunities that university open up for her.[5] Yet such freedom is impaired, if not curtailed, by the racism expressed by white America towards diasporic communities. This appears most overtly at a performance of a David Mamet play which Panna attends with a Polish friend, Imre, and in which she is indignant at the racial stereotyping of Indians:

> Imre says forget it, but I'm going to write David Mamet. So Patels are hard to sell real estate to. You buy them a beer, whisper Glengarry Glen Ross, and they smell swamp instead of sun and surf. They work hard, eat cheap, live ten to a room, stash their savings under futons in Queens, and before you know it they own half of Hoboken. You say, where's the sweet gullibility that made this nation great? (25)

The glib "humour" of the script scarcely conceals the play's fear of the immigrant presence within the nation. Essentialised by a denigrating nomenclature, these "Patels" are the unsophisticated, secretive and wily Easterners of traditional stereotype, people who refuse to enter into the American "way of things" (spurning the "gullibility" of the average consumer), yet who aim for ultimate take-over of American territory (to "own half of Hoboken"). Indeed, the script reveals the typical projections of racialist discourse, with the Indians loathed for the very business acumen and ability to accumulate that is the grounding principle of American capitalism. When the actors go on to mock the appearance of Indian women, and laughter rings out around the theatre, Panna's sinks into misery and rage, emotions of which her breeding denies her expression. Indeed, it is only in the retrospective act of narration, her act of "writing back" against the discourses of the centre, that the marginalised Panna can find her voice. Through this tale of suffering and silencing, Mukherjee reminds us that a hierarchical conception of culture has devastating consequences on migrants' lives, as she expands upon elsewhere. In "Loose Ends," most obviously, a Vietnam veteran unleashes his fear of immigrants through rape and murder; in "The World According to Hsü" a woman lives in fear of racist attacks in Toronto; and in "Isolated Incidents," a Canadian social worker comes into daily contact with complaints about racial discrimination in the workplace, incidents that the police prefer to consider "isolated" and certainly not "racial in nature" (*Darkness* 55).[6]

The superiority felt by the dominant culture, and its mono-perspectivist stance on subordinate ethnicities, does not only reside in the minds of Westerners. The second kind of perspective which emerges in the contact zone is held by migrants themselves, and involves their absorption of exactly these hegemonic ideologies that work to marginalise them. In the post-modern context, this is exemplified by the beguiling hold that American belief and practice can have over the imagination of non-Americans, driving into them a loyalty to its cultural assumptions through insistent displays of wealth and elegance. Again, just as racism is a fundamental denial of hybridity, so ideological assimilation marks a failure of cultural formations to merge and to challenge structures of power. In "A Wife's Story," the issue is crystallised in the outlook of Panna's husband. Arriving in New York for a short visit, he is soon bewitched by the glittering world of consumerism, becoming entranced by the food ("He tries out pizzas, burgers, McNuggets") and captivated by merchandise ("White tube socks with different bands of color delight him") (33-34). On a trip to the Statue of Liberty, the husband insists that Panna takes a photograph of him with the Twin Towers of the city skyline behind him: "He wants to look relaxed, an international businessman at home in all the financial markets" (37-38). The cultural colonisation of the migrant selfhood, which is contrasted to Panna's moment of self-realisation at the close of the story, demonstrates "the tyranny of the American dream" (26) and underlies the familiar immigrant ambition to be "more American than the Americans" (Mukherjee, *Wife* 68).

The subaltern's assimilation of the ideologies of the centre is explored at more length in "Buried Lives." In this story, Mr. Venkatesan is a middle-aged and demure Tamil schoolteacher, sickened by the ongoing civil war that is tearing into all sections of the Sri Lankan community. Indeed, unable to keep himself and his family out of the conflict, the story opens with Venkatesan in the middle of a violent political demonstration, attempting to protect his radicalised younger sister. The conflict, however, is only the most obvious of the schoolteacher's woes. The dullness of his wards, the difficulty of keeping an extended family on his meagre salary, the lack of financial opportunity in a collapsing island economy, all serve to compound his frustration. The only thing that sustains him is his reverential affinity for English culture. For example, as a boy, when Britain still governed Ceylon, his subservience to British rule was so great that even when the imperial police entered his home to arrest an anti-colonial cousin, he "saluted the superintendent smartly" (*Middleman* 155). As an adult, Venkatesan's reverence is symbolised by his love of Matthew Arnold, his "favorite poet" (158),[7] and one whose fondness for all things English is no coincidence. The kind of hegemony the former Empire exerts, in fact, is demonstrated by the profound hold that English literature has over the schoolmaster's imagination. In his more despondent moments, consolation is to be found in reading old imperial romances (with their "fearless young Britons—sailors, soldiers, missionaries—whack[ing] wildernesses into submission" [160]), whose fantasy of mobility, fortune and triumphant masculinity serve as a model for everything that Venkatesan lacks. It is around this time that he decides that flight to the West is the only solution. With his love of British culture quickly displaced by an attraction to America, the new global power, he writes to eight American universities for scholarship application forms, beginning his letter with the honorific, "'Dear Respected Sir.'" The application forms, however, prove tricky:

> He tried to put down in the allotted blanks what it felt like to be born so heartbreakingly far from New York or London. *On this small dead-end island, I feel I am a shadow-man, a nothing. I feel I'm a stranger in my own room. What consoles me is reading. I sink my teeth into fiction by great Englishmen such as G.A. Henty and A.E.W. Mason. I live my life through their imagined lives. And when I put their works down at dawn I ask myself, Hath not a Tamil eyes, heart, ears, nose, throat, to adapt the words of the greatest Briton. Yes, I am a Tamil. If you prick me, do I not bleed? If you tickle me, do I not laugh? Then, if I dream, will you not give me a chance, respected Sir, as only you can?* (161)

Brought up on English literature, Venkatesan's attempts to assimilate Western identity take place in part on the level of language, the teacher filling in the "blanks" (and thus writing the self) via the discourses of the imperial centre; most obviously, via the words of Shakespeare's Shylock, another tale of marginalised ethnicities. Positioning himself within imperial images and motifs ("I live my life through their imagined lives"), the Tamil feels himself transformed into a more substantial self. Yet his inadequate knowledge of English literary trends and his stilted and comic usage of the language merely result in pathos. The outcome of his applications are "eight letters of rejection," a rebuff from the imperial centre that is taken as a denunciation not only of his attempted Englishness but also of his very humanity ("'I am worthless,' Mr. Venkatesan moaned [...]. 'I am a donkey'" [161]). Simultaneously, it seems, the West can assimilate and reject those who heed its sirens. The only course of action left to him, and the course through which he finally achieves his dream, is to exchange legal for illegal migration, paying to be smuggled across to the West (where he eventually reaches Hamburg). Through this dangerous passage, the mobility and adventure once possessed by the colonist is appropriated by the Third World immigrant: it is the latter who now, caught up in their personal odysseys, have to "sail dark, stormy oceans" and who, "[l]ike the blond heroes of the novels," find themselves "chasing dreams of perfect futures" (160).[8] The epic quest is appropriated; the patterns of power and privilege within the Western text are subverted.

Nevertheless, the story dramatises the power of dominant ideology, as Venkatesan is never able to shake off its influence, and hybrid awareness is never developed. The third approach to the cross-cultural encounter, that of faithfulness to the beliefs and practices of the original homeland, may be opposed to the absorption of Western values, but is no less detrimental to the development of hybridity. Here, Mukherjee is not only exploring the lives of immigrants, but also those who have been born into diasporic communities, people for whom the cultural, geo-political and linguistic disparities between their present society and their ethnic roots make the process of establishing loyalty an ongoing problem. Is the concept of "home," in other words, to be found "[i]n the place of birth (*nateo*), the displaced *cultural community* into which the person is born, or in the *nation-state* in which this diasporic community if located?" (Ashcroft, et al. *Post-Colonial Studies* 93). For many of Mukherjee's characters, rejecting the ideologies of the latter, the only option is a fidelity to the codes of the source culture. This conservative allegiance to the past, however, an achievable goal within a close-knit diasporic society, can lead to seclusion and retardation, a denial of the adaptability that the immigrant needs to survive.

The theme, common in Mukherjee's writing, is poignantly explored in "The Management of Grief." Here, an Indo-Canadian woman, Shaila Bhave, narrates the story of her gradual disintegration after her two sons are killed in a plane crash off the coast of Ireland, a tragedy based on the real incidents of the Air India crash of 1985, when a Sikh bomb brought down a passenger plane at the cost of 329 lives. Struggling with her own grief, Shaila is called upon for assistance by a local social worker, who has been appointed to help the grieving families with financial support and counselling. In this way, she finds herself in contact with some of the more elderly of her local Indian community, whose self-imposed isolation is distressing: there are "'some of them [who] speak no English,'" others "'who've never handled money,'" and still others who have never "'gone outside their bedrooms'" (*Middleman* 183). One old Sikh couple that she visits seems particularly desolate; recent arrivals in America, they refuse any help that is offered them, mistrusting the intentions of the social workers, not understanding the legal forms that they need to sign, and going so far as to believe that documents which offer them financial assistance are actually there to extract money. Of this aloofness and withdrawal, their apartment block becomes symbolic, an apparently self-contained "little India," surrounded by sari-clad women and cricket-playing boys, and reeking "of frying ghee" (193). The Sikh couple's apartment is even more resonant:

> The two rooms are dark and stuffy. The lights are off, and an oil lamp sputters on the coffee table. The bent old lady has let us in, and her husband is wrapping a white turban over his oiled, hip-length hair. She immediately goes to the kitchen, and I hear the most familiar sound of an Indian home, tap water hitting and filling a teapot.
>
> They have not paid their utility bills, out of fear and the inability to write a cheque. The telephone is gone; electricity and gas and water are soon to follow. (193)

This abject domestic space is, of course, the grave, with its airlessness, coldness and gloom. The act of cutting oneself off from the vital world around is not merely a denial of hybridity, but a denial of life itself, the establishment of a state in which growth or subsistence is impossible. The same holds true for so many of the elderly characters that populate *The Middleman* and *Darkness*: Charity Chin's uncle, an exile from China, is an "awkward, terrified man" who "doesn't speak much English"; Mr and Mrs Daboo are "bumpkin[s]," with his "Elvis Presley sideburns" and her slovenly "house slippers"; and Dr. Chatterji is "pompous" and "reactionary," a man who "wants to live and work in America but give back nothing except taxes."[9] In so many of these instances, moreover, the rejection of the host culture is the outward sign of a deeper intolerance. In "The Management of Grief," the Sikhs live a life of patriarchal regulation, religious convention and ethnic prejudice, their blunt refusal to "open up to a Hindu woman" reminding Shaila sadly of time "when we all trusted each other in this new country" (193).[10] The mono-perspectivist adherence to the mores of one's homeland lacks what Said calls the exile's potential for "*contrapuntal*" awareness ("Reflections on Exile" 172),[11] and consequently shares the host society's tendency towards racial and sexual hierarchy.

In censuring the practices of some of her Indian characters, Mukherjee was certainly not positioning their communities on a lower level to those of the West. Sangeeta Ray has questioned Mukherjee's treatment of Asian culture, considering her discussions of intra-Indian politics "thoroughly partisan" and accusing her of working within representational patterns "that reinforce the binary opposition between the stagnancy of India and 'the infinite possible geography [...]' of America" (228).[12] With Mukherjee's numerous criticisms of American consumerism, violence and bigotry, it is a difficult argument to maintain. Her refusal to idealise any ethnic grouping and her insistence on viewing blind loyalty to one's community as a deficiency are both evidence, rather, of a suspicion of all monolithic cultural formations, and of her call for hybrid, non-binaristic approaches to identity. This recognition of hybridity, the fourth perspective that can be brought to bear on the cross-cultural encounter, finds continual expression through the short stories and novels, where characters frequently find themselves "shuttl[ing] between identities" (Mukherjee, *Jasmine* 77). In Shaila's journey in "The Management of Grief," for example, it is only through a return to India, and through a re-immersion in Hindu religious tradition, that she can begin to come to terms with her loss and find new direction for her life in America (190-91). At the same time, the story offers a utopian vision of what a society might be like once all hierarchy and intolerance is renounced. Soon after the plane goes down, Shaila travels to Ireland with other grieving families to watch the rescue workers searching the waters for survivors. A local newspaper, discovering that it is a Hindu custom to sprinkle petals on the water in mourning for the dead, entreats its readers to donate flowers to the Indians, and Shaila soon finds that the Irish not only "carry flowers with them," but also "rush to me and give me hugs" (187). The native determination to absorb aspects of their guests' culture, their delight in syncretic identity, is the very antithesis of ethnic bigotry, its beauty and fertility symbolised by the flowers themselves. The experience forms as important a stage in Shaila's mourning as her later reconnection with Hindu tradition in India.

Yet the acceptance of plurality and the development of respect for the other is not the easiest perspective to bring to a contact zone. Within the welter of transcultural relationships that appear in the stories, only a few achieve hybrid awareness, and for these hybridity is far from an absolute, unadulterated state, but is rather a goal that needs to be constantly fought for against the encroachment of cultural hierarchies. The story that perhaps best evokes the precariousness of the condition is "Orbiting," a diasporic fable marking the apex of Mukherjee's short fiction. Another first-person narration, "Orbiting" is told by a young Italian-American woman, Renata deMarco, who holds a Thanksgiving dinner in her apartment for her family and new lover. The fact that the latter is an Afghan refugee, Ro, who has been exiled during the Soviet invasion, causes no end of consternation to her reactionary parents. Mukherjee extends the comedy inherent in the lover-meeting-parents scenario, with its generational misunderstandings, into a much blacker comedy about the clashes of ethnic and national prejudices. What makes the story so important, however, is that the clash of perspectives that I have been outlining up until now is present *within each individual character*, the four perspectives being here perceived as competing and merging in the psyche of the single selfhood. The story not only dramatises social plurality, in other words, but also a plurality within.

The parents, at least initially, appear to display the mono-perspectivism and cultural fidelity that one associates with racism. At the start of the story, as Renata is still getting up, the father arrives at her apartment with the Thanksgiving turkey, immediately revealing a distaste for her untidiness, her failed career, her sexual practices and, most of all, her lack of a dining table, a symbol of the respect for family tradition that he finds wanting in his daughter's life. His veneration for wholesome American values—regular work, financial success, martial stability—is in part an assimilation of hegemonic cultural mores, in part a display of his Italianness. As the grandson of an Italian immigrant, the father finds the European nation a continual "source of pride" (*Middleman* 58), dresses like "an old-world Italian gentleman" (70), is a member of the "Sons of Italy" (67), chooses his electoral candidates on the basis of their Italian ethnicity (67), and has even taken for his wife a Calabrian peasant, a women in whom traditional Italian values are intuitive (58-60). With such overt cultural loyalty, it is no surprise that both he and his wife are riddled with ethnic prejudices. As the story progresses, and other family members arrive, the father's conversation deteriorates: El Salvador is "messy and exotic, at the very rim of comprehension" (61), the Third World is full of indistinguishable crises, both Jews and Muslims are somehow suspect, and even Calabria is defined by "cultural deficiency" (59). A little later, when Ro suddenly appears at the flat, his wife's first instinct is to "scream [...] for the cops" (68). And it is not only the older generation that essentialises the other. Renata's sister has married an Amish man, Brent, who has turned his back on the culture of his childhood and absorbed stridently Italian-American values, changing his name from Schwartzendruber to Schwartz and revealing a fondness for Club Med, gold chains and sport. As for his father-in-law, the Third World for Brent is merely a place of "coups," lacking in any "informed political opinion" (72).

It is into this essentialist milieu that Ro and Renata appear to bring the values of hybrid awareness, although not as successfully as one might suppose. The fact of their relationship certainly seems a recognition, if not celebration, of plurality, particularly with the compromises they need to make in order to unite their very different worlds. Ro, for example, is hardly the easiest choice of lovers for Renata. His is the complex and uncertain life of the political exile: born into a wealthy Afghan family, driven from Kabul by the communist take-over, forced to enter the West illegally, and currently working in the kitchen of a chicken restaurant in constant fear of the American immigration officials.[13] It is suggested that Ro's character is a syncretic merger of the two societies in which he has moved. On the one hand, he is "sophisticated" in a specifically Western manner, a cosmopolitan high-spender who in his more affluent days has "skied in St. Moritz, lost a thousand dollars in a casino in Beirut, knows where to buy Havana Cigars" (72). On the other hand, his beliefs and practices are grounded in Afghan codes of politeness, masculinity and religious duty, and whose demeanour and dress somehow belie his roots. Although the difference is slight, Renata notes at one point how his posture contrasts to that of Brent and her father, and how his clothes, although Western in style, speak more of his Eastern upbringing. "He shows too much white collar and cuff," she muses: "His shirt and his wool-blend flare-leg pants were made to measure in Kabul. The jacket comes from a discount store on Canal Street, part of a discontinued line of two-trousered suits" (70-71). The image is an important one, for despite appearing to symbolise a hybrid mixture of East and West, Ro's outer shell in fact reveals the predominance of Afghanistan, and distinctly lacks American affluence and polish. It is at this point that Ro slowly exhibits increasing loyalty to Afghan mores, especially to codes of maleness. His conversation becomes egocentric, domineering and violent, often focusing on a period of detention and torture that he suffered in Kabul, with its "[e]lectrodes, canes, freezing tanks" (73). Later, he shows an inordinate pleasure at being chosen to carve the Thanksgiving turkey, taking great pride in using his Afghan dagger, which he carries around in his pocket and has already shown off to the family. Here is a man who likes positioning Renata in bars by herself, attracting single men to approach her, in order to "swagger out" and claim her "as soon as someone buys [her] a drink" (65). This loyalty to a "macho culture" (65) does not bode well for their relationship.

The manner in which Ro's character is moulded by cultural discourse is mirrored in that of Renata. Again, she seems initially to represent hybridity, her choice of Ro being an overt rejection of the racism that defines her family, and her attempts to learn about Afghan life, speak a little Pashto and meet Ro's family are all indications that, as she puts it, "traditions change" (61). The kiss that she gives Ro when he arrives at the apartment, just after her mother has screamed for the police, is a clear statement that the parochialism which governed her father's choice of spouse is to be exchanged for the pleasures of miscegenation: "I make the kiss really sexy so they'll know I've slept with this man. Many times" (68). Yet well before the revelation about her character that we find at the end of the story, there are plenty of warning signs that

Renata is closer to her parents than she realises. She openly admits, for example, that she also believed "immigrant [...] children should do better than their parents" (58), and that she recently voted for a certain candidate "because she's a woman and Italian" (66). More worryingly, she admits that before meeting Ro's cousins, the name Abdul always made her "think of a giant black man with goggles on, running down a court" (65), an overt racial stereotype. In the scene in which she notes Ro's posture and clothing, her determination to buy him more Western-looking suits, and her empathy with Brent's daughter's mocking inspection of his appearance, are ominous sign of cultural conformity. This fully emerges at the end of the story. Ro and the family sit down to the meal, and Renata deliberately places the turkey before her lover in order to establish him within the family. She watches him take out his dagger with mounting adoration:

> The turkey is reduced to a drying, whitened skeleton [...]. I realize all in a rush how much I love this man with his blemished, tortured body. I will give him citizenship if he asks [...]. Ro's my chance to heal the world.
>
> I shall teach him how to walk like an American, how to dress like Brent but better, how to fill up a room as Dad does instead of melting and blending but sticking out in the Afghan way. In spite of the funny way he holds himself and the funny way he moves his head from side to side when he wants to say yes, Ro is Clint Eastwood, scared hero and survivor. Dad and Brent are children. I realize Ro's the only circumcised man I've slept with. (74-75)

Renata's determination to change Ro cuts across her presumed hybridity to reveal a range of hegemonic assumption, particularly as she wishes to change him into the two symbols of American convention (Brent and the father) that her relationship was supposed to stand against. In Renata's narrative, contaminated as she is by the discourses of her familial circle, American malehood is posited as the norm, such *easternisms* as Ro's body language a quaint deviance from that norm. Her retention of hegemonic approaches to self and other also displays, via the Eastwood reference, the influence of the masculinist stereotypes of popular culture (with Renata pointedly ignoring what Ro's knife, the weapon of the male, has done to the "tortured body"). At the same time, what she believes to be her love for Ro as an individual merely marks a shift from the Italian-American self-idealisation of her younger days to an essentialising idealisation of the other. Her concept of Ro—and thus of Eastern culture more widely—is grounded in an orientalist eroticisation of the body that reminds us of Edward Said's denunciation of the Western "associat[ion of] the Orient with the escapism of sexual fantasy" (*Orientalism* 190). In other words, the narrator, from whom we receive our data about this family gathering, is profoundly compromised, interpellated by the same discourses as those around her. On this issue, P.A. Abraham is right to remark on *The Middleman's* "characteristically modernist stance," with its lack of "authoritative interpreters" (60). Renata is the unreliable narrator of classic modernist writing, offering a flawed, idiosyncratic perspective on the world of the text which requires as much scrutiny as the perspectives of the characters upon which she comments.

To conclude, "Orbiting" shows the selfhood to be not only hybrid, but also split between hybrid awareness and more hegemonic ideologies. Mukherjee's work is suffused by a sense of the dangers—racism, intolerance, ethnic loyalties, cultural imperialism—that thwart hybridity, and, as "Orbiting" illustrates, is pessimistic about the development of a more heirarchical respect for cultural difference. Nevertheless, some positivity is maintained. Ro and Renata at least attempt to resist the prejudices governing them, and, more significantly, Renata's parents finally accept the Afghan at their Thanksgiving table, ending their exclusivity and symbolising a wider acceptance of the refugee into the national community. While refusing naïve optimism, it is this fluidity within the contact zone that Mukherjee, "the mytho-poet of immigration" (Alam 36), is calling for. On the one hand, hybridity is necessary for the host culture, which, like the Irish in "The Management of Grief," needs to transform itself in order to fully accommodate the migrant; on the other hand, the immigrant must view the selfhood as "as a set of fluid identities," always seeking an opportunity for reincarnation ("Preface," *Darkness* 3).[14] That this is possible Mukherjee has evidence enough from her own life, where hybridity has been a constant attainment, on the literary as much as the social front. By achieving ever-increasing readerships for her immigrant fiction, not only has she helped to reconfigure the idea of America as a hybrid, diasporic space, but also to re-conceive American literature as, in part, an immigrant forum. There are few, for example, who would consider Mukherjee's work, or indeed the writings of the Indian diaspora more widely, as anything but an integral part of mainstream American literature today.

NOTES

1. As Mukherjee dramatises in "The World According to Hsü," this was particularly true in Canada, where the racist epithet "dirty Paki" was not unknown (*Darkness* 41).
2. The subtlety of Mukherjee's analysis of human relations has led Victoria Carchidi to drawn comparison between her work and that of Jane Austen (94).
3. Hybridity leads the way to "an acceptance of difference on equal terms," and to an ending of the hierarchical model of culture, of "the myth of group 'purity,'" which has informed the "apparently endless human history of conquest and annihilation" (Ashcroft, Griffiths, and Tiffin, *Empire Writes Back* 35).
4. On this issue, see also Alam 50-51. For Maya Manju Sharma, it was actually *Darkness* that inaugurated Mukherjee's focus on exuberance (3-22).
5. As she writes: "I've made it. I'm making something of my life. I've left home, my husband, to get a Ph.D." (29). This notion of education as freedom is a common motif in the short stories.
6. As a character in another story in *Darkness* puts it, "Canadians don't want Asian immigrants" ("Tamurlane" 118).
7. See also the reference to Keats and Shelley (168).
8. He finds a more masculine self through the act of journeying, but also learns to give up on the dominant role he had in Sri Lanka, finding that the only way he can remain in the West is to succumb to the advice and assistance of a naturalised Tamil woman (175-76).
9. See "A Wife's Story," "Jasmine," "The Tenant," *Middleman* 31, 128, 106. See also the stories "A Father" and "Nostalgia" in *Darkness*, the

latter having a character who "couldn't pretend he had been reborn when he became an American citizen" (105). Such conservatism particularly effects first generation immigrants; their offspring, or younger relatives, are more likely to be assimilated, as Charity Chin, the Daboos' two daughters and Chatterji's nephew demonstrate.

10. Ethnic prejudice is also seen in "The Tenant," with Dr. Chatterji's "horror" that his nephew has fallen "in love with an African Muslim" (*Middleman* 106).
11. It is not always the case that, as Boehmer has argued about Mukherjee, "dislocation as she represents it is not an impoverishment but an expansion of cultural and aesthetic experience" (241). Indeed, in "The Tenant" Mukherjee is aware that the in-betweenness of the exile can also lead to a sense of inhabiting "dead space" (*Middleman* 110), of being cut off from both source and host culture.
12. See also Banerjee 161-79, and Grewal 180-95.
13. As Renata says, "When I'm with Ro I feel I am looking at America through the wrong end of a telescope. He makes it sound like a police state, with sudden raids, papers, detention centres, deportations, and torture and death waiting in the wings" (66). In its depiction of life for Afghan asylum seekers, "Orbiting" has strong links to the exploration of life in Canada for South Asian immigrants in "Tamurlane" in *Darkness*.
14. As one of the characters in "The Management of Grief" says, admiringly, of the Indian diaspora, "like creatures in epics, they've changed shapes" (192). For Mukherjee, it has been important to avoid being "redefined [...] as an American" and instead "to be part of that long procession of peoples who have over the years redefined America" (Sharma 20).

WORKS CITED

Abraham, P.A. "Crisis of Unbelonging in Some Expatriate Stories from the Canadian and Indian Context." *Writers of Indian Diaspora: Theory and Practice*. Ed. Jasbir Jain. Jaipur and New Delhi: Rawat, 1998. 50-62.

Alam, Fakrul. *Bharati Mukherjee*. New York: Twayne, 1996.

Anderson, Benedict. "Exodus." *Critical Inquiry* 20 (Winter 1994): 314-27.

Ashcroft, Bill, Gareth Griffiths, and Helen Tiffin. *The Empire Writes Back: Theory and Practice in Post-Colonial Literatures*. 2nd ed. London: Routledge, 2002.

——. *Post-Colonial Studies: The Key Concepts*. London and New York: Routledge, 2000.

Banerjee, Debjani. "'In the Presence of History': The Representation of Past and Present Indias in Bharati Mukherjee's Fiction." *Bharati Mukherjee: Critical Perspectives*. Ed. Emmanuel S. Nelson. New York: Garland, 1993. 161-79.

Bhabha, Homi K. *The Location of Culture*. London and New York: Routledge, 1994.

Boehmer, Elleke. *Colonial and Postcolonial Literature: Migrant Metaphors*. Oxford: Oxford University Press, 1995.

Carchidi, Victoria. "'Orbiting': Bharati Mukherjee's Kaleidoscope Vision." *MELUS* 20.4 (Winter 1995): 91-101.

Gandhi, Leela. *Postcolonial Theory: A Critical Introduction*. Edinburgh: Edinburgh University Press, 1998.

Grewal, Gurleen. "Born Again American: The Immigrant Consciousness in *Jasmine*." *Bharati Mukherjee: Critical Perspectives*. Ed. Emmanuel S. Nelson. New York: Garland, 1993. 180-95.

Low, Gail. "The Dis/Embodiment of Culture: The Migrant in V.S. Naipaul and Bharati Mukherjee." *Contemporary Writing and National Identity*. Ed. Tracey Hill and William Hughes. Bath: Sulis, 1995. 112-20.

Mukherjee, Bharati. *Wife*. Boston: Houghton Mifflin, 1975.

——. *Darkness*. New York: Penguin, 1985.

——. *The Middleman and Other Stories*.1988. London: Virago, 1990.

——. *Jasmine*. New ed. London: Virago, 1991.

Nelson, Emmanuel S. Introduction. *Bharati Mukherjee: Critical Perspectives*. Ed. Emmanuel S. Nelson. New York: Garland, 1993. v-xvii.

Ray, Sangeeta. "The Nation in Performance: Bhabha, Mukherjee and Kureishi." *Hybridity and Postcolonialism: Twentieth-Century Indian Literature*. Ed. Monika Fludernik. Tübingen: Stauffenburg Verlag, 1998. 221-39.

Said, Edward, *Orientalism*. New ed. London: Penguin, 1995.

——. "Reflections on Exile." *Granta* 13 (1984): 159-72.

Sharma, Maya Manju. "The Inner World of Bharati Mukherjee: From Expatriate to Immigrant." *Bharati Mukherjee: Critical Perspectives*. Ed. Emmanuel S. Nelson. New York: Garland, 1993. 3-22.

13

A Battle for the Palate or a Feast of Fragrance?—Bulbul Sharma's *The Anger of Aubergines: Stories of Women and Food*[1]

Joel Kuortti

A Playful Break

In the twelve stories of her collection *The Anger of Aubergines* (1997), Bulbul Sharma has ventured to describe female experience and space from the viewpoint of food, cooking and kitchen—each of the stories is followed by one or more recipes related to the foods and drinks in the stories. Even though deeply embedded in Indian (especially Hindu) traditions, the re-inscription of this traditionally feminine domain is not, however, simplistic. In this article, I examine the ways in which these stories may challenge traditionally and culturally assigned gendered positions by looking into a couple of the stories in detail.

The introduction of the collection is a brief autobiographical sketch of Sharma's childhood when she enjoyed Dida's, her grandmother's, cooking and food. It narrates a story of Dida who had been a child bride and who now observes religious regulations of an orthodox Brahmin widow and bewares of pollution. The author, on the other hand, describes herself against such "genuine cooks" as "an armchair cook"—making a playful reference to the legendary armchair anthropologists like E.B. Tylor or James Frazer (Sharma 1997: vii). She also refers to her own cooking somewhat irreverently as "burnt offerings" and some of the recipes as her own "quick and lazy recipes" (Sharma 1997: vii) as in contrast to the tried, successful ones people have shared with her. A break in tradition is thus invoked. These features—playfulness and break in tradition—are features that characterise Sharma's stories.

Already the title of the introduction—"Saying It with Cauliflowers"—is playful. The ironic allusion to the tongue of flowers, together with all the culturally dependent interpretations of floral implications, is replaced by the language of *cauli*flowers. The symbolism and romanticism attached to flowers is supplemented with the domesticity of *cauli*flower. In this case the language of cauliflowers is clear as seen at the end of the story where the author describes her grandmother's advice: "'Eat, eat [...] so thin you are,' she would say as she watched us catch the plates like trained seals. Her simple food, without any garnish or colour, was always special because it was her way of caressing us without getting her hands polluted" (Sharma 1997: vi). The language of cauliflowers is defined as that of caring, traditionally a very feminine domain. After thus describing some of her own culinary history, the author gives a cauliflower recipe that reflects Dida's cooking, being "without any garnish or colour." There is at the same time a warm, affectionate relation to that tradition and also a sense—not necessarily a negative one—of loss, of impossibility to return.

International Kitchen?

In this time of televised kitchen shows and cooking competitions, international cuisine, cross-kitchen, and exotic, *exoticized* trend foods, it might be thought that culinary language is international—just like the language of flowers. That is only partly true, as each dish, each food stuff, is historically and culturally embedded, just like the whole modern culture of gastronomy (see Spang 2000). Thus the idea of "Indian cooking" is itself a construction.

We can take the cauliflower recipe, "Cauliflower with five spices," as an example:

1 small cauliflower, cut into sprigs
2 medium potatoes, cut into small cubes

> 1/2 tsp five spice mixture [*paanch phoron*] (aniseed, cumin, caraway, mustard and fenugreek seeds in equal quantities)
> 1 tbsp cooking oil
> salt to taste
>
> Heat oil in a kadai or deep pan. Add half a teaspoon of the five spice mixture. Let it hiss and crackle. Throw in the potatoes. Saute lightly. Add cauliflower pieces and salt and stir to mix the spices. Cover and cook on a slow fire for five minutes. Take off the cover and keep stirring often to make sure the vegetables are evenly cooked. They should be tender, yet firm. Serve hot with rice or pooris. (Sharma 1997: vi-vii)

The recipe is, first of all, not written in everyday spoken language but formally in a specialist genre, in the applied language of recipes: the list is arranged in a specific order, main ingredients first in order of preparation, followed by spices and other necessary things. Then there are the instructions, complete with serving tips. Through the application of this format, recipes travel easier across cultures—at least when you know how to read them: the terms, methods, appliances, and techniques involved.

> Without going into detail of the very revealing representational aspects, I want to add only that in the Finnish version, the recipes have also been modified to suit Finnish cookery traditions as not all the ingredients are easily available, nor are all the utensils and processes familiar in an ordinary Finnish kitchen. There is also a brief glossary of terms that explains some kitchen terminology as well as terms of family relations to the Finnish readership (Sharma 2003: 155-59). Such practice is common enough in cross-cultural translation.

Another aspect is the list of ingredients. In this particular recipe, the list is short and uncomplicated. There are the basic vegetables—cauliflower and potato—there is oil and salt, and there is a spice mixture. Each of these ingredients has a cultural history of its own but most of all it is the spices that make the difference. The five spice mixture—or *paanch phoron*—is a mix of five types of seeds (there are variants in other sources—such as *nigella*, or onion seed in stead of caraway). The mixture itself is of Bengali origin—not hypothetically "Indian."

In the original Indian edition there is no reference to the national or regional character of the book or the recipes (only one recipe is defined in the title story as a Kashmiri dish). As the primary audience seems to be Indian, there is no need to spell out such obvious demarcations. So, in India the book was subtitled as "stories of women and food." In French translation the subtitle has become "gastronomic stories" (*récits gastronomiques*), forgetting women and elevating the status of food to 'gastronomy.' Even more exotically appealing, in Finnish translation the subtitle is "spicy stories and recipes from India" (*mausteisia tarinoita ja reseptejä Intiasta*). Here, in the Finnish version, women are also removed while spices and India are foregrounded. I consider these shifts in emphasis remarkable. This can be seen for example in the fact that in Finnish bookshops the book has been placed among the cookery books, not fiction.

Traditional Position

The first story, "Jars of Gold," follows up from the introduction. Its theme is the realm of kitchen, reserved for the old grandmother:

> Buaji was seventy-five and the cook a few months older. Both had slightly impaired vision but they never wore their spectacles when they encountered each other inside the storeroom. Each trusted their defective eyes more than any optical lens during this tense moment. Three times a day Buaji doled the rations out to the head cook with such meticulous care that not an extra grain of rice, sugar or dal ever entered the kitchen. (Sharma 1997: 1)

Here we have Buaji watching strictly over the food store and kitchen, "Alert as an eagle on her nest" (Sharma 1997: 2). She deals out the rations to be cooked by the cook and guards the storeroom against any intruders, be they family or servants. The place is tradition embodied: "Nothing ever changed its position in this room" (Sharma 1997: 4). And the main keeper of tradition is the grandmother who controls this particular gendered space.

The recipe connected with this story is for Mango Pickle. This particular pickle has an important role in the story, too. It is a relish of which the narrator's father, Buaji's son," her favourite, got not one but two plump slices" (Sharma 1997: 3), as the narrator remembers with envy. Such traditional favouritism of son's is abundant in Indian texts. What is peculiar here, however, is the father's behaviour that goes somewhat against the grain. The narrator says: "Sometimes my father would give the mango pickle to my mother, though she never asked for it, and Buaji would cough angrily" (Sharma 1997: 4). This subtle incident is again an indication of the strict hierarchies being in a flux, despite the servility of the mother—who would never ask for a favour—and the angry cough of the grandmother—who would never accept such untoward favours.

Here I would like to add another cross-cultural comment. In the instructions for preparation of this pickle it says that "Keep in the sun for 4 to 5 days" (Sharma 1997: 8). In the Finnish translation then, there is an addition: "considering the Finnish sun, this dish remains a curiosity. Whereas over India, sunshine is certain and powerful!" (Sharma, 2003: 19). In an ironic way, this comment emphasises the speciality of the dish and makes a cultural difference between India and Finland on the basis of climate.

Educating and Managing Girls

The next story is "A Taste for Humble Pie." The position of girls and women in India has been under discussion for long. If the previous story pointed at the servility of wives, in this story the attention is on the destiny of an orphan girl Bala. The now 30-plus-old poor Bala had been circulated among relatives who house her for a while before sending her to other relatives. This situation changes gradually as Bala becomes an invaluably skilled domestic hand—she cooks, nurses, and manages the servants. The narrator's mother describes her as "grateful and [she] likes to be useful around the house, unlike some girls I know, who spend all day reading novels" (Sharma 1997: 12). The implication is, even if it is expressed ironically, that educating girls is unproductive as they will waste their time reading worthless novels instead of helping with the housekeeping. This is again an instance where Sharma has sympathetically—without stressing the point—brought up an important issue but has not explicitly given solutions.

The narrator's mother takes on the responsibility to be Bala's "manager" as "[i]t gave her a great sense of power, especially over my [the narrator's] father's relatives" (Sharma 1997: 16). In such moments of domestic care-taking, power relations are articulated and acted out. Just like Buaji in "Jars of Gold," here the mother uses her position in managing domestic affairs in order to influence other matters.

A complex set of allegiances and concerns are released when in one instant a distant male relative, Raj, returns from the United States to attend a wedding. Raj immediately falls for Bala and begins to woo her, to the dismay of the other relatives. The traditional setting of distress over getting marriageable girls married off is turned upside down: nobody wants to let Bala go. She is appreciated for her being what she is, even though everybody tries hard to not to let it show. Especially her spinach pakoras are esteemed high: "'Just taste her pakoras—you will never find another one so delicious and crisp,' [one uncle] said but only when Bala was not around. To her face he continued to shout at her" (Sharma 1997: 16).

The pakoras are so delicious that the narrator's father even says that it is just for them that Raj wants to marry Bala: "Must be the pakoras," he says (Sharma 1997: 21). The ambivalent situation in which Bala has to live—between secret admiration and blatant abuse—never manages to wear her out. She keeps her spirits high and her hands busy. Widows, wives, orphan girls—all of them are bound in servility. Here Bala, however, seems to be enjoying this position and finally, when Raj manages to propose to her, she refuses. All the family is overjoyed for this "victory" of theirs (Sharma 1997: 22) in this inverted Cinderella story: the prince comes to rescue the damsel in distress but she rejects him.

Nowhere in the text has Bala's side of the story been told. The ending, too, leaves this open as the narrator's mother sums the situation up: "I knew Bala would never let us down [...]. How could she, after all that we have done for her" (Sharma 1997: 22). One cannot again escape the ironic twist as it is exactly the opposite what has taken place: it is Bala who had been doing so much for everybody.

Battle for the Palate

If things are left unsaid in Bala's case, the next story "Sandwiched!" is more explicit about matters. Here also the narrative point of view changes from the female first person of the first two stories to the male third person.

In "Sandwiched!" the main character, Vinod, is in a situation between the frying pan and the fire. His mother competes with his wife Nirmala in trying to be the better cook. The competition is described in terms of war: "the battle would begin" (Sharma 1997: 24), "they took their positions for the next attack" (Sharma 1997: 25), "this battle for his palate" (Sharma 1997: 28). "The women prepared a new strategy each day. Sometimes they fought with curries" (Sharma 1997: 28), "his mother would counterattack" (Sharma 1997: 28), "extended battle lines to puddings" (Sharma 1997: 30), and "battle cries (Sharma 1997: 30). Here another traditional condition is defined in stunning rhetoric: that of rivalry between a daughter-in-law and a mother-in-law and the language of war implicitly shows the rivalry to be ridiculous.

Neither of the women of Vinod's life are good cooks, after all, despite all the cooking frenzy, as Vinod regrettably notes: "Both were bad cooks who needed to be praised for every mouthful that choked him. Vinod often wished he could divide his body vertically into two equal parts and give each portion to each woman. He wanted so much to please both" (Sharma 1997: 28). From the moment of first meeting Nirmala during the marriage negotiations, he has suppressed the concern for taste as he is madly in love with her; from the first cups of her "lethal coffee" and the first "shrivelled samosas" (Sharma 1997: 27) he has considered the food she prepares as "nectar to his lovesick tastebuds" (Sharma 1997: 27). The contested ground is Vinod's position between the traditional son's respect of his mother and the more modern husband's love for his wife.

Resolving a Dilemma

In his desperation over the dilemma, he comes to think the unthinkable, that his widowed mother could remarry: "She is only 54. If she were European she could have married again [...] though now even Indian widows [...]" (Sharma 1997: 26). The sentence is left unfinished; Vinod has to abandon his impossible thoughts as he knows such a thing would never happen. He starts to think about falling ill instead as that "would put him on a restricted diet and force the women to call a ceasefire" (Sharma 1997: 31). Ironically enough, when everybody else around him seemed to develop all sorts of conditions from ulcers to blood pressure, he shows no signs of disorder. That day everything changes unexpectedly, though.

During the dinner of another contest for feeding him, Nirmala announces that she is pregnant. This piece of news brings peace to the house for six months as she is resolutely forced to rest. After those months the battle lines would be changed and the women would turn their attention to the baby. Vinod has but one wish: "Vinod wished with all his heart for a healthy, strong son because a daughter, however precious and loved, would not be distraction enough" (Sharma 1997: 33).

Once more there is a playful application of a traditional norm. Indians have favoured sons over daughters so much that in many areas there is a distinct misproportion of boys over girls. Here this traditional desire is replaced with a very personal agenda.

Conclusion: a Feast of Fragrance?

As the cross-cultural features I have discussed also suggest, there is also a feast of fragrance in the stories. It is not only the pressing issues that are brought up but also an outspoken passion for food. This feature especially has made the stories easy to accommodate outside India, a country widely known for its colourful, spicy and fragrant foods.

To conclude, I would like to consider the ways in which these stories have challenged traditionally assigned gendered positions. The discussion of the stories here shows that there is a certain ambivalence between tradition and something else—perhaps we could call it modernity, although it is not spelled out. In the remaining stories, the range of issues expands to resistance to arranged marriage, retributions of a wife, frivolities of family women, budding sexuality of a young woman, attitude towards traditional religiosity, inexpressible spousal devotion, and marital despair and displeasure. In all these, similar questioning is on its way, although the final direction is not revealed.

We can assume that the brevity of the short story genre is important for dealing with the kind of processes that take place in the stories. Whether the genre itself is notably gendered cannot be justified on the basis of the stories but it certainly is open for gendered issues, for the battle for the palate. In the title story "The Anger of Aubergines," the ex-wife of Mr. Kumar prepares him Sunday dinners after which his stomach is disturbed. This unspoken revenge, the anger of aubergines, is interpreted differently by him: "as he lay awake all night, tossing and turning in agony, chewing antacid tablets, he felt justified in leaving his wife" (Sharma 1997: 59).[2]

In the end, it is not indisputable whether the stories of women and food are for a battle or for a feast. But then again, bitter-sweet tastes good, too.

NOTES

1. This work was done the Finnish Academy project no. 205780 "Reconstructing 'America': Racial, Gendered and Diasporic Identities." Extended from a paper given at the International Conference on Interdisciplinary Approaches to Short Fiction Theory and Criticism, March 24-27, 2004, Universidad de Salamanca, Salamanca, Spain.
2. This story is also anthologized in *A Matter of Taste: the Penguin Book of Indian Food Writing*. While the book as a whole is not a critical one

on food writing, in the Introduction, the editor Nilanjana S. Roy outlines the many aspects of Indian food: regional, religious, cultural, literary, and so on (Roy xi-xx).

WORKS CITED

Roy, Nilanjana S. Introduction. *A Matter of Taste: the Penguin Book of Indian Food Writing*. Ed. Nilanjana S. Roy. New Delhi: Penguin, 2004. xi-xx.

Sharma, Bulbul. *The Anger of Aubergines: Stories of Women and Food*. New Delhi: Kali for Women, 1997.

——. *La colère des aubergines; récits gastronomiques*. Trans. Dominique Vitalyos. Picquier Poche, 191. Arles: Éditions Philippe Picquier, 2002.

——. *Munakoisojen Kiukku: Mausteisia Tarinoita ja Reseptejä Intiasta*. Trans. Terhi Kuusisto. Helsinki: Like, 2003.

——. *La vendetta della melanzana*. Trans. Tatiana Moroni and Sara Radaelli. Milano: Marcos Y Marcos, 2001.

Spang, Rebecca L. *The Invention of the Restaurant: Paris and Modern Gastronomic Culture*. Cambridge, Mass. and London: Harvard University Press, 2000.

14 A Home of My Own (?): A Feminist Critique of Lakshmi Kannan's *Going Home*[1]

Mala Pandurang

Lakshmi Kannan is a bi-lingual writer of both English and Tamil fiction, short stories and poetry. Better known by her Tamil pen-name *Kaaveri*, Kannan writes with a stringent anti-patriarchal tone directed particularly at the middle-class, upper caste Tamil Brahmin community to which she belongs. *Going Home* (1995) is a translation by Kannan of her original work in Tamil entitled *Athukku Pogannum.*

In this article, I will read *Going Home* as an intended critique of the stifled and insipid lives lead by educated middle class women of families that appear modern, with "a veneer of a progressive 'with it' kind of atmosphere" (Preface vii). This paper will particularly concentrate on Kannan's use of the leitmotif of the 'house' in order to raise disturbing questions on systemic aspects of patriarchal oppression, within a contemporary urban Indian milieu.

In the preface to the novel, Kannan vents her anger at post-independent Indian society's failure to guarantee property and inheritance rights of Indian women. She points out that while the Hindu Succession Act of 1956 assures the legal rights of a woman to family property, the actual reality of control of assets is another story. Seemingly progressive families, according to Kannan, count upon the "unconditional compliance" of women when it comes to asserting rights over ancestral property (vii). As a consequence of this "tacit silent acceptance of their lot in the unequal equation between them and their male siblings" (vii), the larger number of Indian women neither feel at 'home' in their physical homes, nor within their bodies. 'Home' thus remains an elusive concept. A woman is only a temporary *tenant*, housed in both her physical surroundings and within her own body. Kannan mentions that she had in fact waited for a while before writing the book, with "a kind of hope as uncertain as it was unsure" that the life of the middle class Indian woman would change for the better. *Going Home* is an angry reaction, "not unmixed with guilt and shame" to the "humiliating misogynous and belittling experiences that educated, upper class/caste women face at the hands of their parental and conjugal families" (viii).

Kannan's central protagonist belongs to a Tamil Brahmin family. Gayatri Shankar lives in Delhi in the 1980s, with her husband Shankar and son Arvind. Although Shankar is employed by the Central Government, Gayatri is compelled to work in a private firm to help ends meet. Burdened by emotional pressures from within the home, and physical strain from without, Gayatri's life is representative of the educated middle class Indian woman for whom inflation has left with little choice but to assume the double role of the housewife and the career woman. As her mother comments to her—"there seems to be no way out for the women of your generation" (28).

The story line of *Going Home* is rather thin and traces Gayatri's lack-luster life over a span of perhaps a decade. While Kannan's characters lack depth, interest in the text is sustained by Kannan's exploration of the concept of the 'house' or 'home' as a space occupied, more under compulsion than willingly, by its female inhabitants. The daughter of the family moves from the household of her parents to the household of her parents-in-law. As Gayatri remarks to herself, "one the beginning, the other the end [...]. A strange arbitrary way of marking the order of a woman's life" (63). Neither however really belongs to her, nor does she belong to either.

Gayatri works untiringly to meet monthly loan repayments to sustain Shankar's dream of owning a home of one's own albeit the fact that this will be only be a "matchbox flat with small rooms fitted with tiny windows that look like beady cunning eyes" (10). Frustrated over their cramped existence in a miniscule Delhi flat, Gayatri's mind returns time and again to childhood memories of her grandfather's sprawling mansion in Mysore, called THE RETREAT. The line "Athukku Pogannum" (*I want to go home*) is spoken by the child Gayatri, anxious to return to the expansive space, and liberal atmosphere of her grandfather's home, with its own "distinct personality" (12). The adult Gayatri is well aware that home as an expansive and liberating space is only an illusion, beyond her reach. Still, she cannot reconcile herself to the loss of inheritance of THE RETREAT. Her mother Meenakshi is denied her share in her father's ancestral property, being only a female heir to the property. The daughter's rightful claim to family property under the Act of 1956 remains a mere statement on paper. Gayatri is angered by her mother's refusal to petition the court for the sake of 'family honour.' She cannot reconcile herself to her mother's simple acceptance of the loss of the house. On a visit to her grandfather's house in later years, she stands 'homeless' outside the house. There is a sense of immense pain at the loss of a house that had slipped through the fingers of the daughter of the house: "An elusive house that had become someone else's 'rightful property.' A house that faded away like a dream" (10).

The claustrophobic interior of her Delhi flat in a seven-storied building is in direct contrast to the carefree liberating space of her Thatha's home. Hot and cramped, the flat "agitates on the nerves" (55). Gayatri likens their new home to a rat-trap:

> We have shrunk to adapt ourselves to the narrow limits of this cage—Shankar, Arvind and I. We have learnt to cripple ourselves to a smallness so that we can fit into this rat hole. Or maybe I should call it a rat-trap. For our bodies, Shankar and mine, stiffen like corpses inside this hole as soon as we return from a day at work. (11)

The metaphor of the house is further concentrated and reduced to that of the bathroom. A very basic everyday amenity. "When it comes to designing bathrooms, Delhi architects are suddenly stricken by the most parsimonious instincts. The only way to avoid getting bruised and scratched everywhere in those bathrooms is to squeeze and shrink one's body as small as possible" (51).

Gayatri is unable to share Shankar's excitement at their forthcoming ownership of an equally tiny DDA (Delhi Development Authority) flat, although Shankar tries to convince Gayatri that their feelings of "dislocation," "misgiving" and "restlessness" will all disappear (16). He however places the onus on Gayatri to convert the newly purchased flat into a *happy home*, stating that "only a woman, actually a wife can make it a livable hearth" (85). Kannan's intention to demystify this given of *Grahine Grihim Uchyate—the housewife is the house*. Gayatri asks herself—"how could Shankar be so simplistic?" (16). He fails to recognize that while she might devote her entire life to 'create' a home ("the luxurious softness of our downy nest" 18), it becomes a home more for others rather than the self: "It somehow becomes an arrangement that offers all the conveniences to the man of the house and the children but never to herself. It doesn't ensure her the space she wanted, in the first place" (22).

Part II of the novel opens with the house warming of the new DDA flat. Gayatri is filled with an overwhelming sense of despondency at this final 'refuge,' the "fruit of her hard earned money"—which is so small that it "squeezes the inhabitants and cuts them down to size, so that they become small enough to fit into the tiny spaces" (84). The lack of space has compelled her to give up her keen interest in dance that she had learnt devotedly for many years. The flat constricts the development of her creative and artistic self and increasingly becomes a symbol of repression of all Gayatri's past and present desires.

Going Home is a direct statement on the plight of the married middle class career woman who is compelled to cross over from the private sphere to the public. However, this 'outing' from the inner courtyard into a larger world is not translated into any real freedom for the self. Kannan uses the character of Gayatri's closest friend Rama Doraiswamy, to deconstruct the myth of the working woman as an empowered person equipped to make the necessary transition over her life's courses. Rama is a successful Tamil writer, who has had to struggle against all odds to retain her creativity. She works as a college lecturer, and stoically suffers the indifference of her parents towards their third daughter; a husband who is envious of her fame; and in-laws who are resentful of her career. Like Gayatri, Rama's talents have been buried under the banality of living: "Where is the place for art in the lives of salaried middle class people?" she asks of Gayatri, "Where is the time?" (17). "Doused and dampened by domesticity" on the one hand, and overburdened by professional responsibilities on the other hand, Rama reflects that life "conspires to bring abut a mediocrity, an ordinariness into [our] lives" (21).

There are other women in *Going Home* who are also equally unhappy and unfulfilled. There is the unmarried Sheila whose outstanding looks are a liability in her professional and social interaction with men; Shobha, the mistress of a M.P. who has been installed into a lonely large house "in which time as slowly inexorably wasting away the woman inside"—"she did not belong to the house. Nor did the house belong to her" (138); and the newly-wed Kiran Agarwal whose determination to fight sexual harassment ends in the termination of her services, and who has a husband who suggests that she 'compromises' with her boss. When Gayatri's boss makes subtle advances by repeatedly asking her out to dinner, she opts for vague excuses rather than direct confrontation.

For Gayatri, Rama represents the voice of the suppressed middle class wife. She therefore determinedly tells herself that she will not allow the writer within Rama to die: "[...] because if you die then so will I" (17). However, when Rama tells Gayatri: "We'll have to make ourselves smaller and [...] and [...] learn to fit in, I guess?" (21), it is Gayatri who retorts, "Rama, we'll have to grow a little bigger than all this, even if it hurts. We just have to grow [...] and find the nerve to outgrow this cage" (22). She envies Rama's ability to write: "You can escape from the pressures of the unsaid, the unsayable through your writing. But what about me?" (49). Rama's acclaimed novel *Driftwood* is celebrated for offering a brilliant "paradigm of the lives of thousands of educated but unfortunate working women in India" (71), and Gayatri relates Rama's heightened sensitivity to that of the sandalwood tree—"only when you prick it hard or stab it, or rub it with water, will a sandalwood give off its scent" (76). The reader however only hears discussions by Gayatri and others on Rama's "razor-sharp observations" of a community in which she "continues to search for truth" (116), but does not get to read actual excerpts of the novel. Rama may write with a "sharp incisive mind" and "clarity of vision" of the dilemma of the salaried middle class, but her writing does not lead to personal release. She opts instead to retain the *status quo*, the only luxury she allows herself is a platonic friendship with a colleague and co-writer Damodaran. Therefore her act of breaking of silence through her acclaimed novel *Driftwood* is non-liberatory. Gayatri acknowledges this when she asks herself, "if only Rama had made her choice right in the beginning—what if she had pleaded she could not cope with a job as well as running and tending a family?" (69).

In spite of her string of protests against anti-patriarchal mindsets, Gayatri falls into the trap of a conventional mindset in her resentment against her own daughter-in-law Girija. She protests to Shankar when Girija's mother does not accord them their due respect as in-laws: "Had she no culture or grace, she a mother negotiating a daughter's marriage" (125). Gayatri expresses disappointment at Girija's lack of ambition in life. Gayatri had asked of herself "if only Rama had made her choice right in the beginning—what if she had pleaded she could not cope with a job as well as running and tending a family?" (69)—yet does not concede that Girija might have exercised her choice in opting out of a professional life. She refers to Girija as "an extraordinary dull girl" (128) and goes as far as referring to her as "an aberration of nature" (133). Gayatri fails to concede that Girija's listless ennui could well be due to an equally crippled life within their small flat now shared by four people. Again ironically, if Gayatri does find release of some kind in life, it is through the role traditionally conceived as one of the most basic of life's satisfactions, the arrival of the grandson, perpetuating in turn, the myth of (grand)motherhood.

Kannan spends time in exploring the analogy between the physical house and the human body, and in doing so, deviates from a feminist agenda of activism. While the physical boundaries of a household in the body, the human body in turn houses the *being*. Gayatri talks to Rama about the need to break free of restrictive boundaries, and yet acknowledges the futility of these attempts. Despite attempts to free oneself of both physical and mental fetters, she states, "we only fail in our efforts and return grudgingly to the shell of our body like disappointed tenants, to continue with our lives half-heartedly" (21). After the loss of THE RETREAT, Gayatri is filled with a 'restlessness' and an 'unhoused feeling' takes over her which she cannot verbalize. She feels neither at home in the physical house, nor in her personal 'cage-body.' "Does my body belong to me, or is it something that is holding me down, trying to subdue me?" she asks herself on a number of occasions (88).

As Gayatri ages, she turns to Yoga to strengthen her body so that she may cope with the burden of work. Her involvement with yoga develops within her the gradual detachment from the physical structures of her home and her body: "Tired of living within the body like a tenant, she prepares herself for the final and ultimate 'home.' 'I am ready to leave'" (88), she declares. Ironically yoga and mediation have made her body "indecently tough" such that her body's hold on life "was too firm, too disgracefully, unnecessarily strong" (93). The last scene of the novel is of Gayatri in a state of breathlessness, having helped her young grandson build his own 'home' with plastic building blocks. She has a vision of a mango tree blooming in her grandfather's garden. The reader can surmise from the last paragraph that she is on the verge of death as she tells herself, filled with an overwhelming sense of release:

> Just leave. Run, run [...] run away, breaking through this house that suffocates me, this house that closes in on me, break through this cage that is my body, pressing upon me till I cannot breath, break through my skull, spring up from this centre [...] fight free of it all, and run, run, keep running [...]. (160)

By depicting Gayatri's final release from life as coming only through the pleasurable act of 'running away,' and ultimately through death, Kannan forecloses the option of praxis for her female protagonist. In spite of her feminist intent, Kannan's characters remain conservative in revolt. Protest from within the novel is restricted to the level of verbal articulation. What emerges from this realistic rendering of the lives of educated Tamil Brahmin women, is a sense of victimhood that primarily highlights a sense of powerlessness and helplessness. Kannan's women do not go beyond their status of victims, and the novel thus fails to effectively contest the 'unconditional compliance' of generations of Indian women, that Kannan had so determinedly stated she would, in her preface to the book.

NOTE

1. This paper expands upon an initial review of the novel (*The Elusive Concept of Home: A Feminist Reading of Lakshmi Kannan's Going Home*) published in *The Indian Journal of World Literature and Culture* 1.1 (Jan.–June 2004): 88-90.

WORK CITED

Kannan, Lakshmi. *Going Home*. New Delhi: Disha Books, 1999.

15 Anita Desai's *Diamond Dust and Other Stories*: A Narrative Analysis

Basavaraj Naikar
Joel Kuortti

One of the striking features of the Indian English novelist Anita Desai's collection of nine short stories, *Diamond Dust*, is the feminine point of view expressed through her microscopic observation of life in a very subtle and lyrical language. Whether the setting is in India, Canada or elsewhere, Desai has a remarkable power of evoking the atmosphere in a photographic yet poetic way; as Cressida Connolly notes: "Desai is an excellent mimic, because she can do all the voices" (Connolly online). In our article, we analyse the ways in which Desai has selected a single event or thematic unit and explored its intricacies, highlighting its significance in a very subtle manner. Like a goldsmith or an embroiderer, she deals with superfine aspects of life with microscopic vision. Her stories, therefore, add to the beauty and richness of the genre of Indian short story.

The first story entitled "Royalty" portrays the contrast between east and west, poetic and prosaic life, and nostalgic attachment to one's past. The protagonist of the story, Raja, has returned to India for a visit from California where he teaches Sanskrit and composes poetry. In the story he is returning from South India to Delhi in a train. Though he is used to flying in America, in India he wants to travel by train. His sister Sarla does not understand why he prefers the tedious train journey, but the reason is that Raja has a deep nostalgic attachment to things Indian. He dresses himself in a South Indian dhoti and shirt and travels in train to Delhi in order to relive his past and renew his relation with Indian reality and also to see some (fine and higher) beauty even in drab and ugly everyday things. The nostalgic undertone of the story is emphasised also in the allusive nature of his name and position; Raja's character resembles Ramaswamy in Raja Rao's *The Serpent and the Rope* (1960) as Ramaswamy, too, struggles between two cultures. As a practical woman, Sarla fails to understand Raja's poetic and nostalgic approach to life. Believing in unity of being, Raja ridicules the double standards of Sarla's husband Ravi who pretends to be a patriot although he dresses himself in tweed suit and hats.

Raja finds spiritual peace in his nostalgic engagement with India. On his travels in India, Raja visits the tomb of Nizamuddin and seems to be deeply moved by it. Similarly, he enjoys poetic trance in the observation of the beauty of the Himalayas. Endowed as he is with a poetic and philosophical sensibility—he for example enjoys the Indian music with real passion—he cannot only see but is also able to *show to others* the extraordinary beauty of ordinary things. In the Lodi Gardens it was, as Sarla puts it, exactly "Raja who opened their eyes, who made them see it as they never saw it themselves, as a place of magic, enchantment, of pleasure so immense and rich that it could never be exhausted" (19). Thus his visit to India enables him to have an intense poetic ecstasy and to share it with others. In her delicate sardonic way Desai, thus, explores the psyche of an artist by contrasting it with that of ordinary people, suggesting that perhaps there is no greater royalty than the rich artistic experience one undergoes.

The main theme in the story "Winterscape," then, is the widening gap between people of different generations and cultures, resulting in a sense of alienation and lack of communication the story highlights the contrast between Indian (Hindu) culture and Western (Christian) culture. Whereas in Indian culture filial bonds traditionally transcend the barriers of technical relationships of kinship, in Western culture, they are more often regarded as restricted by technical bonds. Similarly, where Indian culture believes in collective happiness, Western culture believes in the individual happiness. The writer brings out this contrast in a subtle fashion. In the Hindu family in the story, there are two sisters, Asha and Annapurna (or Anu). Asha, the elder sister, gets married but does not have any issue. When the younger sister Anu also gets married little later, she gives birth to a son named Rakesh. Happily and willingly, Anu gives away her child to the care of the childless Asha who nourishes Rakesh very affectionately, experiencing the joy of surrogate motherhood. The two sisters are brought emotionally closer as Asha's husband dies most unexpectedly in a gun-accident. As Rakesh grows into a young man, he cannot differentiate between his mother and aunt on account of their equal affection for him. He, therefore, thinks that he has two mothers instead of one. When he wishes to go to Canada for further education, both the mothers sacrifice their individual pleasure and arrange for the financial support for his education by selling their lands.

In what follows, Indian collectivism is contrasted with Western individualism and its inherent selfishness. After completing his education in Canada, Rakesh, like many ambitious Indian young men, refuses to return to India and settles down in Canada by marrying a Canadian girl called Berth. From the individualistic Western position, Berth cannot understand how Anu could give her baby to her sister. This becomes evident when Rakesh wants to invite his two mothers to Canada for a short trip on the birth of their child. Similarly, Berth's mother Doris wonders at Rakesh's having two mothers. This situation brings out the classical dilemma that the West cannot understand the East.

The overarching theme of cultural contrast is intersected by that of generation gap and time-gap. When the two mothers eventually go to Canada to stay for a few days with Rakesh and try to remind him of his childhood days, he finds that he has forgotten the past because of the long interval of time as well as his long stay in a foreign land and culture. The lack of communication with his two mothers is supplemented by the fact that his personality has matured: he is no longer a boy but an adult, highly educated man who finds it difficult to communicate with his illiterate mothers. Likewise the mothers feel a sense of alienation. Although Rakesh and Berth try their best to take care of the two mothers by clothing and entertaining them, they begin to feel tired of the Canadian way of life. Their nostalgic yearnings and actual displeasures become a dilemma, "as complete, and as fragile, after all, as a snow crystal" (46). Even if they watch the Canadian winter with curiosity mostly through the window—as is captured in Rakesh's photographs—they fall ill because of the cold weather. The winter, here, is not only factual but grows into metaphorical proportions for them: the relationship has become cold, there is no real communication between the two mothers and their son. After the realisation of this communication breakdown, Rakesh sends his mothers back to India and his wife heaves a sigh of relief when they leave. In this story, from her own privileged position between two cultures, Desai has managed to show the contrast between Indian collectivism and Western individualism, between Indian and Western concepts of motherhood, in a very delicate fashion. "Tepoztlan Tomorrow" tells a somewhat parallel story as Desai highlights the generation gap, nostalgic attachment to one's native city, and the continuous deterioration of the same. The protagonist, Louis, goes to the town of Tepoztlan in Mexico and meets his aunt Dona Celia. The story shows a picture of decadence of the city in various ways, quite in line with Nirad Chaudhuri's picture of American decadence as part of global decadence.

The title story, "Diamond Dust: A Tragedy," depicts the theme of unusually intimate relationship between man and animal, between Mr. Das, the protagonist, and his pet dog called Diamond. Although loved by its owner, the mongrel dog is a terror to the neighbours. People who are scared of it try to avoid going to Mr. Das's compound. The postman does this by throwing the mail into the hedge. Once the dog manages to break its chain and goes out for a mating bout with stray bitches and comes back with bloodstains on its genitalia. Mr. Das is relieved on its return after the first outing.

When it goes out for the second time, it is caught by the police and taken away in the police van. Mr. Das grows anxious about its absence and despite his wife's warning—"Give him up before this search kills you" (63)—begins to search for it at every possible corner of the city. Finally he finds it in the police van, but when he climbs the rear side of it, the vehicle jerking back kills him. Deep attachment for the pet dog had made Mr. Das vulnerable and costs him his life in the end. What Desai seems to question is the extent of love: how far it should stretch? Is love a tragic delusive mania as the title suggests?[1]

Within a wonderful scenic portrayal, the story "Underground" describes a desperate search. Jack Higgins and his wife Meg go in a car in search of a hotel on a hot sandy beach in Cornwall. Meg has recently been hospitalised and needs rest after being released. Her husband has brought her to enjoy the hot sun and searches for a hotel. But everywhere he gets a negative answer. Finally, he has to be satisfied with an underground room. Invisible to Jack and Meg is the tragic intertwined story of the unsuccessful hotel proprietor Bob McTaggart whose White House Hotel stands persistently empty after the death of his wife Helen. Like Mr. Das in "Diamond Dust," McTaggart is possessed by love and hope. He "felt himself dissolve, become one with the silent evening, having no existence apart from it, there is still hope" (81). The story is episodic and the motif is reminiscent of the Biblical story of Joseph and Mary looking for lodging in Bethlehem, ending up in the legendary manger. One could say that Desai has managed to show how sublime narratives like the Biblical story can become reality in ordinary lives. Together with the love-story, this realisation enhances the importance of telling stories.

"The Man Who Saw Himself Drowned" is a psychological fantasy. It tells about the death by drowning of the protagonist's *doppelgänger*. The nameless protagonist attends his double's funeral and wonders: "Now I was truly perplexed. My previous life had ended, but did that mean I now had to construct a new one?" (91). The story has the quality of a fable and is conspicuous for its psychological significance, as the figure of the double is a recurring phenomenon in literary and cinematic art. Furthermore, it easily brings the strange, nightmarish novels and stories of Franz Kafka to one's mind. With this story, Desai is taking part in the tradition of the literature of the uncanny.

"The Artist's Life" presents a picture of the paradox of an artist's life. Miss Polly attends a summer school where she is taught by Miss Abigail to paint according to her dreams. It shows her, a budding artist, trying to create beauty amidst physical and behavioural ugliness: "Those unpredictable roseate dreams were cruelly limited, encroached upon by the undeniable reality of the house, yard, suburb—enemies, all, of Art" (104). Polly's mother's tenant Miss Mabel Dodd is another artist teaching the delinquents in a school. Problems arise as Miss Mabel, in spite of being an artist, does not clean the surroundings of her cabin. Miss Polly's mother is puzzled by Miss Mabel's negligence and wishes to remind her of the need for cleaning. She, therefore, leaves a few garbage cans outside her cabin. Miss Mabel perhaps takes a cue from this and brings a black youth and cleans the surroundings every Sunday. But one day, Miss Polly and her mother are surprised to see that somebody has written "PIG" on her car with excrement. They cannot guess as to who might have done the filthy thing. The police are called to investigate the matter. It is suspected that one of Miss Mabel's delinquent students or the black youth must have done the heinous thing. Like in her novel *Baumgartner's Bombay* (1988), Desai writes superbly about the irredeemable dilemma between everyday tedium and higher artistic dreams and ambitions.

"Five Hours to Simla or Faisla" is perhaps the most clearly focused story in this collection. It is a humorous story about obstinacy. With another five hours ahead, a family is travelling to Simla in a car. On the way, they are forced to stop as an unexpected difficulty crops up. While a *sardarji* had been driving his truck along the road, some goatherd pelted a stone at his vehicle, shattering the windscreen of his truck. The *sardarji* gets angry, parks his truck across the road, thereby blocking the traffic from both the sides and causing a good deal of trouble to the travellers on the way to Simla. He demands compensation from the goatherd. The traffic jam extends for two miles, but the *sardarji* sits leisurely on the bridge wall. The travellers do not know how to deal with him because of his seemingly irrational demand. Some people go in search of the goatherd while others go to the nearest city to find a police station. Meanwhile a temporary market forms there and beggars, hawkers, tea-vendors and toy-vendors gather and make the best of the situation. The members of the family in the car feel restless and helpless and during the four or five hours of tension and waiting, they gradually compromise with the situation. Necessity impels them to neglect the ideal of hygiene. They eat and drink the cheap stuff that is available with the hawkers and vendors. After the long and tedious waiting, they are surprised to see a police van come from a nearby town. The travellers expect an exchange of words between the *sardarji* and the police officers. But to their surprise, the *sardarji*, irrationally and humorously, instead of asking for any compensation, climbs into his truck, starts it and drives away without any demur. The family heaves a sigh of relief. The Bakhtinian carnivalesque character of the story is marked, and as Margaret Ball notes: "the trivial dialogue of the family raises questions about identity" (Ball online).

The final story of the collection, "The Rooftop Dwellers," deals with the problems of an unmarried working woman in Delhi. Moyna is a young lady who has passed her M.A. in English and wants to earn her livelihood in the metropolitan city. She joins the literary magazine *Books* as a sub-editor. Moyna cannot afford to hire a proper house or apartment. As finding any living-space at all is problematic in the overcrowded city, Moyna ends up hiring a rooftop *barsati* where she has to get up early in the morning to collect water from the tap, as there is no facility for storing it. She suffers from the insecurity and minimalism of her everyday life, as well as from lack of social life. The owners of the house suspect her morals when she brings male friends to her room. Once when she returns in the evening, she is surprised and shocked to learn that the things in her room are stolen by somebody. In course of time, she realises the impracticability of running a literary magazine. The politician who is financing the magazine decides to wind it up.

When things are deteriorating for Moyna, her mother calls her to meet a bridegroom who had returned from America. Although Desai's depiction of women's problems has a ring of authenticity and sympathy, Moyna's response to her mother's call is at the same time both assuring and problematic: "Moyna flung herself backward at the same time throwing the letter into the air with a shout of laughter. She rolled her head about on the pillow, spluttering, 'Oh, Mama, re-a-ll-y, Mama [...],' she was free, she was determined, she had made her decision, and she sat up, laughing" (207). In its simplicity, the story throws light upon the contemporary Indian society by highlighting the problems of an unmarried working woman; even an educated woman in India has to face many odds in the pursuit of her independence and identity.

On the whole, the stories in *Diamond Dust* are written from an omniscient point of view. They are conspicuous for their remarkable and microscopic description, evocation of relevant mood and atmosphere and insight into the subtle workings of the human mind. Sometimes her virtues become her vices in that the abundance of descriptive element tends to slacken the pace of the stories. As the blurb says, "in this brilliant new collection of funny, sad, compassionate and charming stories, Anita Desai shows us ordinary lives in a disconcerting world, where hopes and dreams clash with disappointment and the human spirit shines strongly from India to Canada, England, and elsewhere." Obviously, the stories of *Diamond Dust* add to the beauty and richness of the genre of Indian English short story.

NOTE

1. Madhoo Kamra, and Ananya, "*Diamond Dust*: Echoes of Dissonance and Despair," Available at <www.lit-india.org/criticism/litcrit/diamonddust.php>. (25 Oct. 2005)

WORKS CITED

Ball, Magdalena. "A Hundred Possible Answers: Anita Desai's *Diamond Dust*." Available at <www.compulsivereader.com/html/modules.php?op=modload&name=News&file=article&sid=82>. (25 Oct. 2005)

Connolly, Cressida. "Mixed Blessings: *Diamond Dust* by Anita Desai." *New Statesman* 5 June 2000. Available at <www.newstatesman.com/200006050050>. (25 Oct. 2005)

Desai, Anita. *Baumgartner's Bombay*. London: Penguin, 1988.

——. *Diamond Dust and Other Stories*. London: Chatto & Windus, 2000. London: Vintage, 2001.

Kamra, Madhoo and Ananya. "*Diamond Dust*: Echoes of Dissonance and Despair." Available at <www.lit-india.org/criticism/litcrit/diamonddust.php>. (25 Oct. 2005)

Rao, Raja. *The Serpent and the Rope*. London: Murray, 1960.

Contributors

Damai, Puspa: Writing, Rhetoric and American Cultures, Michigan State University, 235 Bessey Hall, East Lansing, MI 48824 USA. **Mailing address**: 1420 Spartan Village, Apt. # C, East Lansing, MI 48823, USA.
E-mail: puspadamai@myway.com and pldamai@yahoo.com

Dengel-Janic, Ellen: Provencweg 12, 72072 Tuebingen, Germany.
E-mail: ellen.dengel-janic@student.uni-tuebingen.de

Govinden, Betty: Department of Curriculum Studies, University of Durban-Westville, Private Bag X54001, Durban 4000 South Africa. E-mail: herbyg@absamail.co.za

Hammond, Andrew: Faculty of Humanities, Swansea Institute of Higher Education, University of Wales, Townhill Road, Swansea, SA2 OUT, Wales, UK. **Mailing address**: 30 Bayview Terrace, Brynmill, Swansea, SA1 4LT, Wales, UK. Email: andrew.hammond@sihe.ac.uk and ahammond@mail5.freeserve.co.uk

Hand, Felicity: Departament de Filologia Anglesa, Edifici B, Universitat Autònoma de Barcelona 08193 BELLATERRA, Barcelona, Spain. E-mail: felicity.hand@uab.es

Jahan, Husne: 3570 Rue Chene d'or, San Jose, CA 95148-4303, USA. E-mail: hjahan@sbcglobal.net

Kuortti, Joel: Ketostenkatu 50, 33300 Tampere, Finland.
E-mail: joel.kuortti@tintti.net

Mittapalli, Rajeshwar: Department of English, Kakatiya University, Vidyaranyapuri, Warangal 506009, AP, India.
E-mail: rajeshwar9@yahoo.com

Naidu, Samantha: Department of English, Rhodes University, P.O. Box 94, Grahamstown 6140 South Africa. E-mail: s.naidu@ru.ac.za

Naikar, Basavaraj: Department of English, Karnatak University, Dharwad 580003 Karnataka, India. E-mail: bsnaikar@yahoo.com

Navarro-Tejero, Antonia: Dpto. Filologias Inglesa y Alemana, Facultad de Filosofia y Letras, Universidad de Cordoba, Plaza Cardenal Salazar, Cordoba, Spain. **Mailing address:** Calle Sanlucar de Guadiana, 42. Bajo B. 21007 Huelva, Spain. E-mail: anavarrotejero@yahoo.com

Pandey, Beerendra: Central Department of English, Tribhuvan University, Kathmandu, Nepal. E-mail: bpandeykpandey@yahoo.com

Pandurang, Mala: Department of English, Dr BMN College of Home Science, 338 Kidwai Road, Matunga, Mumbai 400019 India. E-mail: mpandu@yahoo.com

Sahu, Nandini: Department of English, IACR, Rayagada 765001 Orissa, India. E-mail: kavinandini@rediffmail.com

Sultana, Rebecca: 24 Mabelle Ave, Apartment 317, Toronto, M9A 4X7, Canada. E-mail:rsultana456@hotmail.com